Contents

Introduction

The central theme of this book is GraphQL in modern applications. While GraphQL is only a specification that can be used in many programming languages, this book focuses on GraphQL in JavaScript. Facebook, the company behind the GraphQL specification, didn't release without a reason GraphQL's reference implementation in JavaScript. It is the most compelling programming language for companies and their client-server architecture nowadays. Using Facebook's specification as their blueprint, other programming languages like Python and Java followed.

GraphQL is a query language that can be used anywhere, but it often bridges the gap between client and server applications. It isn't opinionated about which network layer is used, so data can be read and written between client and server applications. It is used to complement the network stack for many libraries and frameworks in JavaScript. The client side takes advantage of popular solutions like React, Angular, and Vue, while the server side can use middleware libraries like Express, Koa, and Hapi in a Node.js environment. It is just a matter of sending GraphQL operations with HTTP across the wire to connect both sides.

The emergence of GraphQL introduces a new era in web development. RESTful applications were the industry favorite for data transfers between client and server applications, but modern requirements have shifted. Applications have to deal with multiple clients–i.e. desktop, web, mobile, wearables–which are all interested in APIs exposed by server applications. The choice becomes one between using multiple client-specific APIs with REST, or just one API with GraphQL for all client applications, which hardly seems like a choice at all. GraphQL is more than just a unified interface, though; its ecosystem offers powerful capabilities and even more potential as its open source community grows.

For me, it was a lucky coincidence that a former coworker open-sourced the GraphQL implementation for Java. He worked to become one of GraphQL's first open source contributors, eventually creating the go-to implementations for Java. The experience shaped my own thinking about GraphQL, which was expanded when my employer evaluated GraphQL for their enterprise application. The glue between our client and server application was initially largely influenced by REST; we had API endpoints for all our RESTful resources in place, eventually running into issues like Facebook for API-consuming client-side applications. The API endpoints were too rigid, so they required aggregations and modifications. An aggregation means putting resources into a singular API endpoint, where a modification is to offer variations of an API endpoint to request different representations of a resource. We introduced our own implementation to request resources from the server and ended up with our own naive implementation of GraphQL. From a client-side perspective, only Relay for React was released these days as a sophisticated library in terms of consuming GraphQL APIs, so we invested time in this as well. In the end, GraphQL was too early in its development, so we postponed introducing it to our technology stack. Admittedly, none of us knew it would become so powerful or popular.

This book starts with GraphQL in client-side applications, so you will use React as a UI library to consume your a third-party GraphQL API, which happens to be GitHub's GraphQL API. It is a popular choice among developers for a couple reasons: GitHub was one of few popular companies to release a GraphQL API to the public; GitHub's subsequent growth has granted some credibility to GraphQL itself; and a third-party API usually focuses on client-side GraphQL application in the beginning. This book teaches how to consume the GraphQL API in a client application without having to build the GraphQL server yourself.

When we shift gears in this book toward GraphQL on the server side, we will implement a GraphQL API that can eventually be consumed by a GraphQL client application. You will implement powerful features such as authentication, database connections and pagination. By the end, you should have a firm grasp about using GraphQL in your JavaScript applications.

About the Author

I am a German software and web engineer dedicated to learning and teaching programming in JavaScript. After obtaining my Master's Degree in computer science, I continued learning on my own. I gained experience from the startup world, where I used JavaScript intensively during both my professional life and spare time, which eventually led to a desire to teach others about these topics.

For a few years, I worked closely with an exceptional team of engineers at a company called Small Improvements, developing large scale applications. The company offered a SaaS product that enables customers to give feedback to businesses. This application was developed using JavaScript on its frontend, and Java as its backend. The first iteration of Small Improvements' frontend was written in Java with the Wicket Framework and jQuery. When the first generation of SPAs became popular, the company migrated to Angular 1.x for its frontend application. After using Angular for over two years, it became clear that Angular wasn't the best solution to work with state intense applications, so they made the jump to React and Redux. This enabled it to operate on a large scale successfully.

During my time in the company, I regularly wrote articles about web development on my website. I received great feedback from people learning from my articles which allowed me to improve his writing and teaching style. Article after article, I grew my ability to teach others. I felt that my first articles were packed with too much information, quite overwhelming for students, but I improved by focusing on one subject at a time.

Currently, I am a self-employed software engineer and educator. I find it a fulfilling pastime to see students thrive by giving them clear objectives and short feedback loops. You can find more information about me and ways to support and work with me on my website[1].

---

[1] https://www.robinwieruch.de/about

Requirements

To get the most out of this book, you should be familiar with the basics of web development, which includes some knowledge of HTML, CSS and JavaScript. You will also need to be familiar with the term API[2], because they are discussed frequently. I encourage you to join the official Slack Group[3] for the book, help or get help from others.

Editor and Terminal

For the development environment, use a running editor or IDE and terminal (command line tool), and follow my setup guide[4]. It is adjusted for MacOS users, but you can find a Windows setup guide, too. There are lots of articles about setting up a web development environment for your OS.

React

On the client-side, this book uses React to teach about GraphQL in JavaScript. My other book called The Road to learn React teaches you all the fundamentals about React. It also teaches you to make the transition from JavaScript ES5 to JavaScript ES6. The book is available for free and after having read the Road to learn React, you should possess all the knowledge to implement the GraphQL client-side application with this book.

Node

On the server-side, this book uses Node with Express as library to teach about GraphQL in JavaScript. You don't need to know much about those technologies before using them for your first GraphQL powered applications. The book will guide you through the process of setting up a Node application with Express and shows you how to weave GraphQL into the mix. Afterward, you should be able to consume the GraphQL API provided by your server-side application in your client-side application.

Node and NPM

You will need to have node and npm[5] installed, which are used to manage the libraries we'll use along the way. In this book, you will install external node packages via npm (node package manager). These node packages can be libraries or whole frameworks. You can verify which node and npm versions you have in the command line. If you don't see output in the terminal, you will need to install node and npm. These are the versions used for this publication:

---

[2]https://www.robinwieruch.de/what-is-an-api-javascript/
[3]https://slack-the-road-to-learn-react.wieruch.com/
[4]https://www.robinwieruch.de/developer-setup/
[5]https://nodejs.org/en/

Command Line

```
node --version
*v10.11.0
npm --version
*v6.4.1
```

If you read the Road to learn React, you should be familiar with the setup already, since it introduces the npm ecosystem as well.

FAQ

Why does the book use React to teach about GraphQL?

GraphQL is often used in modern applications to connect client and server applications. These applications are often built with solutions such as React, Angular and Vue. To teach about GraphQL, it makes sense to apply it in a real world context like React for your client application. I picked React because it has only a slim API and a good learning curve. It is only the view layer in your tech stack. You can learn about it in the Road to learn React[6]. However, you can apply your learnings about GraphQL in other client-side applications, too.

Why does it use Node/Express to teach about GraphQL?

You can consume third-party GraphQL APIs with a client application, but you can also implement your own GraphQL API on the server-side. Since it is more efficient to stick to one programming language (JavaScript), I picked Node.js. Express.js is the most popular choice for Node.js applications, which is why I picked it over alternatives like Hapi or Koa.

How do I get updates?

I have two channels where I share updates about my content. You can subscribe to updates by email[7] or follow me on Twitter[8]. Regardless of the channel, my objective is to only share quality content. Once you receive notification the book has changed, you can download a new version of it.

How do I gain access to the source code projects?

If you bought the complete course that grants access to the source code projects or any other add-on, you should find these on your course dashboard[9]. If you bought the course other than the official Road to React[10] course platform, create an account on the platform, and then go to the Admin page and contact me with one of the email templates. After that I can unlock the course for you. If you haven't bought the complete course, you can reach out any time to upgrade your content to access the other material.

Can I get a copy of the book if I bought it on Amazon?

If you have bought the book on Amazon, you may have seen that the book is available on my website too. Since I use Amazon as one way to monetize my often free content, I honestly thank you for your support and invite you to sign up on Road to React[11]. There you can write me an email (Admin page) about your purchase, so that I can unlock the whole course package for you. In addition, you can always download the latest ebook version of the book on the platform.

How can I get help while reading the book?

---

[6]https://roadtoreact.com
[7]https://www.getrevue.co/profile/rwieruch
[8]https://twitter.com/rwieruch
[9]https://roadtoreact.com/my-courses
[10]https://roadtoreact.com
[11]https://roadtoreact.com

The book has a Slack Group[12] for people who want to follow along with fellow students and experienced readers. You can join the channel to get help or to help others. You might find that helping others learn programming helps you internalize your own lessons. If there are no other options, you can always reach out to me.

Is there any troubleshoot area?

If you run into problems, please join the Slack Group. Also, check the open issues on GitHub[13] or in the GitHub repositories of the applications you will build along the way to see if any solutions are listed for specific issue. If your problem wasn't mentioned, open a new issue where you can explain your problem, provide a screenshot, and offer more details (e.g. book page, node version).

What if I cannot afford the complete course?

If you cannot afford the complete course but want to learn about the topic, you can reach out to me. It could be that you are still a student, or that the complete course would be too expensive in your country. I want to support any cause to improve diversity in our culture of developers. If you belong to a minority, or are in an organization that supports diversity, please reach out to me.

Can I help to improve the content?

Yes, I would love to hear your feedback. You can open an issue on GitHub[14] and express improvements to the technical aspects or the text content. You can also open pull requests on GitHub for documents or repositories.

How do I support the project?

If you find my lessons useful and would like to contribute, seek my website's About Page[15] for information about how to offer support. It is also very helpful for my readers spread the word about how my books helped them, so others might discover ways to improve their web development skillsets. Contributing through any of the provided channels gives me the freedom to create in-depth courses, and to continue offering free material.

Is there a money back guarantee?

Yes, there is 100% money back guarantee for two months if you don't think it's a good fit. Please contact me directly to seek a refund.

What's your motivation behind the book?

I want to teach about this topic consistently. I often find materials online that don't receive update, or only applies to a small part of a topic. Sometimes people struggle to find consistent and up-to-date resources to learn from. I want to provide this consistent and up-to-date learning experience. Also, I hope I can support the less fortunate with my projects by giving them the content for free or by having other impacts[16]. Recently, I've found myself fulfilled when teaching others about programming, as it's a meaningful activity I prefer over any 9-to-5 job. I hope to continue this path in the future.

---

[12]https://slack-the-road-to-learn-react.wieruch.com/
[13]https://github.com/the-road-to-graphql/the-road-to-graphql/issues
[14]http://github.com/rwieruch/the-road-to-graphql
[15]https://www.robinwieruch.de/about/
[16]https://www.robinwieruch.de/giving-back-by-learning-react/

How to read this book

No one has ever learned programming from reading a book. Programming is about practical experiences, and conquering challenges to strengthen your skills as a developer long-term. Paradigms like functional programming and object-oriented programming require more extensive practice to use practically. Complex concepts like state management in modern web applications and libraries like React and Express will take more than a weekend to master. You will only learn these concepts by practicing them consistently.

I want this book to provide you with more hands on experience and challenges to help you grow as a programmer. The challenges are meant to create a flow experience, a scenario where challenges are met by your skills and tools. If the book manages to keep the balance of challenging you and respecting your skill level, you might experience a state of flow[17]. I found this insight astonishing when I read about myself, so I hope I can induce it in this book.

Tips & Tricks

As mentioned, there are practical tasks in the book, where be guided to solve problems using the techniques you learned in previous sections. It should let you experience practical uses for the lessons you've learned in these chapters, and provide deeper understanding of the more abstract content for your own projects.

Make sure to internalize each lesson before you continue with the next sections. The book is written in a way that the lessons build on the one before. Your knowledge of these topics scales horizontally using different techniques side-by-side, and vertically using technique-on-technique. Internalizing becomes much easier if you take notes as you move through the lessons. Consider writing down questions that aren't covered in the text so you can look them up afterward. These notes can also become feedback, which I use to improve future versions.

I encourage you to write the code examples out yourself instead of copy/pasting it. Typing out code teaches you how find syntax errors and bugs, so you can fix errors on your own after you've moved on to trying the examples with your own data. Don't get discouraged if you encounter bugs, though. Bugs will usually appear in any application that gets complex enough, but it's acceptable to find them in learning scenarios because you'll have a chance to learn how to fix them.

The materials that follow should be absorbed with an IDE open to type out the examples and observe the output. I will provide additional tools like GraphQL Playground[18] that show how the code examples would function in real-world situations. Try to find time between the lessons to experiment with your own applications and apply the tools you've acquired. Without applying what you've learned in these chapters, you can never master them. If you having difficulty coming up with project ideas, this article[19] could help.

---

[17]https://www.robinwieruch.de/lessons-learned-deep-work-flow/
[18]https://github.com/prisma/graphql-playground
[19]https://www.robinwieruch.de/how-to-learn-framework/

Challenge

I write a lot about lessons I've learned. That's how I got where I am. Since teaching has helped me a lot in my career, I want you to experience the same effects. First, you have to teach yourself. For this book, my challenge is for you to teach others while you are learning. Here are a couple of tips on how to achieve it:

- Write a blog post about a specific topic from this book. It's not about copying and pasting the material, but teaching the topic your own way. Find your own words to explain the concepts, solve a problem, and dive even further into every detail of the topic. You will see how it fills your own knowledge gaps, and how it can open doors for your career in the long term.
- If you are active on social media, consider sharing some tricks you've learned from this book with your friends. You can tweet hot tips about your latest experiment from the book which may be interesting, or show off your skills in web development Facebook groups. Take quality screenshots of your progress so viewers can follow along.
- If you feel confident recording your learning adventures, share your way through the book on Facebook Live, YouTube Live, or Twitch. You might have many people following your live sessions, but you can always post the recording on YouTube afterward. It is a great way to verbalize problems and their solutions. If parts between recordings are take longer, cut the video or use timelapse to show the highlights. Also, consider keeping bugs and mishaps in the videos, as these can be valuable learning tools for viewers who run into the same issues. These are a few tips for a quality video:
- Record the audio in your native language. English is preferable, since it will reach the largest audience.
- Verbalize your thoughts, actions, and the problems you are running into. A visual video is only part of the challenge; the other part is narrating through implementation. The production values don't need to be perfect, and the result should include all the ups and downs of your process. If you run into bugs, embrace the trouble. Try to fix the problem yourself and search online for help. Speak about the problem, and your plan to solve it. This helps others to follow your thought process.
- Check your audio before you record a long video to make sure it records clearly, and make sure the environment has acoustics that won't hinder vocal clarity. Make sure to increase the font size in your IDE or command line terminal so viewers can see any text you'd like to be featured.
- Edit the video before you put it on YouTube. Try to keep it concise for your audience, leaving out the reading passages while summarizing the steps in your own words.

You can reach out to me to promote anything you released. If your content turns out well, I may even include it with future versions of the book as official supplementary materials. I hope you accept these challenges to enhance your learning experience.

GraphQL

When it comes to network requests between client and server applications, REST[20] is one of the most popular choices to connect both worlds. In REST, everything evolves around the idea of having resources that are accessible by URLs. You can read a resource with a HTTP GET request, create a resource with a HTTP POST request, and update or delete it with HTTP PUT and DELETE requests. These are called CRUD (Create, Read, Update, Delete) operations. Resources can be anything from authors, articles, or users. The format for transferring data is not opinionated with REST, but most often people will use JSON for it. In the end, REST enables applications to communicate with each other by using plain HTTP with URLs and HTTP methods.

Code Playground

```
// a RESTful request with HTTP GET
https://api.domain.com/authors/7

// the response in JSON
{
  "id": "7",
  "name": "Robin Wieruch",
  "avatarUrl": "https://domain.com/authors/7",
  "firstName": "Robin",
  "lastName": "Wieruch"
}
```

Though REST was the status quo for a long time, a Facebook technology called GraphQL has recently emerged as a potential successor. The following sections introduce GraphQL's advantages and disadvantages, as well as possible alternatives for developers who need options.

---

[20]https://en.wikipedia.org/wiki/Representational_state_transfer

What is GraphQL?

In short, GraphQL is an open source **query language** created by Facebook, a company that unsurprisingly remains at the pinnacle of web-based software development. Before GraphQL went open source in 2015, Facebook used it internally for their mobile applications since 2012, as an alternative to the common REST architecture. It allows requests for specific data, giving clients more control over what information is sent. This is more difficult with a RESTful architecture because the backend defines what data is available for each resource on each URL, while the frontend always has to request all the information in a resource, even if only a part of it is needed. This problem is called overfetching. In the worst case scenario, an client application has to read multiple resources through multiple network requests. This is overfetching, but also adds the need for waterfall network requests. A query language like GraphQL on the server-side and client-side lets the client decide which data it needs by making a single request to the server. Network usage was reduced dramatically for Facebook's mobile applications as a result, because GraphQL made it more efficient with data transfers.

Facebook open-sourced the GraphQL specification and its reference implementation in JavaScript, and multiple major programming languages implemented the specification have followed since then. The ecosystem around GraphQL is growing horizontally by offering multiple programming languages, but also vertically, with libraries on top of GraphQL like Apollo and Relay.

A GraphQL operation is either a query (read), mutation (write), or subscription (continuous read). Each of those operations is only a string that needs to be constructed according to the GraphQL query language specification. Fortunately, GraphQL is evolving all the time, so there may be other operations in the future.

Once this GraphQL operation reaches the backend application, it can be interpreted against the entire GraphQL schema there, and resolved with data for the frontend application. GraphQL is not opinionated about the network layer, which is often HTTP, nor about the payload format, which is usually JSON. It isn't opinionated about the application architecture at all. It is only a query language.

Code Playground

```
// a GraphQL query
author(id: "7") {
  id
  name
  avatarUrl
  articles(limit: 2) {
    name
    urlSlug
  }
}
```

```
// a GraphQL query result
{
  "data": {
    "author": {
      "id": "7",
      "name": "Robin Wieruch",
      "avatarUrl": "https://domain.com/authors/7",
      "articles": [
        {
          "name": "The Road to learn React",
          "urlSlug": "the-road-to-learn-react"
        },
        {
          "name": "React Testing Tutorial",
          "urlSlug": "react-testing-tutorial"
        }
      ]
    }
  }
}
```

One query already requests multiple resources (author, article), called fields in GraphQL, and only a particular set of nested fields for these fields (name, urlSlug for article), even though the entity itself offers more data in its GraphQL schema (e.g. description, releaseData for article). A RESTful architecture needs at least two waterfall requests to retrieve the author entity and its articles, but the GraphQL query made it happen in one. In addition, the query only selected the necessary fields instead of the whole entity.

That's GraphQL in a nutshell. The server application offers a GraphQL schema, where it defines all available data with its hierarchy and types, and a client application only queries the required data.

GraphQL Advantages

The following list shows the major advantages of using GraphQL in an application.

Declarative Data Fetching

As you've seen, GraphQL embraces declarative data fetching with its queries. The client selects data along with its entities with fields across relationships in one query request. GraphQL decides which fields are needed for its UI, and it almost acts as UI-driven data fetching, like how Airbnb uses it. A search page at Airbnb usually has a search result for homes, experiences, and other domain-specific things. To retrieve all data in one request, a GraphQL query that selects only the part of the data for the UI makes perfect sense. It offers a great separation of concerns: a client knows about the data requirements; the server knows about the data structure and how to resolve the data from a data source (e.g. database, microservice, third-party API).

No Overfetching with GraphQL

There is no overfetching in GraphQL. A mobile client usually overfetches data when there is an identical API as the web client with a RESTful API. With GraphQL, the mobile client can choose a different set of fields, so it can fetch only the information needed for what's onscreen.

GraphQL for React, Angular, Node and Co.

GraphQL is not just exciting for React developers, though. While Facebook showcased GraphQL on a client-side application with React, it is decoupled from any frontend or backend solution. The reference implementation of GraphQL is written in JavaScript, so the usage of GraphQL in Angular, Vue, Express, Hapi, Koa and other JavaScript libraries on the client-side and server-side is possible, and that's just the JavaScript ecosystem. GraphQL does mimic REST's programming language-agnostic interface between two entities, such as client or server.

Who is using GraphQL?

Facebook is the driving company behind the GraphQL specification and reference implementation in JavaScript, but other well-known companies are also it for their applications. They are invested in the GraphQL ecosystem due to the huge demand for modern applications. Beyond Facebook, GraphQL has also been used by these well-known companies:

- GitHub [1][21] [2][22]

---

[21]https://githubengineering.com/the-github-graphql-api/
[22]https://youtu.be/lj41qhtkggU

- Shopify [1][23] [2][24]
- Twitter[25]
- Coursera[26]
- Yelp[27]
- Wordpress[28]
- The New York Times[29]
- Samsara[30]
- and more[31] ...

When GraphQL was developed and open sourced by Facebook, other companies ran into similar issues for their mobile applications. That's how Netflix came up with Falcor[32], an alternative to GraphQL. It shows again that modern applications demanded solutions like GraphQL and Falcor.

Single Source of Truth

The GraphQL schema is the single source of truth in GraphQL applications. It provides a central location, where all available data is described. The GraphQL schema is usually defined on server-side, but clients can read (query) and write (mutation) data based on the schema. Essentially, the server-side application offers all information about what is available on its side, and the client-side application asks for part of it by performing GraphQL queries, or alters part of it using GraphQL mutations.

GraphQL embraces modern Trends

GraphQL embraces modern trends on how applications are built. You may only have one backend application, but multiple clients on the web, phones, and smartwatches depending on its data. GraphQL can be used to connect both worlds, but also to fulfil the requirements of each client application–network usage requirements, nested relationships of data, fetching only the required data–without a dedicated API for each client. On the server side, there might be one backend, but also a group of microservices that offer their specific functionalities. This defines the perfect use for GraphQL schema stitching, which lets you aggregate all functionalities into one GraphQL schema.

---

[23]https://shopifyengineering.myshopify.com/blogs/engineering/solving-the-n-1-problem-for-graphql-through-batching
[24]https://youtu.be/2It9NofBWYg
[25]https://www.youtube.com/watch?v=Baw05hrOUNM
[26]https://youtu.be/F329W0PR6ds
[27]https://youtu.be/bqcRQYTNCOA
[28]https://youtu.be/v3xY-rCsUYM
[29]https://youtu.be/W-u-vZUSnIk
[30]https://youtu.be/g-asVW9JFPw
[31]https://graphql.org/users/
[32]https://github.com/Netflix/falcor

GraphQL Schema Stitching

Schema stitching makes it possible to create one schema out of multiple schemas. Think about a microservices architecture for your backend where microservice handles the business logic and data for a specific domain. In this case, each microservice can define its own GraphQL schema, after which you'd use schema stitching to weave them into one that is accessed by the client. Each microservice can have its own GraphQL endpoint, where one GraphQL API gateway consolidates all schemas into one global schema.

GraphQL Introspection

A GraphQL introspection makes it possible to retrieve the GraphQL schema from a GraphQL API. Since the schema has all the information about data available through the GraphQL API, it is perfect for autogenerating API documentation. It can also be used to mock the GraphQL schema client-side, for testing or retrieving schemas from multiple microservices during schema stitching.

Strongly Typed GraphQL

GraphQL is a strongly typed query language because it is written in the expressive GraphQL Schema Definition Language (SDL). Being strongly-typed makes GraphQL less error prone, can be validated during compile-time and can be used for supportive IDE/editor integrations such as auto-completion and validation.

GraphQL Versioning

In GraphQL there are no API versions as there used to be in REST. In REST it is normal to offer multiple versions of an API (e.g. api.domain.com/v1/, api.domain.com/v2/), because the resources or the structure of the resources may change over time. In GraphQL it is possible to deprecate the API on a field level. Thus a client receives a deprecation warning when querying a deprecated field. After a while, the deprecated field may be removed from the schema when not many clients are using it anymore. This makes it possible to evolve a GraphQL API over time without the need for a versioning.

A growing GraphQL Ecosystem

The GraphQL ecosystem is growing. There are not only integrations for the strongly typed nature of GraphQL for editors and IDEs, but also standalone applications for GraphQL itself. What you may remember as Postman[33] for REST APIs is now GraphiQL[34] or GraphQL Playground[35] for GraphQL

---

[33]https://www.getpostman.com
[34]https://github.com/graphql/graphiql
[35]https://github.com/prismagraphql/graphql-playground

APIs. There are various libraries like Gatsby.js[36], a static website generator for React using GraphQL. With Gatsby.js, you can build a blog engine by providing your blog content at build-time with a GraphQL API, and you have headless content management systems (CMS) (e.g. GraphCMS[37]) for providing (blog) content with a GraphQL API. More than just technical aspects are evolving; there are conferences, meetups, and communities forming for GraphQL, as well as newsletters and podcasts.

Should I go all in GraphQL?

Adopting GraphQL for an existing tech stack is not an "all-in" process. Migrating from a monolithic backend application to a microservice architecture is the perfect time to offer a GraphQL API for new microservices. With multiple microservices, teams can introduce a GraphQL gateway with schema stitching to consolidate a global schema. The API gateway is also used for the monolithic REST application. That's how APIs are bundled into one gateway and migrated to GraphQL.

---

[36]https://www.gatsbyjs.org/
[37]https://graphcms.com

GraphQL Disadvantages

The following topics show you some of the disadvantages for using GraphQL.

GraphQL Query Complexity

People often mistake GraphQL as a replacement for server-side databases, but it's just a query language. Once a query needs to be resolved with data on the server, a GraphQL agnostic implementation usually performs database access. GraphQL isn't opinionated about that. Also, GraphQL doesn't take away performance bottlenecks when you have to access multiple fields (authors, articles, comments) in one query. Whether the request was made in a RESTful architecture or GraphQL, the varied resources and fields still have to be retrieved from a data source. As a result, problems arise when a client requests too many nested fields at once. Frontend developers are not always aware of the work a server-side application has to perform to retrieve data, so there must be a mechanism like maximum query depths, query complexity weighting, avoiding recursion, or persistent queries for stopping inefficient requests from the other side.

GraphQL Rate Limiting

Another problem is rate limiting. Whereas in REST it is simpler to say "we allow only so many resource requests in one day", it becomes difficult to make such a statement for individual GraphQL operations, because it can be everything between a cheap or expensive operation. That's where companies with public GraphQL APIs come up with their specific rate limiting calculations[38] which often boil down to the previously mentioned maximum query depths and query complexity weighting.

GraphQL Caching

Implementing a simplified cache with GraphQL is more complex than implementing it in REST. In REST, resources are accessed with URLs, so you can cache on a resource level because you have the resource URL as identifier. In GraphQL, this becomes complex because each query can be different, even though it operates on the same entity. You may only request just the name of an author in one query, but want to know the email address in the next. That's where you need a more fine-grained cache at field level, which can be difficult to implement. However, most of the libraries built on top of GraphQL offer caching mechanisms out of the box.

---

[38]https://developer.github.com/v4/guides/resource-limitations/

Why not REST?

GraphQL is an alternative to the commonly used RESTful architecture that connects client and server applications. Since REST comes with a URL for each resource, it often leads to inefficient waterfall requests. For instance, imagine you want to fetch an author entity identified by an id, and then you fetch all the articles by this author using the author's id. In GraphQL, this is a single request, which is more efficient. If you only want to fetch the author's articles without the whole author entity, GraphQL lets you to select only the parts you need. In REST, you would overfetch the entire author entity.

Today, client applications are not made for RESTful server applications. The search result on Airbnb's platform shows homes, experiences, and other related things. Homes and experiences would already be their own RESTful resources, so in REST you would have to execute multiple network requests. Using a GraphQL API instead, you can request all entities in one GraphQL query, which can request entities side by side (e.g. homes and experiences) or in nested relationships (e.g. articles of authors). GraphQL shifts the perspective to the client, which decides on the data it needs rather than the server. This is the primary reason GraphQL was invented in the first place, because a Facebook's mobile client required different data than their web client.

There are still cases where REST is a valuable approach for connecting client and server applications, though. Applications are often resource-driven and don't need a flexible query language like GraphQL. However, I recommend you to give GraphQL a shot when developing your next client server architecture to see if it fits your needs.

GraphQL Alternatives

REST is the most popular alternative for GraphQL, as it is still the most common architectures for connecting client and server applications. It became more popular than networking technologies like RPC[39] and SOAP[40] because it used the native features of HTTP, where other protocols like SOAP tried to build their own solution on top of it.

Falcor by Netflix is another alternative, and it was developed at the same time as GraphQL. Netflix ran into similar issues as Facebook, and eventually open-sourced their own solution. There isn't too much traction around Falcor, maybe because GraphQL got so popular, but developers at Netflix have shown great engineering efforts in the past, so it may be worth looking into it.

There are plenty of reasons to adopt GraphQL for your JavaScript applications instead of implementing yet another RESTful architecture. It has many advantages, and plays nicely with modern software architecture. This book will introduce how it can be used for many practical, real-life solutions, so you should have an idea if it works for you by the time you've read through the chapters.

[39]https://en.wikipedia.org/wiki/Remote_procedure_call
[40]https://simple.wikipedia.org/wiki/SOAP_(protocol)

Apollo

Finding the right solution a given problem is not always simple, and web applications build with GraphQL are a good example of how changing times make for constantly evolving challenges. Moreover, evolving challenges create a scenario where the solutions must also evolve, so even the number of choices becomes a task. This article will decipher the pros and cons of one such solution: Apollo for GraphQL, with alternative solutions in case you decide against it.

GraphQL is only the query language that has a reference implementation in JavaScript, and Apollo builds its ecosystem on top to make GraphQL available for a wider audience. This includes the client-side as well as the server-side, because they provide a large ecosystem of libraries for both. The libraries provide an intermediate layer too: Apollo Engine, which is a GraphQL gateway. Essentially there's a reason Apollo is one of the most popular choices for using GraphQL in JavaScript applications

Apollo Advantages

The following topics show you some of the advantages of using Apollo, to provide a well-rounded pro and con list. Feel free to contact me if you think anything is missing from either list.

Apollo's Ecosystem

While GraphQL is in its early stages, the Apollo ecosystem offers solutions for many of its challenges. Beyond that we can see how much the ecosystem is growing, because the company announces an update for Apollo or another library that can be used with Apollo's tech stack at every other technology conference. Apollo isn't just covering GraphQL, though; they also have effort invested in REST interfaces for backward compatibility to RESTful architectures. This even takes GraphQL beyond the network layer and remote data, offering a state management solution for local data, too.

The Company and Community behind Apollo

The company behind Apollo is pouring lots of resources into its success. They are also active in open source, offering in-depth articles about their products, supported by an established presence at the conferences. In general, the GraphQL ecosystem seems to be in good shape for the future[41]. The community behind GraphQL is growing, as more developers are adopt it and use Apollo for client and server-side JavaScript applications.

Who is using Apollo?

Tech-savvy companies are taking advantage of Apollo already. Many were familiar with the popular Meteor framework before, but new and extremely popular companies like Airbnb and Twitch are using it. These are just a few of their stories:

- Airbnb [1][42] [2][43]
- Twitch[44]
- The New York Times[45]
- KLM[46]
- Medium[47]

---

[41]https://techcrunch.com/2018/05/15/prisma
[42]https://medium.com/airbnb-engineering/reconciling-graphql-and-thrift-at-airbnb-a97e8d290712
[43]https://youtu.be/oBOSJFkrNqc
[44]https://about.sourcegraph.com/graphql/twitch-our-graphql-transformation
[45]https://open.nytimes.com/the-new-york-times-now-on-apollo-b9a78a5038c
[46]https://youtu.be/T2njjXHdKqw
[47]https://www.infoq.com/news/2018/05/medium-reactjs-graphql-migration

Apollo's Documentation

While Apollo continues to evolve, the team and community behind it keeps the documentation up to date, and they have plenty of insight about how to build applications. In fact, they cover so many areas it can be overwhelming for beginners.

Apollo Libraries

Apollo offers plenty of libraries for implementing an effective GraphQL tech stack for JavaScript applications, and their libraries are open-sourced to be more manageable. For instance, Apollo Link[48] provides an API for chaining different features into a GraphQL control flow. This makes it possible for automatic network retries or RESTful API endpoints instead of a GraphQL endpoints (the endpoints can be used together. too).

Apollo is also offering exchangeable libraries which can be seen in the Apollo Client Cache. The Apollo Client itself is not biased toward its cache, where the data is stored, as any cache advertised by Apollo or its community works. There are already caches available that can be used to setup a Apollo Client instance.

Apollo's Features

Apollo comes with built-in features to pull all the complexity out of applications and handle the intersection between client and server applications. For instance, Apollo Client caches requests, which are not made twice when the result is already in the cache. The function provides a performance boost for applications, saving valuable network traffic. Also, Apollo Client normalizes data, so nested data from a GraphQL query is stored in a normalized data structure in the Apollo Client Cache. Data can be read from the Apollo Client Cache by an identifier, without looking up a "article" entity in an "author" entity. Beyond caching and normalization, Apollo Client comes with many more features like error management, support for pagination and optimistic UI, prefetching of data, and connection of the data layer (Apollo Client) to the view layer (e.g. React).

Interoperability with other Frameworks

One of Apollo's libraries makes it possible to connect Apollo Client to React. Just like libraries like Redux and MobX, the React-Apollo library has higher-order and render prop components to connect both worlds. However, there are other libraries out there that bridge not only Apollo Client to React, but also Apollo to Angular or Apollo to Vue. That's what makes Apollo Client view layer agnostic, which is great for the growing JavaScript ecosystem.

Apollo is also library agnostic on the server-side, and it offers several solutions to connect with Node.js libraries. Apollo Server for Express.js is one of the most popular choices among developers and companies, and there are other solutions for Koa and Hapi on Node.js for Apollo Server as well.

---

[48]https://www.apollographql.com/docs/link/

Modern Data Handling with Apollo

Remember back when we had to trigger data fetching in a component's lifecycle methods imperatively? Apollo Client solves this, because its data queries are declarative. React often employs a higher-order component or render prop to trigger a query automatically when a component renders. The GraphQL mutations are triggered imperatively, but that's only because a higher-order component or render prop grants access to the function which executes the mutation (e.g. on a button click). Essentially, Apollo embraces declarative programming over imperative programming.

Modern State Management with GraphQL and Apollo

With the rise of GraphQL in JavaScript applications, state management entered another state of confusion. Even though lots of pain points are eliminated using a GraphQL library like Apollo Client, since it takes care of state management for remote data, some developers are confused about where to put state management libraries like Redux or MobX now. However, it can be made simple using these libraries for local data only and leaving the remote data to Apollo. There is no longer a need to fetch data with asynchronous actions in Redux, so it becomes a predictable state container for all the remaining application state (e.g. local data/view data/UI data). In fact, the remaining application state may be simple enough to be managed by React's local state instead of Redux.

Meanwhile, Apollo has already released their own solution to manage local state–which is supposed to be managed by React's local state, Redux or MobX–by embracing GraphQL for everything. The Apollo Link State library lets us manage local data with GraphQL operations, except on the client-side in Apollo Client. It's Apollo saying: "You don't need any other state management library, we take care of your data." These are exciting times for developing JavaScript applications.

Convenient Development Experience

Using Apollo for JavaScript applications is becoming easier every day. The community is pushing out tools for implementation. There are development tools available as browser extensions, third-party tools to perform GraphQL operations such as GraphiQL, and libraries to simplify developing Apollo applications. For instance, the Apollo Boost library provides an almost zero-configuration Apollo Client setup to get started with GraphQL for client-side applications. Apollo takes away all the boilerplate implementation that comes with GraphQL reference implementation in JavaScript.

Apollo Disadvantages

The following topics show you some of the disadvantages of using Apollo, to provide a well-rounded pro and con list. Feel free to contact me if you think anything is missing from either list.

Bleeding Edge

GraphQL is in its early stages. Apollo users and all early GraphQL adopters are working with brand new technology. The Apollo team is developing a rich ecosystem around GraphQL, providing the basics as well as advanced features like caching and monitoring. This comes with pitfalls, however, mainly because everything isn't set in stone. There are sporadic changes that can pose challenges when you are updating GraphQL-related libraries. In contrast, some libraries in GraphQL might be more conservative than the Apollo team, but the features usually aren't as powerful.

The ability for developers to continue learning is also hindered by fast-pace development. Tutorials for GraphQL and Apollo are sometimes outdated, and finding an answer may require external resources. The same is true for most new technology, though.

Under Construction

The Apollo team and community implements many new features in a rapid pace, but going so fast comes with a price. Searching for solutions often leads to GitHub, because there is little other information on the subject. While you may indeed find a GitHub issue for your problem, there is often no solution for it.

Rapid development also comes with the price of neglecting obsolete earlier versions. In my experience, people seemed confused when Apollo abandoned Redux[49] as their internal state management solution. Apollo isn't opinionated about how Redux should be used side by side with it, but since it has been abandoned as internal state management solution, many people didn't know how to proceed when Apollo 2.0 was released. I think the team behind Apollo might be struggling to keep up with the fast-paced GraphQL ecosystem, and it's not always easy to heed all voices in open source development.

It is Bold and Fashionable

Apollo is bold, because it is moving beyond being a network layer ecosystem between client and server for GraphQL in JavaScript, but positioning itself as the data management solution of tomorrow. It connects client and backend applications with GraphQL, apollo-link-rest for RESTful APIs, and apollo-link-state for local state management. Some experts are skeptical about the "GraphQL everything" mentality, but time will tell if it corners that market.

---

[49]https://github.com/apollographql/apollo-client/issues/2593

Apollo is fashionable, because it keeps up with the latest trends. In React, the latest trend was render prop components. Because of this, and arguably the benefits of render prop components over higher-order components, the React Apollo library introduced render prop components[50] next to higher-order components. It was a smart move to offer multiple solutions since both higher-order and render prop components come with their own sets of pros and cons. However, Apollo does advocate for render props over higher-order components, and it's not clear if this was hype-driven development or marketing or if they truly believe that this is the way of the future. Render props are relatively new in React, so it will take time for developers to realize they come with their own pitfalls (see: higher-order components). I have seen React applications become too verbose by using multiple render prop components in one React component, even though one render prop didn't depend on another render prop, rather than having those co-located to the React component by using higher-order components. After all, Apollo offers both solutions, render props and higher-order components, so the developer decides on a case by case basis for their applications. It's a good sign for users that the Apollo team is keeping up with the recent trends from other libraries, and not confining themselves to a bubble.

Missing Competition

Most of these concerns are about the newness of GraphQL, concerns that could be applied to virtually any other open source solution in the same field. One major concern, though, is the missing competition in the GraphQL in JavaScript domain. A couple of alternatives to Apollo are listed in the next section, but they are limited compared to the Apollo ecosystem. While it is possible to write your own library for GraphQL (e.g. a simple GraphQL in React client[51]), not many developers have attempted it yet. Some problems solved by Apollo are not trivial, but I think competition would be a healthy push for GraphQL in JavaScript ecosystem. There is huge potential in GraphQL now, and open source developers would be wise to take advantage.

---

[50]https://www.robinwieruch.de/react-render-props-pattern/
[51]https://github.com/rwieruch/react-graphql-client

Apollo Alternatives for JavaScript, React and Node.js

Some disadvantages stem from using GraphQL as an alternative to a RESTful-driven architecture. There are some alternatives for Apollo Client and Apollo Server that can consume GraphQL APIs in JavaScript. The following list should grant insights about solutions in the JavaScript ecosystem, used for React on the client-side and Node.js on the server-side.

Apollo Client Alternatives for React

When it comes to Apollo Client[52] for React, Angular, Vue, or similar applications, there are several alternatives to check out. Like Apollo, these come with their own advantages and disadvantages.

- plain HTTP request: Even though sophisticated GraphQL libraries can be used to perform your GraphQL operations, GraphQL itself isn't opinionated about the network layer. So it is possible for you to use GraphQL with plain HTTP methods using only one endpoint with an opinionated payload structure for GraphQL queries and mutations.
- Relay[53]: Relay is Facebook's library for consuming GraphQL on the client-side in React applications. It was among the first GraphQL client libraries before Apollo emerged.
- urql[54]: urql is a GraphQL client library from Formidable Labs for consuming GraphQL in React applications. It was open-sourced as minimalistic alternative to the growing Apollo behemoth.
- graphql.js[55]: graphql.js shouldn't be mistaken for the GraphQL reference implementation. It's a simple GraphQL client for applications without powerful libraries such as Vue, React, or Angular.
- AWS Amplify - GraphQL Client[56]: The AWS Amplify family offers libraries for cloud-enabled applications. One of the modules is a GraphQL client used for general GraphQL servers or AWS AppSync APIs.

Apollo Server Alternatives for Node.js

When it comes to Apollo Server[57] for Node.js with Express, Koa, Hapi or something else, there are several alternatives you can checkout. Obviously these come with their own advantages and disadvantages whereas these things are not covered here.

- express-graphql[58]: The library provides a lower-level API to connect GraphQL layers to Express middleware. It takes the pure GraphQL.js reference implementation for defining GraphQL schemas, where Apollo Server simplifies it for developers.

---

[52]https://github.com/apollographql/apollo-client
[53]https://github.com/facebook/relay
[54]https://github.com/FormidableLabs/urql
[55]https://github.com/f/graphql.js/
[56]https://github.com/aws/aws-amplify
[57]https://github.com/apollographql/apollo-server
[58]https://github.com/graphql/express-graphql

- graphql-yoga[59]: A fully-featured GraphQL Server with focus on easy setup, performance & great developer experience. It builds on top of other GraphQL libraries to take away even more boilerplate code from you.

There are many reasons to use Apollo and its striving ecosystem for JavaScript applications, when you want to use a GraphQL interface over a RESTful interface. Their libraries are framework agnostic, so they can be used with a wide variety of frameworks on the client-side like React, Angular, Vue, and server-side applications like Express, Koa, Hapi.

[59]https://github.com/prisma/graphql-yoga

GraphQL Setup, Tools and APIs

Step-by-step is often the easiest way learn something new, so it's fortunate that learning GraphQL in JavaScript teaches both the client and the server-side of an application. Seeing both sides of the web transactions is useful, but the catch is you have to learn two environments. The step-by-step mentality can be difficult to apply here, so I encourage beginners to start with a client-side application by consuming a third-party GraphQL API before the server side, which uses a GraphQL server.

GitHub[60] is one of the first major tech brands to adopt GraphQL. They even managed to release[61] a public GraphQL API (official documentation)[62], which is quite popular among developers, because most are familiar enough with GitHub from using it for their own projects.

In this chapter, I hope to cover everything you need to get started with GitHub's GraphQL API, and learning to use GraphQL in JavaScript from a client-side perspective by consuming their API. You should gain understanding about GitHub's terminology, and how to consume account data using its GraphQL API. There are a few applications we will implement with this GraphQL API from a client perspective, so it makes sense to invest time into this section to avoid any fundamental mistakes. Afterward, we will transition to the server-side by implementing our own GraphQL server.

---

[60]https://github.com
[61]https://githubengineering.com/the-github-graphql-api
[62]https://developer.github.com/v4

Feeding the API with Data on GitHub

If you don't have an account on GitHub yet, and don't know much about its ecosystem, follow this official GitHub Learning Lab[63]. If you want to dive deeper into Git and its essential commands, checkout this guide[64] about it. This might come in handy if you decide to share projects with others on GitHub in the future. It is a good way to showcase a development portfolio to potential clients or hiring companies.

For our interactions with GitHub's GraphQL API, you will use your own account with information to read/write from/to this data. Before that, complete your GitHub profile by providing additional information so you can recognize it later when it is read by the API.

Exercises:

- Create a GitHub account if you don't have one
- Provide additional information for your GitHub profile

GitHub Repositories

You can also create repositories on GitHub. In the words of their official glossary: *"A repository is the most basic element of GitHub. They're easiest to imagine as a project's folder. A repository contains all of the project files (including documentation), and stores each file's revision history. Repositories can have multiple collaborators and can be either public or private."* GitHub's glossary[65] will explain the key terms–repository, issue, clone, fork, push–which are necessary to follow along with the upcoming chapters to learn about GraphQL. Basically a repository is the place for application source code that can be shared with others. I encourage you to put a few of your projects into GitHub repositories, so you can access them all later with what you've learned about their GraphQL API.

If you don't have any projects to upload, you can always 'fork' repositories from other GitHub users and work on copies of them. A fork is basically a clone of a repository where you can add changes without altering the original. There are many public repositories on GitHub that can be cloned to your local machine or forked to your list so you can get an understanding of the mechanic through experimentation. For example, if you visit my GitHub profile[66], you can see all my public repositories, though not all of these are mine, because some of them are just forks of others. Feel free to fork these repositories if you'd like to use them as practice, and if you'd like them to be accessible via GitHub's GraphQL API from your own account.

---

[63]https://lab.github.com/
[64]https://www.robinwieruch.de/git-essential-commands/
[65]https://help.github.com/articles/github-glossary/
[66]https://github.com/rwieruch

Exercises:

- Create/Fork a couple of GitHub repositories, and verify that they show in your account as copies. Copies are indicated by the username that proceeds the repository name in all its titles; for example, a repo called *OriginalAuthor/TestRepo* would be renamed to *YourUser-Name/TestRepo* once you've forked it.

Paginated Data

GitHub's GraphQL API allows you to request multiple repositories at once, which is useful for pagination. Pagination is a programming mechanic invented to work with large lists of items. For example, imagine you have more than a hundred repositories in your GitHub account, but your UI only only shows ten of them. Transferring the whole list across the wire for each request is impractical and inefficient, because only a subset is needed at a time, which pagination allows.

Using pagination with GitHub's GraphQL API lets you adjust the numbers to your own needs, so make sure to adjust the numbers (e.g. limit, offset) to your personal requirements (e.g. available repositories of your GitHub account or available repositories of a GitHub organization). You at least want to have enough repositories in your collection to see the pagination feature in action, so recommend more than twenty (20), assuming each page will display ten (10), or use five(5) repositories when displaying two (2.)

Issues and Pull Requests

Once you dive deeper into GitHub's GraphQL API and you start to request nested relationships (e.g. issues of repositories, pull requests of repositories), make sure that the repositories have a few issues or pull requests. This is so you'll see something when we implement the feature to show all the issues in a repository. It might be better to request repositories from a GitHub organization where there will be plenty of issues and pull requests.

Exercises:

- Read more about the different terms in GitHub's glossary[67]. Consider these questions:
    - What is a GitHub organization and GitHub user?
    - What are repositories, issues and pull requests?
    - What are GitHub repository stars and GitHub repository watchers?
- Create or fork enough repositories to use the pagination feature.
- Create pull requests and issues in a few of your GitHub repositories.

---

[67]https://help.github.com/articles/github-glossary/

Read/Write Data with GitHub's Personal Access Token

To use GitHub's GraphQL API, you need to generate a personal access token on their website. The access token authorizes users to interact with data, to read and write it under your username. Follow their step by step instructions[68] to obtain the personal access token, and be sure to check the necessary scopes (permissions) for it, as you will need them to implement a well-rounded GitHub client later.

---

[68]https://help.github.com/articles/creating-a-personal-access-token-for-the-command-line

☑ **repo**	Full control of private repositories
☑ repo:status	Access commit status
☑ repo_deployment	Access deployment status
☑ public_repo	Access public repositories
☑ repo:invite	Access repository invitations
☑ **admin:org**	Full control of orgs and teams
☑ write:org	Read and write org and team membership
☑ read:org	Read org and team membership
☐ **admin:public_key**	Full control of user public keys
☐ write:public_key	Write user public keys
☐ read:public_key	Read user public keys
☐ **admin:repo_hook**	Full control of repository hooks
☐ write:repo_hook	Write repository hooks
☐ read:repo_hook	Read repository hooks
☐ **admin:org_hook**	Full control of organization hooks
☐ **gist**	Create gists
☑ **notifications**	Access notifications
☑ **user**	Update all user data
☑ read:user	Read all user profile data
☑ user:email	Access user email addresses (read-only)
☑ user:follow	Follow and unfollow users
☐ **delete_repo**	Delete repositories
☐ **write:discussion**	Read and write team discussions
☐ read:discussion	Read team discussions
☐ **admin:gpg_key**	Full control of user gpg keys (Developer Preview)
☐ write:gpg_key	Write user gpg keys
☐ read:gpg_key	Read user gpg keys

Later, the personal access token can be used to interact with GitHub's GraphQL API. Be careful not to share these authorizations with any third parties.

Interacting with GitHub's GraphQL API

There are two common ways to interact with the GitHub GraphQL API without writing any source code for it. First, you can use GitHub's GraphQL Explorer[69]. You only need to sign up with your GitHub account to perform a query or mutation to their GraphQL API, and its a good way to simplify you first experience. Second, you can use a generic client in the form of an application. GraphiQL is a client that makes GraphQL requests as integration or as a standalone application. The former can be accomplished by setting up GraphiQL directly in your application[70]; the latter may be more convenient for you by using GraphiQL as standalone application[71]. It's a lightweight shell around GraphiQL that can be downloaded and installed manually or by the command line.

GitHub's GraphQL Explorer knows about your credentials, since you need to sign up using it, but the GraphiQL application needs to know about the personal access token you created. You can add it in your HTTP header for every request in the headers configuration.

In the next step, we add a new header with a name and value to your GraphiQL configuration. To communicate with GitHub's GraphQL API, fill in the header name with "Authorization" and the header value with "bearer [your personal access token]". Save this new header for your GraphiQL application. Finally, you are ready to make requests to GitHub's GraphQL API with your GraphiQL application.

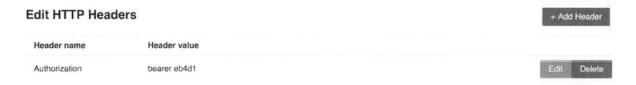

If you use your own GraphiQL application, you'll need to provide the GraphQL endpoint for GitHub's GraphQL API: `https://api.github.com/graphql`. For GitHub's GraphQL API, use the POST HTTP method[72] for queries and mutations, and to transfer data as a payload to your GraphQL endpoint.

This section provided you with two ways to interact with GitHub's GraphQL API. Where GitHub's GraphQL Explorer can only be used for GitHub's API, GraphiQL integrated into an application or standalone can be used for any GraphQL API. The difference is that it requires a bit more setup. The GitHub GraphQL Explorer is really nothing more than a hosted standalone GraphiQL application tailored to use GitHub's GraphQL API.

---

[69]https://developer.github.com/v4/explorer/

[70]https://github.com/skevy/graphiql-app

[71]https://github.com/skevy/graphiql-app

[72]https://en.wikipedia.org/wiki/Hypertext_Transfer_Protocol#Request_methods

After you've set up GitHub to use their GraphQL API to learn about GraphQL, you should be ready to implement your first GraphQL client interactions. Follow along and create your first GraphQL client-side application with the tools you have just set up but also with React.

GraphQL Fundamentals

Before we start to build full-fledged GraphQL applications, on the client- and server-side, let's explore GraphQL with the tools we have installed in the previous sections. You can either use GraphiQL or the GitHub's GraphQL Explorer. In the following, you will learn about GraphQL's fundamentals by executing your first GraphQL queries, mutations and even by exploring features such as pagination, in context of GitHub's GraphQL API.

GraphQL Operation: Query

In this section, you will interact with the GitHub API using queries and mutations without React, so you can use your GraphiQL application or GitHub's GraphQL Explorer to make GraphQL query requests to GitHub's API. Both tools should be authorized to make request using a personal access token. On the left-hand side of your GraphiQL application, you can fill in GraphQL queries and mutations. Add the following query to request data about yourself.

GitHub GraphQL Explorer

```
{
  viewer {
    name
    url
  }
}
```

The `viewer` object can be used to request data about the currently authorized user. Since you are authorized by your personal access token, it should show data about your account. The `viewer` is an **object** in GraphQL terms. Objects hold data about an entity. This data is accessed using a so-called **field** in GraphQL. Fields are used to ask for specific properties in objects. For instance, the `viewer` object exposes a wide range of fields. Two fields for the object—`name` and `url`—were used in the query. In its most basic form, a query is just objects and fields, and objects can also be called fields.

Once you run the query in GraphiQL, you should see output similar to the one below, where your name and url are in the place of mine:

GitHub GraphQL Explorer

```
{
  "data": {
    "viewer": {
      "name": "Robin Wieruch",
      "url": "https://github.com/rwieruch"
    }
  }
}
```

Congratulations, you have performed your first query to access fields from your own user data. Now, let's see how to request data from another source other than yourself, like a public GitHub organization. To specify a GitHub organization, you can pass an **argument** to fields:

GitHub GraphQL Explorer

```
{
  organization(login: "the-road-to-learn-react") {
    name
    url
  }
}
```

When using GitHub's API, an organization is identified with a `login`. If you have used GitHub before, you might know this is a part of the organization URL:

Code Playground

```
https://github.com/the-road-to-learn-react
```

By providing a `login` to identify the organization, you can request data about it. In this example, you have specified two fields to access data about the organization's `name` and `url`. The request should return something similar to the following output:

GitHub GraphQL Explorer

```
{
  "data": {
    "organization": {
      "name": "The Road to learn React",
      "url": "https://github.com/the-road-to-learn-react"
    }
  }
}
```

In the previous query you passed an argument to a field. As you can imagine, you can add arguments to various fields using GraphQL. It grants a great deal of flexibility for structuring queries, because you can make specifications to requests on a field level. Also, arguments can be of different types. With the organization above, you provided an argument with the type `String`, though you can also pass types like enumerations with a fixed set of options, integers, or booleans.

If you ever wanted to request data about two identical objects, you would have to use **aliases** in GraphQL. The following query wouldn't be possible, because GraphQL wouldn't know how to resolve the two organization objects in a result:

GitHub GraphQL Explorer

```
{
  organization(login: "the-road-to-learn-react") {
    name
    url
  }
  organization(login: "facebook") {
    name
    url
  }
}
```

You'd see an error such as `Field 'organization' has an argument conflict`. Using aliases, you can resolve the result into two blocks:

GitHub GraphQL Explorer

```
{
  book: organization(login: "the-road-to-learn-react") {
    name
    url
  }
  company: organization(login: "facebook") {
    name
    url
  }
}
```

The result should be similar to the following:

GitHub GraphQL Explorer

```
{
  "data": {
    "book": {
      "name": "The Road to learn React",
      "url": "https://github.com/the-road-to-learn-react"
    },
    "company": {
      "name": "Facebook",
      "url": "https://github.com/facebook"
    }
  }
}
```

Next, imagine you want to request multiple fields for both organizations. Re-typing all the fields for each organization would make the query repetitive and verbose, so we'll use **fragments** to extract the query's reusable parts. Fragments are especially useful when your query becomes deeply nested and uses lots of shared fields.

GitHub GraphQL Explorer

```
{
  book: organization(login: "the-road-to-learn-react") {
    ...sharedOrganizationFields
  }
  company: organization(login: "facebook") {
    ...sharedOrganizationFields
  }
}

fragment sharedOrganizationFields on Organization {
  name
  url
}
```

As you can see, you have to specify on which **type** of object the fragment should be used. In this case, it is the type Organization, which is a custom type defined by GitHub's GraphQL API. This is how you use fragments to extract and reuse parts of your queries. At this point, you might want to open "Docs" on the right side of your GraphiQL application. The documentation gives you access to the GraphQL **schema**. A schema exposes the GraphQL API used by your GraphiQL application, which is Github's GraphQL API in this case. It defines the GraphQL **graph** that is accessible via the GraphQL API using queries and mutations. Since it is a graph, objects and fields can be deeply nested in it, which we'll certainly encounter as we move along.

Since we're exploring queries and not mutations at the moment, select "Query" in the "Docs" sidebar. Afterward, traverse the objects and fields of the graph, explore their optional arguments. By clicking them, you can see the accessible fields within those objects in the graph. Some fields are common GraphQL types such as String, Int and Boolean, while some other types are **custom types** like the Organization type we used. In addition, you can see whether arguments are required when requesting fields on an object. It can be identified by the exclamation point. For instance, a field with a String! argument requires that you pass in a String argument whereas a field with a String argument doesn't require you to pass it.

In the previous queries, you provided arguments that identified an organization to your fields; but you **inlined these arguments** in your query. Think about a query like a function, where it's important to provide dynamic arguments to it. That's where the **variable** in GraphQL comes in, as it allows arguments to be extracted as variables from queries. Here's how an organization's login argument can be extracted to a dynamic variable:

GitHub GraphQL Explorer

```
query ($organization: String!) {
  organization(login: $organization) {
    name
    url
  }
}
```

It defines the `organization` argument as a variable using the $ sign. Also, the argument's type is defined as a `String`. Since the argument is required to fulfil the query, the `String` type has an exclamation point.

In the "Query Variables" panel, the variables would have the following content for providing the `organization` variable as argument for the query:

GitHub GraphQL Explorer

```
{
  "organization": "the-road-to-learn-react"
}
```

Essentially, variables can be used to create dynamic queries. Following the best practices in GraphQL, we don't need manual string interpolation to structure a dynamic query later on. Instead, we provide a query that uses variables as arguments, which are available when the query is sent as a request to the GraphQL API. You will see both implementations later in your React application.

Sidenote: You can also define a **default variable** in GraphQL. It has to be a non-required argument, or an error will occur about a **nullable variable** or **non-null variable**. For learning about default variables, we'll make the `organization` argument non-required by omitting the exclamation point. Afterwards, it can be passed as a default variable.

GitHub GraphQL Explorer

```
query ($organization: String = "the-road-to-learn-react") {
  organization(login: $organization) {
    name
    url
  }
}
```

Try to execute the previous query with two sets of variables: once with the `organization` variable that's different from the default variable, and once without defining the `organization` variable.

Now, let's take a step back to examine the structure of the GraphQL query. After you introduced variables, you encountered the `query` statement in your query structure for the first time. Before, you used the **shorthand version of a query** by omitting the `query` statement, but the `query` statement has to be there now that it's using variables. Try the following query without variables, but with the query statement, to verify that the long version of a query works.

GitHub GraphQL Explorer

```
query {
  organization(login: "the-road-to-learn-react") {
    name
    url
  }
}
```

While it's not the shorthand version of the query, it still returns the same data as before, which is the desired outcome. The query statement is also called **operation type** in GraphQL lingua. For instance, it can also be a `mutation` statement. In addition to the operation type, you can also define an **operation name**.

GitHub GraphQL Explorer

```
query OrganizationForLearningReact {
  organization(login: "the-road-to-learn-react") {
    name
    url
  }
}
```

Compare it to anonymous and named functions in your code. A **named query** provides a certain level of clarity about what you want to achieve with the query in a declarative way, and it helps with debugging multiple queries, so it should be used when you want to implement an application. Your final query, without showing the variables panel again, could look like the following:

GitHub GraphQL Explorer

```
query OrganizationForLearningReact($organization: String!) {
  organization(login: $organization) {
    name
    url
  }
}
```

So far you've only accessed one object, an organization with a couple of its fields. The GraphQL schema implements a whole graph, so let's see how to access a **nested object** from within the graph with a query. It's not much different from before:

GitHub GraphQL Explorer

```
query OrganizationForLearningReact(
  $organization: String!,
  $repository: String!
) {
  organization(login: $organization) {
    name
    url
    repository(name: $repository) {
      name
    }
  }
}
```

Provide a second variable to request a specific repository of the organization:

GitHub GraphQL Explorer

```
{
  "organization": "the-road-to-learn-react",
  "repository": "the-road-to-learn-react-chinese"
}
```

The organization that teaches about React has translated versions of its content, and one of its repositories teaches students about React in simplified Chinese. Fields in GraphQL can be nested objects again, and you have queried two associated objects from the graph. The requests are made on a graph that can have a deeply nested structure. While exploring the "Docs" sidebar in GraphiQL before, you might have seen that you can jump from object to object in the graph.

A **directive** can be used to query data from your GraphQL API in a more powerful way, and they can be applied to fields and objects. Below, we use two types of directives: an **include directive**, which includes the field when the Boolean type is set to true; and the **skip directive**, which excludes it instead. With these directives, you can apply conditional structures to your shape of query. The following query showcases the include directive, but you can substitute it with the skip directive to achieve the opposite effect:

GitHub GraphQL Explorer

```
query OrganizationForLearningReact(
  $organization: String!,
  $repository: String!,
  $withFork: Boolean!
) {
  organization(login: $organization) {
    name
    url
    repository(name: $repository) {
      name
      forkCount @include(if: $withFork)
    }
  }
}
```

Now you can decide whether to include the information for the forkCount field based on provided variables.

GitHub GraphQL Explorer

```
{
  "organization": "the-road-to-learn-react",
  "repository": "the-road-to-learn-react-chinese",
  "withFork": true
}
```

The query in GraphQL gives you all you need to read data from a GraphQL API. The last section may have felt like a whirlwind of information, so these exercises provide additional practice until you feel comfortable.

Exercises:

- Read more about the Query in GraphQL[73].
- Explore GitHub's query schema by using the "Docs" sidebar in GraphiQL.
- Create several queries to request data from GitHub's GraphQL API using the following features:
    - objects and fields
    - nested objects
    - fragments
    - arguments and variables
    - operation names
    - directives

---

[73]http://graphql.org/learn/queries

GraphQL Operation: Mutation

This section introduces the GraphQL mutation. It complements the GraphQL query because it is used for writing data instead of reading it. The mutation shares the same principles as the query: it has fields and objects, arguments and variables, fragments and operation names, as well as directives and nested objects for the returned result. With mutations you can specify data as fields and objects that should be returned after it 'mutates' into something acceptable. Before you start making your first mutation, be aware that you are using live GitHub data, so if you follow a person on GitHub using your experimental mutation, you will follow this person for real. Fortunately this sort of behavior is encouraged on Github.

In this section, you will star a repository on GitHub, the same one you used a query to request before, using a mutation from GitHub's API[74]. You can find the addStar mutation in the "Docs" sidebar. The repository is a project for teaching developers about the fundamentals of React, so starring it should prove useful.

You can visit the repository[75] to see if you've given a star to the repository already. We want an unstarred repository so we can star it using a mutation. Before you can star a repository, you need to know its identifier, which can be retrieved by a query:

GitHub GraphQL Explorer

```
query {
  organization(login: "the-road-to-learn-react") {
    name
    url
    repository(name: "the-road-to-learn-react") {
      id
      name
    }
  }
}
```

In the results for the query in GraphiQL, you should see the identifier for the repository:

Code Playground

```
MDEwOlJlcG9zaXRvcnk2MzM1MjkwNw==
```

Before using the identifier as a variable, you can structure your mutation in GraphiQL the following way:

---

[74]https://developer.github.com/v4/mutation/addstar
[75]https://github.com/the-road-to-learn-react/the-road-to-learn-react

GitHub GraphQL Explorer

```
mutation AddStar($repositoryId: ID!) {
  addStar(input: { starrableId: $repositoryId }) {
    starrable {
      id
      viewerHasStarred
    }
  }
}
```

The mutation's name is given by GitHub's API: `addStar`. You are required to pass it the `starrableId` as `input` to identify the repository; otherwise, the GitHub server won't know which repository to star with the mutation. In addition, the mutation is a named mutation: `AddStar`. It's up to you to give it any name. Last but not least, you can define the return values of the mutation by using objects and fields again. It's identical to a query. Finally, the variables tab provides the variable for the mutation you retrieved with the last query:

GitHub GraphQL Explorer

```
{
  "repositoryId": "MDEwOlJlcG9zaXRvcnk2MzM1MjkwNw=="
}
```

Once you execute the mutation, the result should look like the following. Since you specified the return values of your mutation using the `id` and `viewerHasStarred` fields, you should see them in the result.

GitHub GraphQL Explorer

```
{
  "data": {
    "addStar": {
      "starrable": {
        "id": "MDEwOlJlcG9zaXRvcnk2MzM1MjkwNw==",
        "viewerHasStarred": true
      }
    }
  }
}
```

The repository is starred now. It's visible in the result, but you can verify it in the repository on GitHub[76]. Congratulations, you made your first mutation.

---

[76]https://github.com/the-road-to-learn-react/the-road-to-learn-react

Exercises:

- Read more about the Mutation in GraphQL[77]
- Explore GitHub's mutations by using the "Docs" sidebar in GraphiQL
- Find GitHub's addStar mutation in the "Docs" sidebar in GraphiQL
    - Check its possible fields for returning a response
- Create a few other mutations for this or another repository such as:
    - Unstar repository
    - Watch repository
- Create two named mutations side by side in the GraphiQL panel and execute them
- Read more about the schema and types[78]
    - Make yourself a picture of it, but don't worry if you don't understand everything yet

---

[77]http://graphql.org/learn/queries/#mutations
[78]http://graphql.org/learn/schema

GraphQL Pagination

This is where we return to the concept of **pagination** mentioned in the first chapter. Imagine you have a list of repositories in your GitHub organization, but you only want to retrieve a few of them to display in your UI. It could take ages to fetch a list of repositories from a large organization. In GraphQL, you can request paginated data by providing arguments to a **list field**, such as an argument that says how many items you are expecting from the list.

GitHub GraphQL Explorer

```
query OrganizationForLearningReact {
  organization(login: "the-road-to-learn-react") {
    name
    url
    repositories(first: 2) {
      edges {
        node {
          name
        }
      }
    }
  }
}
```

A `first` argument is passed to the `repositories` list field that specifies how many items from the list are expected in the result. The query shape doesn't need to follow the `edges` and `node` structure, but it's one of a few solutions to define paginated data structures and lists with GraphQL. Actually, it follows the interface description of Facebook's GraphQL client called Relay. GitHub followed this approach and adopted it for their own GraphQL pagination API. Later, you will learn in the exercises about other strategies to implement pagination with GraphQL.

After executing the query, you should see two items from the list in the repositories field. We still need to figure out how to fetch the next two repositories in the list, however. The first result of the query is the first **page** of the paginated list, the second query result should be the second page. In the following, you will see how the query structure for paginated data allows us to retrieve meta information to execute successive queries. For instance, each edge comes with its own cursor field to identify its position in the list.

GitHub GraphQL Explorer

```
query OrganizationForLearningReact {
  organization(login: "the-road-to-learn-react") {
    name
    url
    repositories(first: 2) {
      edges {
        node {
          name
        }
        cursor
      }
    }
  }
}
```

The result should be similar to the following:

GitHub GraphQL Explorer

```
{
  "data": {
    "organization": {
      "name": "The Road to learn React",
      "url": "https://github.com/the-road-to-learn-react",
      "repositories": {
        "edges": [
          {
            "node": {
              "name": "the-road-to-learn-react"
            },
            "cursor": "Y3Vyc29yOnYyOpHOA8awSw=="
          },
          {
            "node": {
              "name": "hackernews-client"
            },
            "cursor": "Y3Vyc29yOnYyOpHOBGhimw=="
          }
        ]
      }
    }
```

```
    }
}
```

Now, you can use the cursor of the first repository in the list to execute a second query. By using the `after` argument for the `repositories` list field, you can specify an entry point to retrieve your next page of paginated data. What would the result look like when executing the following query?

GitHub GraphQL Explorer

```
query OrganizationForLearningReact {
  organization(login: "the-road-to-learn-react") {
    name
    url
    repositories(first: 2, after: "Y3Vyc29yOnYyOpHOA8awSw==") {
      edges {
        node {
          name
        }
        cursor
      }
    }
  }
}
```

In the previous result, only the second item is retrieved, as well as a new third item. The first item isn't retrieved because you have used its cursor as `after` argument to retrieve all items after it. Now you can imagine how to make successive queries for paginated lists:

- execute the initial query without a cursor argument
- execute every following query with the cursor of the **last** item's cursor from the previous query result

To keep the query dynamic, we extract its arguments as variables. Afterward, you can use the query with a dynamic `cursor` argument by providing a variable for it. The `after` argument can be `undefined` to retrieve the first page. In conclusion, that would be everything you need to fetch pages of lists from one large list by using a feature called pagination. You need a mandatory argument specifying how many items should be retrieved and an optional argument, in this case the `after` argument, specifying the starting point for the list.

There are also a couple helpful ways to use meta information for your paginated list. Retrieving the `cursor` field for every repository may be verbose when using only the `cursor` of the last repository, so you can remove the `cursor` field for an individual edge, but add the `pageInfo` object with its `endCursor` and `hasNextPage` fields. You can also request the `totalCount` of the list.

GitHub GraphQL Explorer

```
query OrganizationForLearningReact {
  organization(login: "the-road-to-learn-react") {
    name
    url
    repositories(first: 2, after: "Y3Vyc29yOnYyOpHOA8awSw==") {
      totalCount
      edges {
        node {
          name
        }
      }
      pageInfo {
        endCursor
        hasNextPage
      }
    }
  }
}
```

The `totalCount` field discloses the total number of items in the list, while the `pageInfo` field gives you information about two things:

- **endCursor** can be used to retrieve the successive list, which we did with the `cursor` field, except this time we only need one meta field to perform it. The cursor of the last list item is sufficient to request the next page of list.
- **hasNextPage** gives you information about whether or not there is a next page to retrieve from the GraphQL API. Sometimes you've already fetched the last page from your server. For applications that use infinite scrolling to load more pages when scrolling lists, you can stop fetching pages when there are no more available.

This meta information completes the pagination implementation. Information is made accessible using the GraphQL API to implement paginated lists[79] and infinite scroll[80]. Note, this covers GitHub's GraphQL API; a different GraphQL API for pagination might use different naming conventions for the fields, exclude meta information, or employ different mechanisms altogether.

Exercises:

- Extract the `login` and the `cursor` from your pagination query as variables.

---

[79]https://www.robinwieruch.de/react-paginated-list/
[80]https://www.robinwieruch.de/react-infinite-scroll/

- Exchange the `first` argument with a `last` argument.
- Search for the `repositories` field in the GraphiQL "Docs" sidebar which says: "A list of repositories that the ... owns."
    - Explore the other arguments that can be passed to this list field.
    - Use the `orderBy` argument to retrieve an ascending or descending list.
- Read more about pagination in GraphQL[81].
    - The cursor approach is only one solution which is used by GitHub.
    - Make sure to understand the other solutions, too.

Interacting with GitHub's GraphQL API via GraphiQL or GitHub's GraphQL Explorer is only the beginning. You should be familiar with the fundamental GraphQL concepts now. But there are a lot more exciting concepts to explore. In the next chapters, you will implement fully working GraphQL client application with React that interacts with GitHub's API.

---

[81]http://graphql.org/learn/pagination

React with GraphQL

In this client-sided GraphQL application we'll build together, you will learn how to combine React with GraphQL. There is no clever library like Apollo Client[82] or Relay[83] to help you get started yet, so instead, you will perform GraphQL queries and mutations with basic HTTP requests. Later, in the next application we are going to build together, I'll introduce Apollo as a GraphQL client for your React.js application. For now, the application we build should should only show how to use GraphQL in React with HTTP.

Along the way, you will build a simplified GitHub client, basically an issue tracker for GitHub, that consumes GitHub's GraphQL API[84]. You will perform GraphQL queries and mutations to read and write data, and by the end, you should be able to showcase a GraphQL in React example that can be used by other developers as a learning tool. The final application you are going to build can be found in this repository on GitHub[85].

---

[82]https://github.com/apollographql/apollo-client
[83]https://github.com/facebook/relay
[84]https://developer.github.com/v4/
[85]https://github.com/rwieruch/react-graphql-github-vanilla

Writing your first React GraphQL Client

After the last sections, you should be ready to use queries and mutations in your React application. In this section, you will create a React application that consumes the GitHub GraphQL API. The application should show open issues in a GitHub repository, making it a simple issue tracker. Again, if you lack experience with React, see the Road to learn React[86] to learn more about it. After that you should be well set up for the following section.

For this application, no elaborate React setup is needed. You will simply use create-react-app[87] to create your React application with zero-configuration. Install it with npm by typing the following instructions on the command line: `npm install -g create-react-app`. If you want to have an elaborated React setup instead, read this setup guide for using Webpack with React[88].

Now, let's create the application with create-react-app. In your general projects folder, type the following instructions:

Command Line

```
create-react-app react-graphql-github-vanilla
cd react-graphql-github-vanilla
```

After your application has been created, you can test it with `npm start` and `npm test`. Again, after you have learned about plain React in *the Road to learn React*, you should be familiar with npm, create-react-app, and React itself.

The following application will focus on the *src/App.js* file. It's up to you to split out components, configuration, or functions to their own folders and files. Let's get started with the App component in the mentioned file. In order to simplify it, you can change it to the following content:

src/App.js

```
import React, { Component } from 'react';

const TITLE = 'React GraphQL GitHub Client';

class App extends Component {
  render() {
    return (
      <div>
        <h1>{TITLE}</h1>
      </div>
    );
  }
}
```

---

[86]https://www.robinwieruch.de/the-road-to-learn-react
[87]https://github.com/facebook/create-react-app
[88]https://www.robinwieruch.de/minimal-react-webpack-babel-setup/

```
}
```

```
export default App;
```

The component only renders a `title` as a headline. Before implementing any more React components, let's install a library to handle GraphQL requests, executing queries and mutations, using a HTTP POST method. For this, you will use axios[89]. On the command line, type the following command to install axios in the project folder:

Command Line

```
npm install axios --save
```

Afterward, you can import axios next to your App component and configure it. It's perfect for the following application, because somehow you want to configure it only once with your personal access token and GitHub's GraphQL API.

First, define a base URL for axios when creating a configured instance from it. As mentioned before, you don't need to define GitHub's URL endpoint every time you make request because all queries and mutations point to the same URL endpoint in GraphQL. You get the flexibility from your query and mutation structures using objects and fields instead.

src/App.js

```
import React, { Component } from 'react';
import axios from 'axios';

const axiosGitHubGraphQL = axios.create({
  baseURL: 'https://api.github.com/graphql',
});

...

export default App;
```

Second, pass the personal access token as header to the configuration. The header is used by each request made with this axios instance.

---

[89]https://github.com/axios/axios

src/App.js

```
...

const axiosGitHubGraphQL = axios.create({
  baseURL: 'https://api.github.com/graphql',
  headers: {
    Authorization: 'bearer YOUR_GITHUB_PERSONAL_ACCESS_TOKEN',
  },
});

...
```

Replace the YOUR_GITHUB_PERSONAL_ACCESS_TOKEN string with your personal access token. To avoid cutting and pasting your access token directly into the source code, you can create a *.env* file to hold all your environment variables on the command line in your project folder. If you don't want to share the personal token in a public GitHub repository, you can add the file to your *.gitignore*.

Command Line

```
touch .env
```

Environment variables are defined in this *.env* file. Be sure to follow the correct naming constraints when using create-react-app, which uses REACT_APP as prefix for each key. In your *.env* file, paste the following key value pair. The key has to have the REACT_APP prefix, and the valueÂ has to be your personal access token from GitHub.

.env

```
REACT_APP_GITHUB_PERSONAL_ACCESS_TOKEN=xxxXXX
```

Now, you can pass the personal access token as environment variable to your axios configuration with string interpolation (template literals[90]) to create a configured axios instance.

---

[90]https://developer.mozilla.org/en-US/docs/Web/JavaScript/Reference/Template_literals

src/App.js

```
. . .

const axiosGitHubGraphQL = axios.create({
  baseURL: 'https://api.github.com/graphql',
  headers: {
    Authorization: `bearer ${
      process.env.REACT_APP_GITHUB_PERSONAL_ACCESS_TOKEN
    }`,
  },
});

. . .
```

The initial axios setup is essentially the same as we completed using GraphiQL application before to access GitHub's GraphQL API, when you had to set a header with a personal access token and endpoint URL as well.

Next, set up a form for capturing details about a GitHub organization and repository from a user. It should be possible to fill out an input field to request a paginated list of issues for a specific GitHub repository. First, there needs to be a form with an input field to enter the organization and repository. The input field has to update React's local state. Second, the form needs a submit button to request data about the organization and repository that the user provided in the input field, which located in the component's local state. Third, it would be convenient to have an initial local state for the organization and repository to request initial data when the component mounts for the first time.

Let's tackle implementing this scenario in two steps. The render method has to render a form with an input field. The form has to have an onSubmit handler, and the input field needs an onChange handler. The input field uses the path from the local state as a value to be a controlled component. The path value in the local state from the onChange handler updates in the second step.

src/App.js

```
class App extends Component {
  render() {
    return (
      <div>
        <h1>{TITLE}</h1>

        <form onSubmit={this.onSubmit}>
          <label htmlFor="url">
            Show open issues for https://github.com/
          </label>
          <input
```

```
            id="url"
            type="text"
            onChange={this.onChange}
            style={{ width: '300px' }}
          />
          <button type="submit">Search</button>
        </form>

        <hr />

        {/* Here comes the result! */}
      </div>
    );
  }
}
```

Declare the class methods to be used in the render method. The componentDidMount() lifecycle method can be used to make an initial request when the App component mounts. There needs to be an initial state for the input field to make an initial request in this lifecycle method.

src/App.js

```
class App extends Component {
  state = {
    path: 'the-road-to-learn-react/the-road-to-learn-react',
  };

  componentDidMount() {
    // fetch data
  }

  onChange = event => {
    this.setState({ path: event.target.value });
  };

  onSubmit = event => {
    // fetch data

    event.preventDefault();
  };

  render() {
    ...
```

```
  }
}
```

The previous implementation uses a React class component syntax you might have not used before. If you are not familiar with it, check this GitHub repository[91] to gain more understanding. Using **class field declarations** lets you omit the constructor statement for initializing the local state, and eliminates the need to bind class methods. Instead, arrow functions will handle all the binding.

Following a best practice in React, make the input field a controlled component. The input element shouldn't be used to handle its internal state using native HTML behavior; it should be React.

src/App.js

```
class App extends Component {
  ...

  render() {
    const { path } = this.state;

    return (
      <div>
        <h1>{TITLE}</h1>

        <form onSubmit={this.onSubmit}>
          <label htmlFor="url">
            Show open issues for https://github.com/
          </label>
          <input
            id="url"
            type="text"
            value={path}
            onChange={this.onChange}
            style={{ width: '300px' }}
          />
          <button type="submit">Search</button>
        </form>

        <hr />

        {/* Here comes the result! */}
      </div>
    );
```

---

[91]https://github.com/the-road-to-learn-react/react-alternative-class-component-syntax

```
    }
}
```

The previous setup for the form–using input field(s), a submit button, onChange() and onSubmit() class methods–is a common way to implement forms in React. The only addition is the initial data fetching in the componentDidMount() lifecycle method to improve user experience by providing an initial state for the query to request data from the backend. It is a useful foundation for fetching data from a third-party API in React[92].

When you start the application on the command line, you should see the initial state for the path in the input field. You should be able to change the state by entering something else in the input field, but nothing happens with componentDidMount() and submitting the form yet.

You might wonder why there is only one input field to grab the information about the organization and repository. When opening up a repository on GitHub, you can see that the organization and repository are encoded in the URL, so it becomes a convenient way to show the same URL pattern for the input field. You can also split the organization/repository later at the / to get these values and perform the GraphQL query request.

Exercises:

- Confirm your source code for the last section[93]
- If you are unfamiliar with React, check out *The Road to learn React*

---

[92]https://www.robinwieruch.de/react-fetching-data/
[93]https://github.com/the-road-to-graphql/react-graphql-github-vanilla/tree/ca7b278b8f602c46dfac64a1304d39a8e8e0006b

GraphQL Query in React

In this section, you are going to implement your first GraphQL query in React, fetching issues from an organization's repository, though not all at once. Start by fetching only an organization. Let's define the query as a variable above of the App component.

src/App.js

```
const GET_ORGANIZATION = `
  {
    organization(login: "the-road-to-learn-react") {
      name
      url
    }
  }
`;
```

Use template literals in JavaScript to define the query as string with multiple lines. It should be identical to the query you used before in GraphiQL or GitHub Explorer. Now, you can use axios to make a POST request to GitHub's GraphiQL API. The configuration for axios already points to the correct API endpoint and uses your personal access token. The only thing left is passing the query to it as payload during a POST request. The argument for the endpoint can be an empty string, because you defined the endpoint in the configuration. It will execute the request when the App component mounts in `componentDidMount()`. After the promise from axios has been resolved, only a console log of the result remains.

src/App.js

```
...

const axiosGitHubGraphQL = axios.create({
  baseURL: 'https://api.github.com/graphql',
  headers: {
    Authorization: `bearer ${
      process.env.REACT_APP_GITHUB_PERSONAL_ACCESS_TOKEN
    }`,
  },
});

const GET_ORGANIZATION = `
  {
    organization(login: "the-road-to-learn-react") {
      name
      url
```

```
    }
  }
`;

class App extends Component {
  ...

  componentDidMount() {
    this.onFetchFromGitHub();
  }

  onSubmit = event => {
    // fetch data

    event.preventDefault();
  };

  onFetchFromGitHub = () => {
    axiosGitHubGraphQL
      .post('', { query: GET_ORGANIZATION })
      .then(result => console.log(result));
  };

  ...
}
```

You used only axios to perform a HTTP POST request with a GraphQL query as payload. Since axios uses promises, the promise resolves eventually and you should have the result from the GraphQL API in your hands. There is nothing magical about it. It's an implementation in plain JavaScript using axios as HTTP client to perform the GraphQL request with plain HTTP.

Start your application again and verify that you have got the result in your developer console log. If you get a 401 HTTP status code[94], you didn't set up your personal access token properly. Otherwise, if everything went fine, you should see a similar result in your developer console log.

---

[94]https://en.wikipedia.org/wiki/List_of_HTTP_status_codes

Developer Tools

```
{
  "config": ...,
  "data":{
    "data":{
      "organization":{
        "name":"The Road to learn React",
        "url":"https://github.com/the-road-to-learn-react"
      }
    }
  },
  "headers": ...,
  "request": ...,
  "status": ...,
  "statusText": ...
}
```

The top level information is everything axios returns you as meta information for the request. It's all axios, and nothing related to GraphQL yet, which is why most of it is substituted with a placeholder. Axios has a `data` property where that shows the result of your axios request. Then again comes a `data` property which reflects the GraphQL result. At first, the `data` property seems redundant in the first result, but once you examine it you will know that one `data` property comes from axios, while the other comes from the GraphQL data structure. Finally, you find the result of the GraphQL query in the second `data` property. There, you should find the organization with its resolved name and url fields as string properties.

In the next step, you're going to store the result holding the information about the organization in React's local state. You will also store potential errors in the state if any occur.

src/App.js

```
class App extends Component {
  state = {
    path: 'the-road-to-learn-react/the-road-to-learn-react',
    organization: null,
    errors: null,
  };

  ...

  onFetchFromGitHub = () => {
    axiosGitHubGraphQL
      .post('', { query: GET_ORGANIZATION })
      .then(result =>
```

```
        this.setState(() => ({
          organization: result.data.data.organization,
          errors: result.data.errors,
        })),
      );
  }

  ...

}
```

In the second step, you can display the information about the organization in your App component's
render() method:

src/App.js

```
class App extends Component {
  ...

  render() {
    const { path, organization } = this.state;

    return (
      <div>
        <h1>{TITLE}</h1>

        <form onSubmit={this.onSubmit}>
          ...
        </form>

        <hr />

        <Organization organization={organization} />
      </div>
    );
  }
}
```

Introduce the Organization component as a new functional stateless component to keep the render
method of the App component concise. Because this application is going to be a simple GitHub issue
tracker, you can already mention it in a short paragraph.

src/App.js

```
class App extends Component {

  ...

}


const Organization = ({ organization }) => (
  <div>
    <p>
      <strong>Issues from Organization:</strong>
      <a href={organization.url}>{organization.name}</a>
    </p>
  </div>
);
```

In the final step, you have to decide what should be rendered when nothing is fetched yet, and what should be rendered when errors occur. To solve these edge cases, you can use conditional rendering[95] in React. For the first edge case, simply check whether an organization is present or not.

src/App.js

```
class App extends Component {
  ...

  render() {
    const { path, organization, errors } = this.state;

    return (
      <div>

        ...

        <hr />

        {organization ? (
          <Organization organization={organization} errors={errors} />
        ) : (
          <p>No information yet ...</p>
        )}
      </div>
    );
  }
}
```

---

[95]https://www.robinwieruch.de/conditional-rendering-react/

For the second edge case, you have passed the errors to the Organization component. In case there are errors, it should simply render the error message of each error. Otherwise, it should render the organization. There can be multiple errors regarding different fields and circumstances in GraphQL.

src/App.js

```
const Organization = ({ organization, errors }) => {
  if (errors) {
    return (
      <p>
        <strong>Something went wrong:</strong>
        {errors.map(error => error.message).join(' ')}
      </p>
    );
  }

  return (
    <div>
      <p>
        <strong>Issues from Organization:</strong>
        <a href={organization.url}>{organization.name}</a>
      </p>
    </div>
  );
};
```

You performed your first GraphQL query in a React application, a plain HTTP POST request with a query as payload. You used a configured axios client instance for it. Afterward, you were able to store the result in React's local state to display it later.

GraphQL Nested Objects in React

Next, we'll request a nested object for the organization. Since the application will eventually show the issues in a repository, you should fetch a repository of an organization as the next step. Remember, a query reaches into the GraphQL graph, so we can nest the `repository` field in the `organization` when the schema defined the relationship between these two entities.

src/App.js

```
const GET_REPOSITORY_OF_ORGANIZATION = `
  {
    organization(login: "the-road-to-learn-react") {
      name
      url
      repository(name: "the-road-to-learn-react") {
        name
        url
      }
    }
  }
`;

class App extends Component {
  ...

  onFetchFromGitHub = () => {
    axiosGitHubGraphQL
      .post('', { query: GET_REPOSITORY_OF_ORGANIZATION })
      .then(result =>
          ...
      );
  };

  ...

}
```

In this case, the repository name is identical to the organization. That's okay for now. Later on, you can define an organization and repository on your own dynamically. In the second step, you can extend the Organization component with another Repository component as child component. The result for the query should now have a nested repository object in the organization object.

src/App.js

```
const Organization = ({ organization, errors }) => {
  if (errors) {
    ...
  }

  return (
    <div>
      <p>
        <strong>Issues from Organization:</strong>
        <a href={organization.url}>{organization.name}</a>
      </p>
      <Repository repository={organization.repository} />
    </div>
  );
};

const Repository = ({ repository }) => (
  <div>
    <p>
      <strong>In Repository:</strong>
      <a href={repository.url}>{repository.name}</a>
    </p>
  </div>
);
```

The GraphQL query structure aligns perfectly with your component tree. It forms a natural fit to continue extending the query structure like this, by nesting other objects into the query, and extending the component tree along the structure of the GraphQL query. Since the application is an issue tracker, we need to add a list field of issues to the query.

If you want to follow the query structure more thoughtfully, open the "Docs" sidebar in GraphiQL to learn out about the types Organization, Repository, Issue. The paginated issues list field can be found there as well. It's always good to have an overview of the graph structure.

Now let's extend the query with the list field for the issues. These issues are a paginated list in the end. We will cover these more later; for now, nest it in the repository field with a last argument to fetch the last items of the list.

src/App.js

```
const GET_ISSUES_OF_REPOSITORY = `
  {
    organization(login: "the-road-to-learn-react") {
      name
      url
      repository(name: "the-road-to-learn-react") {
        name
        url
        issues(last: 5) {
          edges {
            node {
              id
              title
              url
            }
          }
        }
      }
    }
  }
`;
```

You can also request an id for each issue using the id field on the issue's node field, to use a key attribute for your list of rendered items in the component, which is considered best practice in React[96]. Remember to adjust the name of the query variable when its used to perform the request.

src/App.js

```
class App extends Component {
  ...

  onFetchFromGitHub = () => {
    axiosGitHubGraphQL
      .post('', { query: GET_ISSUES_OF_REPOSITORY })
      .then(result =>

        ...

      );
  };

  ...

}
```

---

[96]https://reactjs.org/docs/lists-and-keys.html

The component structure follows the query structure quite naturally again. You can add a list of rendered issues to the Repository component. It is up to you to extract it to its own component as a refactoring to keep your components concise, readable, and maintainable.

src/App.js

```
const Repository = ({ repository }) => (
  <div>
    <p>
      <strong>In Repository:</strong>
      <a href={repository.url}>{repository.name}</a>
    </p>

    <ul>
      {repository.issues.edges.map(issue => (
        <li key={issue.node.id}>
          <a href={issue.node.url}>{issue.node.title}</a>
        </li>
      ))}
    </ul>
  </div>
);
```

That's it for the nested objects, fields, and list fields in a query. Once you run your application again, you should see the last issues of the specified repository rendered in your browser.

GraphQL Variables and Arguments in React

Next we'll make use of the form and input elements. They should be used to request the data from GitHub's GraphQL API when a user fills in content and submits it. The content is also used for the initial request in componentDidMount() of the App component. So far, the organization login and repository name were inlined arguments in the query. Now, you should be able to pass in the path from the local state to the query to define dynamically an organization and repository. That's where variables in a GraphQL query came into play, do you remember?

First, let's use a naive approach by performing string interpolation with JavaScript rather than using GraphQL variables. To do this, refactor the query from a template literal variable to a function that returns a template literal variable. By using the function, you should be able to pass in an organization and repository.

src/App.js

```
const getIssuesOfRepositoryQuery = (organization, repository) => `
  {
    organization(login: "${organization}") {
      name
      url
      repository(name: "${repository}") {
        name
        url
        issues(last: 5) {
          edges {
            node {
              id
              title
              url
            }
          }
        }
      }
    }
  }
`;
```

Next, call the onFetchFromGitHub() class method in the submit handle, but also when the component mounts in componentDidMount() with the initial local state of the path property. These are the two essential places to fetch the data from the GraphQL API on initial render, and on every other manual submission from a button click.

src/App.js

```
class App extends Component {
  state = {
    path: 'the-road-to-learn-react/the-road-to-learn-react',
    organization: null,
    errors: null,
  };

  componentDidMount() {
    this.onFetchFromGitHub(this.state.path);
  }

  onChange = event => {
    this.setState({ path: event.target.value });
```

```
    };

    onSubmit = event => {
      this.onFetchFromGitHub(this.state.path);

      event.preventDefault();
    };

    onFetchFromGitHub = () => {
      ...
    }

    render() {
      ...
    }
}
```

Lastly, call the function that returns the query instead of passing the query string directly as payload. Use the JavaScript's split method on a string[97] to retrieve the prefix and suffix of the / character from the path variable where the prefix is the organization and the suffix is the repository.

src/App.js

```
class App extends Component {
  ...

  onFetchFromGitHub = path => {
    const [organization, repository] = path.split('/');

    axiosGitHubGraphQL
      .post('', {
        query: getIssuesOfRepositoryQuery(organization, repository),
      })
      .then(result =>
        this.setState(() => ({
          organization: result.data.data.organization,
          errors: result.data.errors,
        })),
      );
  };


  ...

}
```

[97]https://developer.mozilla.org/en-US/docs/Web/JavaScript/Reference/Global_Objects/String/split

Since the split returns an array of values and it is assumed that there is only one slash in the path, the array should consist of two values: the organization and the repository. That's why it is convenient to use a JavaScript array destructuring to pull out both values from an array in the same line.

Note that the application is not built for to be robust, but is intended only a learning experience. It is unlikely anyone will ask a user to input the organization and repository with a different pattern than *organization/repository*, so there is no validation included yet. Still, it is a good foundation for you to gain experience with the concepts.

If you want to go further, you can extract the first part of the class method to its own function, which uses axios to send a request with the query and return a promise. The promise can be used to resolve the result into the local state, using `this.setState()` in the `then()` resolver block of the promise.

src/App.js

```
const getIssuesOfRepository = path => {
  const [organization, repository] = path.split('/');

  return axiosGitHubGraphQL.post('', {
    query: getIssuesOfRepositoryQuery(organization, repository),
  });
};

class App extends Component {
  ...

  onFetchFromGitHub = path => {
    getIssuesOfRepository(path).then(result =>
      this.setState(() => ({
        organization: result.data.data.organization,
        errors: result.data.errors,
      })),
    );
  };

  ...
}
```

You can always split your applications into parts, be they functions or components, to make them concise, readable, reusable and testable[98]. The function that is passed to `this.setState()` can be

---
[98]https://www.robinwieruch.de/react-testing-tutorial/

extracted as higher-order function. It has to be a higher-order function, because you need to pass the result of the promise, but also provide a function for the `this.setState()` method.

src/App.js

```
const resolveIssuesQuery = queryResult => () => ({
  organization: queryResult.data.data.organization,
  errors: queryResult.data.errors,
});

class App extends Component {
  ...

  onFetchFromGitHub = path => {
    getIssuesOfRepository(path).then(queryResult =>
      this.setState(resolveIssuesQuery(queryResult)),
    );
  };

  ...
}
```

Now you've made your query flexible by providing dynamic arguments to your query. Try it by starting your application on the command line and by filling in a different organization with a specific repository (e.g. *facebook/create-react-app*).

It's a decent setup, but there was nothing to see about variables yet. You simply passed the arguments to the query using a function and string interpolation with template literals. Now we'll use GraphQL variables instead, to refactor the query variable again to a template literal that defines inline variables.

src/App.js

```
const GET_ISSUES_OF_REPOSITORY = `
  query ($organization: String!, $repository: String!) {
    organization(login: $organization) {
      name
      url
      repository(name: $repository) {
        name
        url
        issues(last: 5) {
          edges {
            node {
              id
```

```
            title
            url
          }
        }
      }
    }
  }
}
`;
```

Now you can pass those variables as argument next to the query for the HTTP POST request:

src/App.js

```
const getIssuesOfRepository = path => {
  const [organization, repository] = path.split('/');

  return axiosGitHubGraphQL.post('', {
    query: GET_ISSUES_OF_REPOSITORY,
    variables: { organization, repository },
  });
};
```

Finally, the query takes variables into account without detouring into a function with string interpolation. I strongly suggest practicing with the exercises below before continuing to the next section. We've yet to discuss features like fragments or operation names, but we'll soon cover them using Apollo instead of plain HTTP with axios.

Exercises:

- Confirm your source code for the last section[99]
- Explore and add fields to your organization, repository and issues
  - Extend your components to display the additional information
- Read more about serving a GraphQL API over HTTP[100]

---

[99]https://github.com/the-road-to-graphql/react-graphql-github-vanilla/tree/c08126a9ec91dde4198ae85bb2f194fa7767c683
[100]http://graphql.org/learn/serving-over-http/

GraphQL Pagination in React

Last section you implemented a list field in your GraphQL query, which fit into the flow of structuring the query with nested objects and a list responsible for showing partial results of the query in React.

In this section, you will explore pagination with list fields with GraphQL in React in more detail. Initially, you will learn more about the arguments of list fields. Further, you will add one more nested list field to your query. Finally, you will fetch another page of the paginated issues list with your query.

Let's start by extending the issues list field in your query with one more argument:

src/App.js

```
const GET_ISSUES_OF_REPOSITORY = `
  query ($organization: String!, $repository: String!) {
    organization(login: $organization) {
      name
      url
      repository(name: $repository) {
        name
        url
        issues(last: 5, states: [OPEN]) {
          edges {
            node {
              id
              title
              url
            }
          }
        }
      }
    }
  }
`;
```

If you read the arguments for the issues list field using the "Docs" sidebar in GraphiQL, you can explore which arguments that you can pass to the field. One of these is the states argument, which defines whether or not to fetch open or closed issues. The previous implementation of the query has shown you how to refine the list field, in case you only want to show open issues. You can explore more arguments for the issues list field, but also for other list fields, using the documentation from Github's API.

Now we'll implement another nested list field that could be used for pagination. Each issue in a repository can have reactions, essentially emoticons like a smiley or a thumbs up. Reactions can be seen as another list of paginated items. First, extend the query with the nested list field for reactions:

src/App.js

```
const GET_ISSUES_OF_REPOSITORY = `
  query ($organization: String!, $repository: String!) {
    organization(login: $organization) {
      name
      url
      repository(name: $repository) {
        name
        url
        issues(last: 5, states: [OPEN]) {
          edges {
            node {
              id
              title
              url
              reactions(last: 3) {
                edges {
                  node {
                    id
                    content
                  }
                }
              }
            }
          }
        }
      }
    }
  }
`;
```

Second, render the list of reactions in one of your React components again. Implement dedicated List and Item components, such as ReactionsList and ReactionItem for it. As an exercise, try keeping the code for this application readable and maintainable.

src/App.js

```
const Repository = ({ repository }) => (
  <div>
    ...

    <ul>
      {repository.issues.edges.map(issue => (
        <li key={issue.node.id}>
          <a href={issue.node.url}>{issue.node.title}</a>

          <ul>
            {issue.node.reactions.edges.map(reaction => (
              <li key={reaction.node.id}>{reaction.node.content}</li>
            ))}
          </ul>
        </li>
      ))}
    </ul>
  </div>
);
```

You extended the query and React's component structure to render the result. It's a straight forward implementation when you are using a GraphQL API as your data source which has a well defined underlying schema for these field relationships.

Lastly, you will implement real pagination with the issues list field, as there should be a button to fetch more issues from the GraphQL API to make it a function of a completed application. Here is how to implement a button:

src/App.js

```
const Repository = ({
  repository,
  onFetchMoreIssues,
}) => (
  <div>
    ...

    <ul>
      ...
    </ul>

    <hr />
```

```
    <button onClick={onFetchMoreIssues}>More</button>
  </div>
);
```

The handler for the button passes through all the components to reach the Repository component:

src/App.js

```
const Organization = ({
  organization,
  errors,
  onFetchMoreIssues,
}) => {
  ...

  return (
    <div>
      <p>
        <strong>Issues from Organization:</strong>
        <a href={organization.url}>{organization.name}</a>
      </p>
      <Repository
        repository={organization.repository}
        onFetchMoreIssues={onFetchMoreIssues}
      />
    </div>
  );
};
```

Logic for the function is implemented in the App component as class method. It passes to the Organization component as well.

src/App.js

```
class App extends Component {
  ...

  onFetchMoreIssues = () => {
    ...
  };

  render() {
    const { path, organization, errors } = this.state;
```

```
    return (
      <div>
        ...

        {organization ? (
          <Organization
            organization={organization}
            errors={errors}
            onFetchMoreIssues={this.onFetchMoreIssues}
          />
        ) : (
          <p>No information yet ...</p>
        )}
      </div>
    );
  }
}
```

Before implementing the logic for it, there needs to be a way to identify the next page of the paginated list. To extend the inner fields of a list field with fields for meta information such as the pageInfo or the totalCount information, use pageInfo to define the next page on button-click. Also, the totalCount is only a nice way to see how many items are in the next list:

src/App.js

```
const GET_ISSUES_OF_REPOSITORY = `
  query ($organization: String!, $repository: String!) {
    organization(login: $organization) {
      name
      url
      repository(name: $repository) {
        ...
        issues(last: 5, states: [OPEN]) {
          edges {
            ...
          }
          totalCount
          pageInfo {
            endCursor
            hasNextPage
          }
        }
      }
    }
```

```
  }
`;
```

Now, you can use this information to fetch the next page of issues by providing the cursor as a variable to your query. The cursor, or the `after` argument, defines the starting point to fetch more items from the paginated list.

src/App.js

```
class App extends Component {
  ...

  onFetchMoreIssues = () => {
    const {
      endCursor,
    } = this.state.organization.repository.issues.pageInfo;

    this.onFetchFromGitHub(this.state.path, endCursor);
  };

  ...
}
```

The second argument wasn't introduced to the `onFetchFromGitHub()` class method yet. Let's see how that turns out.

src/App.js

```
const getIssuesOfRepository = (path, cursor) => {
  const [organization, repository] = path.split('/');

  return axiosGitHubGraphQL.post('', {
    query: GET_ISSUES_OF_REPOSITORY,
    variables: { organization, repository, cursor },
  });
};

class App extends Component {
  ...

  onFetchFromGitHub = (path, cursor) => {
    getIssuesOfRepository(path, cursor).then(queryResult =>
      this.setState(resolveIssuesQuery(queryResult, cursor)),
    );
```

```
  };

  . . .

}
```

The argument is simply passed to the `getIssuesOfRepository()` function, which makes the GraphQL API request, and returns the promise with the query result. Check the other functions that call the `onFetchFromGitHub()` class method, and notice how they don't make use of the second argument, so the cursor parameter will be `undefined` when it's passed to the GraphQL API call. Either the query uses the cursor as argument to fetch the next page of a list, or it fetches the initial page of a list by having the cursor not defined at all:

src/App.js

```
const GET_ISSUES_OF_REPOSITORY = `
  query (
    $organization: String!,
    $repository: String!,
    $cursor: String
  ) {
    organization(login: $organization) {
      name
      url
      repository(name: $repository) {
        . . .
        issues(first: 5, after: $cursor, states: [OPEN]) {
          edges {
            . . .
          }
          totalCount
          pageInfo {
            endCursor
            hasNextPage
          }
        }
      }
    }
  }
`;
```

In the previous template string, the `cursor` is passed as variable to the query and used as `after` argument for the list field. The variable is not enforced though, because there is no exclamation mark next to it, so it can be `undefined`. This happens for the initial page requests for a paginated list, when you only want to fetch the first page. Further, the argument `last` has been changed to `first` for the `issues` list field, because there won't be another page after you fetched the last item in the initial request. Thus, you have to start with the first items of the list to fetch more items until you reach the end of the list.

That's it for fetching the next page of a paginated list with GraphQL in React, except one final step. Nothing updates the local state of the App component about a page of issues yet, so there are still only the issues from the initial request. You want to merge the old pages of issues with the new page of issues in the local state of the App component, while keeping the organization and repository information in the deeply nested state object intact. The perfect time for doing this is when the promise for the query resolves. You already extracted it as a function outside of the App component, so you can use this place to handle the incoming result and return a result with your own structure and information. Keep in mind that the incoming result can be an initial request when the App component mounts for the first time, or after a request to fetch more issues happens, such as when the "More" button is clicked.

src/App.js

```
const resolveIssuesQuery = (queryResult, cursor) => state => {
  const { data, errors } = queryResult.data;

  if (!cursor) {
    return {
      organization: data.organization,
      errors,
    };
  }

  const { edges: oldIssues } = state.organization.repository.issues;
  const { edges: newIssues } = data.organization.repository.issues;
  const updatedIssues = [...oldIssues, ...newIssues];

  return {
    organization: {
      ...data.organization,
      repository: {
        ...data.organization.repository,
        issues: {
          ...data.organization.repository.issues,
          edges: updatedIssues,
        },
      },
    },
    errors,
```

```
    };
};
```

The function is a complete rewrite, because the update mechanism is more complex now. First, you passed the cursor as an argument to the function, which determines whether it was an initial query or a query to fetch another page of issues. Second, if the cursor is undefined, the function can return early with the state object that encapsulates the plain query result, same as before. There is nothing to keep intact in the state object from before, because it is an initial request that happens when the App component mounts or when a user submits another request which should overwrite the old state anyway. Third, if it is a fetch more query and the cursor is there, the old and new issues from the state and the query result get merged in an updated list of issues. In this case, a JavaScript destructuring alias is used to make naming both issue lists more obvious. Finally, the function returns the updated state object. Since it is a deeply nested object with multiple levels to update, use the JavaScript spread operator syntax to update each level with a new query result. Only the edges property should be updated with the merged list of issues.

Next, use the hasNextPage property from the pageInfo that you requested to show a "More" button (or not). If there are no more issues in the list, the button should disappear.

src/App.js

```
const Repository = ({ repository, onFetchMoreIssues }) => (
  <div>
    ...

    <hr />

    {repository.issues.pageInfo.hasNextPage && (
      <button onClick={onFetchMoreIssues}>More</button>
    )}
  </div>
);
```

Now you've implemented pagination with GraphQL in React. For practice, try more arguments for your issues and reactions list fields on your own. Check the "Docs" sidebar in GraphiQL to find out about arguments you can pass to list fields. Some arguments are generic, but have arguments that are specific for to lists. These arguments should show you how finely-tuned requests can be with a GraphQL query.

Exercises:

- Confirm your source code for the last section[101]

---

[101]https://github.com/the-road-to-graphql/react-graphql-github-vanilla/tree/060677346e8955fb1a6c7579859ce92e62e1f406

- Explore further arguments, generic or specific for the type, on the `issues` and `reactions` list fields
  - Think about ways to beautify the updating mechanism of deeply nested state objects and contribute your thoughts to it[102]

---

[102]https://github.com/rwieruch/react-graphql-github-apollo/pull/14

GraphQL Mutation in React

You fetched a lot of data using GraphQL in React, the larger part of using GraphQL. However, there are always two sides to such an interface: read and write. That's were GraphQL mutations complement the interface. Previously, you learned about GraphQL mutations using GraphiQL without React. In this section, you will implement such a mutation in your React GraphQL application.

You have executed GitHub's addStar mutation before in GraphiQL. Now, let's implement this mutation in React. Before implementing the mutation, you should query additional information about the repository, which is partially required to star the repository in a mutation.

src/App.js

```
const GET_ISSUES_OF_REPOSITORY = `
  query (
    $organization: String!,
    $repository: String!,
    $cursor: String
  ) {
    organization(login: $organization) {
      name
      url
      repository(name: $repository) {
        id
        name
        url
        viewerHasStarred
        issues(first: 5, after: $cursor, states: [OPEN]) {
          ...
        }
      }
    }
  }
`;
```

The viewerHasStarred field returns a boolean that tells whether the viewer has starred the repository or not. This boolean helps determine whether to execute a addStar or removeStar mutation in the next steps. For now, you will only implement the addStar mutation. The removeStar mutation will be left off as part of the exercise. Also, the id field in the query returns the identifier for the repository, which you will need to clarify the target repository of your mutation.

The best place to trigger the mutation is a button that stars or unstars the repository. That's where the viewerHasStarred boolean can be used for a conditional rendering to show either a "Star" or

"Unstar" button. Since you are going to star a repository, the Repository component is the best place to trigger the mutation.

src/App.js

```
const Repository = ({
  repository,
  onFetchMoreIssues,
  onStarRepository,
}) => (
  <div>
    ...

    <button
      type="button"
      onClick={() => onStarRepository()}
    >
      {repository.viewerHasStarred ? 'Unstar' : 'Star'}
    </button>

    <ul>
      ...
    </ul>
  </div>
);
```

To identify the repository to be starred, the mutation needs to know about the id of the repository. Pass the viewerHasStarred property as a parameter to the handler, since you'll use the parameter to determine whether you want execute the star or unstar mutation later.

src/App.js

```
const Repository = ({ repository, onStarRepository }) => (
  <div>
    ...

    <button
      type="button"
      onClick={() =>
        onStarRepository(repository.id, repository.viewerHasStarred)
      }
    >
      {repository.viewerHasStarred ? 'Unstar' : 'Star'}
    </button>
```

```
      . . .
    </div>
);
```

The handler should be defined in the App component. It passes through each component until it reaches the Repository component, also reaching through the Organization component on its way.

src/App.js

```
const Organization = ({
  organization,
  errors,
  onFetchMoreIssues,
  onStarRepository,
}) => {
  . . .

  return (
    <div>
      . . .
      <Repository
        repository={organization.repository}
        onFetchMoreIssues={onFetchMoreIssues}
        onStarRepository={onStarRepository}
      />
    </div>
  );
};
```

Now it can be defined in the App component. Note that the id and the viewerHasStarred information can be destructured from the App's local state, too. This is why you wouldn't need to pass this information in the handler, but use it from the local state instead. However, since the Repository component knew about the information already, it is fine to pass the information in the handler, which also makes the handler more explicit. It's also good preparation for dealing with multiple repositories and repository components later, since the handler will need to be more specific in these cases.

src/App.js

```
class App extends Component {
  ...

  onStarRepository = (repositoryId, viewerHasStarred) => {
    ...
  };

  render() {
    const { path, organization, errors } = this.state;

    return (
      <div>
        ...

        {organization ? (
          <Organization
            organization={organization}
            errors={errors}
            onFetchMoreIssues={this.onFetchMoreIssues}
            onStarRepository={this.onStarRepository}
          />
        ) : (
          <p>No information yet ...</p>
        )}
      </div>
    );
  }
}
```

Now, you can implement the handler. The mutation can be outsourced from the component. Later, you can use the viewerHasStarred boolean in the handler to perform a addStar or removeStar mutation. Executing the mutation looks similar to the GraphQL query from before. The API endpoint is not needed, because it was set in the beginning when you configured axios. The mutation can be sent in the query payload, which we'll cover later. The variables property is optional, but you need to pass the identifier.

src/App.js

```
const addStarToRepository = repositoryId => {
  return axiosGitHubGraphQL.post('', {
    query: ADD_STAR,
    variables: { repositoryId },
  });
};

class App extends Component {
  ...

  onStarRepository = (repositoryId, viewerHasStarred) => {
    addStarToRepository(repositoryId);
  };

  ...
}
```

Before you define the addStar mutation, check GitHub's GraphQL API again. There, you will find all information about the structure of the mutation, the required arguments, and the available fields for the result. For instance, you can include the viewerHasStarred field in the returned result to get an updated boolean of a starred or unstarred repository.

src/App.js

```
const ADD_STAR = `
  mutation ($repositoryId: ID!) {
    addStar(input:{starrableId:$repositoryId}) {
      starrable {
        viewerHasStarred
      }
    }
  }
`;
```

You could already execute the mutation in the browser by clicking the button. If you haven't starred the repository before, it should be starred after clicking the button. You can visit the repository on GitHub to get visual feedback, though you won't see any results reflected yet. The button still shows the "Star" label when the repository wasn't starred before, because the viewerHasStarred boolean wasn't updated in the local state of the App component after the mutation. That's the next thing you are going to implement. Since axios returns a promise, you can use the then() method on the promise to resolve it with your own implementation details.

src/App.js

```
const resolveAddStarMutation = mutationResult => state => {
  ...
};

class App extends Component {
  ...

  onStarRepository = (repositoryId, viewerHasStarred) => {
    addStarToRepository(repositoryId).then(mutationResult =>
      this.setState(resolveAddStarMutation(mutationResult)),
    );
  };

  ...
}
```

When resolving the promise from the mutation, you can find out about the `viewerHasStarred` property in the result. That's because you defined this property as a field in your mutation. It returns a new state object for React's local state, because you used the function in `this.setState()`. The spread operator syntax is used here, to update the deeply nested data structure. Only the `viewerHasStarred` property changes in the state object, because it's the only property returned by the resolved promise from the successful request. All other parts of the local state stay intact.

src/App.js

```
const resolveAddStarMutation = mutationResult => state => {
  const {
    viewerHasStarred,
  } = mutationResult.data.data.addStar.starrable;

  return {
    ...state,
    organization: {
      ...state.organization,
      repository: {
        ...state.organization.repository,
        viewerHasStarred,
      },
    },
  };
};
```

Now try to star the repository again. You may have to go on the Github page and unstar it first. The button label should adapt to the updated viewerHasStarred property from the local state to show a "Star" or "Unstar" label. You can use what you've learned about starring repositories to implement a removeStar mutation.

We also want to show the current number of people who have starred the repository, and update this count in the addStar and removeStar mutations. First, retrieve the total count of stargazers by adding the following fields to your query:

src/App.js

```
const GET_ISSUES_OF_REPOSITORY = `
  query (
    $organization: String!,
    $repository: String!,
    $cursor: String
  ) {
    organization(login: $organization) {
      name
      url
      repository(name: $repository) {
        id
        name
        url
        stargazers {
          totalCount
        }
        viewerHasStarred
        issues(first: 5, after: $cursor, states: [OPEN]) {
          ...
        }
      }
    }
  }
`;
```

Second, you can show the count as a part of your button label:

src/App.js

```
const Repository = ({
  repository,
  onFetchMoreIssues,
  onStarRepository,
}) => (
  <div>
    ...

    <button
      type="button"
      onClick={() =>
        onStarRepository(repository.id, repository.viewerHasStarred)
      }
    >
      {repository.stargazers.totalCount}
      {repository.viewerHasStarred ? ' Unstar' : ' Star'}
    </button>

    <ul>
      ...
    </ul>
  </div>
);
```

Now we want the count to update when you star (or unstar) a repository. It is the same issue as the missing update for the `viewerHasStarred` property in the local state of the component after the `addStar` mutation succeeded. Return to your mutation resolver and update the total count of stargazers there as well. While the stargazer object isn't returned as a result from the mutation, you can increment and decrement the total count after a successful mutation manually using a counter along with the `addStar` mutation.

src/App.js

```
const resolveAddStarMutation = mutationResult => state => {
  const {
    viewerHasStarred,
  } = mutationResult.data.data.addStar.starrable;

  const { totalCount } = state.organization.repository.stargazers;

  return {
    ...state,
```

```
  organization: {
    ...state.organization,
    repository: {
      ...state.organization.repository,
      viewerHasStarred,
      stargazers: {
        totalCount: totalCount + 1,
      },
    },
  },
};
};
```

You have implemented your first mutation in React with GraphQL. So far, you have just implemented the addStar mutation. Even though the button already reflects the viewerHasStarred boolean by showing a "Star" or "Unstar" label, the button showing "Unstar" should still execute the addStar mutation. The removeStar mutation to unstar the repository is one of the practice exercises mentioned below.

Exercises:

- Confirm your source code for the last section[103]
- Implement the removeStar mutation, which is used analog to the addStar mutation.
    - The onStarRepository class method has already access to the viewerHasStarred property.
    - Conditionally execute a addStar or removeStar mutation in the class handler.
    - Resolve the new state after removing a star from a repository.
    - Align your final thoughts with this implementation[104].
- Implement the addReaction mutation for an issue
- Implement more fine-grained components (e.g. IssueList, IssueItem, ReactionList, Reaction-Item)
    - Extract components to their own files and use import and export statements to use them again in the App or other extracted components

---

[103]https://github.com/the-road-to-graphql/react-graphql-github-vanilla/tree/3dcd95e32ef24d9e716a1e8ac144b62c0f41ca3c
[104]https://github.com/rwieruch/react-graphql-github-vanilla

Shortcomings of GraphQL in React without Apollo

We implemented a simple GitHub issue tracker that uses React and GraphQL without a dedicated library for GraphQL, using only axios to communicate with the GraphQL API with HTTP POST methods. I think it is important to work with raw technologies, in this case GraphQL, using plain HTTP methods, before introducing another abstraction. The Apollo library offers an abstraction that makes using GraphQL in React much easier, so you will use Apollo for your next application. For now, using GraphQL with HTTP has shown you two important things before introducing Apollo:

- How GraphQL works when using a puristic interface such as HTTP.
- The shortcomings of using no sophisticated GraphQL Client library in React, because you have to do everything yourself.

Before we move on, I want to address the shortcomings of using puristic HTTP methods to read and write data to your GraphQL API in a React application:

- **Complementary**: To call a GraphQL API from your client application, use HTTP methods. There are several quality libraries out there for HTTP requests, one of which is axios. That's why you have used axios for the previous application. However, using axios (or any other HTTP client library) doesn't feel like the best fit to complement a GraphQL centred interface. For instance, GraphQL doesn't use the full potential of HTTP. It's just fine to default to HTTP POST and only one API endpoint. It doesn't use resources and methods on those resources like a RESTful interface, so it makes no sense to specify a HTTP method and an API endpoint with every request, but to set it up once in the beginning instead. GraphQL comes with its own constraints. You could see it as a layer on top of HTTP when it's not as important for a developer to know about the underlying HTTP.
- **Declarative**: Every time you make a query or mutation when using plain HTTP requests, you have to make a dedicated call to the API endpoint using a library such as axios. It's an imperative way of reading and writing data to your backend. However, what if there was a declarative approach to making queries and mutations? What if there was a way to co-locate queries and mutations to your view-layer components? In the previous application, you experienced how the query shape aligned perfectly with your component hierarchy shape. What if the queries and mutations would align in the same way? That's the power of co-locating your data-layer with your view-layer, and you will find out more about it when you use a dedicated GraphQL client library for it.
- **Feature Support**: When using plain HTTP requests to interact with your GraphQL API, you are not leveraging the full potential of GraphQL. Imagine you want to split your query from the previous application into multiple queries that are co-located with their respective components where the data is used. That's when GraphQL would be used in a declarative way in your view-layer. But when you have no library support, you have to deal with multiple queries on your own, keeping track of all of them, and trying to merge the results in your state-layer. If you consider the previous application, splitting up the query into multiple queries would add a

whole layer of complexity to the application. A GraphQL client library deals with aggregating the queries for you.

- **Data Handling**: The naive way for data handling with puristic HTTP requests is a subcategory of the missing feature support for GraphQL when not using a dedicated library for it. There is no one helping you out with normalizing your data and caching it for identical requests. Updating your state-layer when resolving fetched data from the data-layer becomes a nightmare when not normalizing the data in the first place. You have to deal with deeply nested state objects which lead to the verbose usage of the JavaScript spread operator. When you check the implementation of the application in the GitHub repository again, you will see that the updates of React's local state after a mutation and query are not nice to look at. A normalizing library such as normalizr[105] could help you to improve the structure of your local state. You learn more about normalizing your state in the book Taming the State in React[106]. In addition to a lack of caching and normalizing support, avoiding libraries means missing out on functionalities for pagination and optimistic updates. A dedicated GraphQL library makes all these features available to you.

- **GraphQL Subscriptions**: While there is the concept of a query and mutation to read and write data with GraphQL, there is a third concept of a GraphQL **subscription** for receiving real-time data in a client-sided application. When you would have to rely on a plain HTTP requests as before, you would have to introduce WebSockets[107] next to it. It enables you to introduce a long-lived connection for receiving results over time. In conclusion, introducing GraphQL subscriptions would add another tool to your application. However, if you would introduce a GraphQL library for it on the client-side, the library would probably implement GraphQL subscriptions for you.

I am looking forward to introducing Apollo as a GraphQL client library to your React application. It will help with the aforementioned shortcomings. However, I do strongly believe it was good to learn about GraphQL in React without a GraphQL library in the beginning.

You can find the final repository on GitHub[108]. The repository showcases most of the exercise tasks too. The application is not feature complete since it doesn't cover all edge cases and isn't styled. However, I hope the implementation walkthrough with plain GraphQL in React has helped you to understand using only GraphQL client-side in React using HTTP requests. I feel it's important to take this step before using a sophisticated GraphQL client library such as Apollo or Relay.

I've shown how to implement a React application with GraphQL and HTTP requests without using a library like Apollo. Next, you will continue learning about using GraphQL in React using Apollo instead of basic HTTP requests with axios. The Apollo GraphQL Client makes caching your data, normalizing it, performing optimistic updates, and pagination effortless. That's not all by a long

---

[105]https://github.com/paularmstrong/normalizr
[106]https://roadtoreact.com
[107]https://developer.mozilla.org/en-US/docs/Web/API/WebSockets_API
[108]https://github.com/rwieruch/react-graphql-github-vanilla

shot, so stay tuned for the next applications you are are going to build with GraphQL.

Apollo Client

Apollo is an entire ecosystem built by developers as an infrastructure for GraphQL applications. You can use it on the client-side for a GraphQL client application, or server-side for a GraphQL server application. At the time of writing this tutorial, Apollo offers the richest and most popular ecosystem around GraphQL in JavaScript. There are other libraries for React applications like Relay[109] and Urql[110], but they are just for React applications, and they are not as popular as the Apollo Client. Apollo is framework agnostic, meaning you can use it with other libraries than react. It can be coupled with other libraries/frameworks like Vue and Angular as well, so everything you learn in this tutorial is likely transferable to the others.

---

[109]http://facebook.github.io/relay
[110]https://github.com/FormidableLabs/urql

Starting with Apollo Boost on the Command Line

This application starts by introducing Apollo Client with Apollo Boost. The latter allows you to create a zero-configuration Apollo Client to get started the fastest and most convenient way. This section focuses on the Apollo Client instead of React for the sake of learning. To get started, find the Node.js boilerplate project and its installation instructions[111]. You will use Apollo Client on the command line in a Node.js environment for now. On top of the minimal Node.js project, you will introduce the Apollo Client with Apollo Boost to experience the GraphQL client without a view-layer library.

In the following, you will consume GitHub's GraphQL API, and then output the queries and mutation results in the command line. To do this, you need a personal access token on GitHub's website, which we covered in a previous chapter. If you haven't done it yet, head to GitHub's instructions[112] to generate a personal access token with sufficient permissions.

After you've cloned and installed the Node.js boilerplate project and created your personal access token, install these two packages in the command line from the root folder of the new project:

Command Line

```
npm install apollo-boost graphql --save
```

The apollo-boost[113] package gives access to a zero-configuration Apollo Client, and the graphql[114] package allows GraphQL queries, mutations, and subscriptions on both the client and server. It is JavaScript's reference implementation of Facebook's GraphQL specification[115].

In the next steps, you will configure and use the Apollo Client that comes with Apollo Boost in the *src/index.js* file of the project. The project stays small, and you will only implement it in this section, so for now we can have everything in one file for the sake of learning.

In your *src/index.js* file, you can import the Apollo Client from Apollo Boost. After that, you can create a client instance by calling its constructor with a URI. The client needs to know where the data comes from, and where it should be written, so you can pass GitHub's API endpoint to it.

---

[111]https://github.com/rwieruch/node-babel-server
[112]https://help.github.com/articles/creating-a-personal-access-token-for-the-command-line/
[113]https://github.com/apollographql/apollo-client/tree/master/packages/apollo-boost
[114]https://github.com/graphql/graphql-js
[115]https://github.com/facebook/graphql

src/index.js

```
import ApolloClient from 'apollo-boost';

const client = new ApolloClient({
  uri: 'https://api.github.com/graphql',
});
```

The Apollo Client already works this way. Remember, however, that GitHub's GraphQL API requires a personal access token. That's why you have to define it once when creating the Apollo Client instance. Therefore, you can use the `request` property to define a function which has access to the context of each request made through the Apollo Client. There, you pass the authorization header using Apollo Boost as one of its default headers.

src/index.js

```
import ApolloClient from 'apollo-boost';

const client = new ApolloClient({
  uri: 'https://api.github.com/graphql',
  request: operation => {
    operation.setContext({
      headers: {
        authorization: `Bearer YOUR_GITHUB_PERSONAL_ACCESS_TOKEN`,
      },
    });
  },
});
```

You did the same for the previous application, using only axios for plain HTTP requests. You configured axios once with the GraphQL API endpoint to default all requests to this URI, and set up the authorization header. The same happened here, because it's enough to configure your client once for all the following GraphQL requests.

Remember, replace the YOUR_GITHUB_PERSONAL_ACCESS_TOKEN string with your personal access token you created on GitHub's website before. However, you may not want to put your access token directly into the source code, so you can create a *.env* file which holds all of your environment variables in your project folder. If you don't want to share the personal token in a public GitHub repository, you can also add the file to your *.gitignore* file. In the command line, you can create this file:

Command Line

```
touch .env
```

Simply define your environment variables in this *.env* file. In your *.env* file, paste the following key value pair whereas the naming for the key is up to you and the valueÂ has to be your personal access token from GitHub.

.env

```
GITHUB_PERSONAL_ACCESS_TOKEN=xxxXXX
```

In any Node.js application, use the key as environment variable in your source code with the following package: dotenv[116]. Follow their instructions to install it for your project. Usually, the process is only a npm install dotenv, followed by including import 'dotenv/config'; at the top of your *index.js* file. Afterward, you can use the personal access token from the *.env* file in your *index.js* file. If you run into an error, just continue reading this section to learn how to fix it.

src/index.js

```
import ApolloClient from 'apollo-boost';

import 'dotenv/config';

const client = new ApolloClient({
  uri: 'https://api.github.com/graphql',
  request: operation => {
    operation.setContext({
      headers: {
        authorization: `Bearer ${process.env.GITHUB_PERSONAL_ACCESS_TOKEN}`,
      },
    });
  },
});
```

Note: There may be additional configuration steps for the previously installed dotenv package. Since the installation instructions may vary with different dotenv versions, check their GitHub website after you have installed it to find the best configurations.

When you start your application with npm start without query or mutation and just Apollo Client, you might see the following error: *"Error: fetch is not found globally and no fetcher passed, to fix pass a fetch for your environment ...".* The error occurs because the native fetch API[117], which is used to make requests to remote APIs on a promise basis, is only available in the browser. You can't access

---

[116]https://github.com/motdotla/dotenv
[117]https://developer.mozilla.org/en-US/docs/Web/API/Fetch_API

it in a Node.js application that runs only in the command line. However, the Apollo Client uses the fetch API to perform queries and mutations, usually from a browser environment and not Node.js environment. As you may remember, a query or mutation can be performed with a simple HTTP request, so the Apollo Client uses the native fetch API from a browser to perform these requests. The solution is to use a node package to make fetch available in a Node.js environment. Fortunately, there are packages to address this issue, which can be installed via the command line:

Command Line

```
npm install cross-fetch --save
```

Second, import it anonymously in your project:

src/index.js

```
import 'cross-fetch/polyfill';
import ApolloClient from 'apollo-boost';
```

The error should disappear when you start the application from the command line, but nothing happens just yet. An instance of the Apollo Client is created with a configuration. In the following, you will perform your first query with Apollo Client.

Exercises:

- Confirm your source code for the last section[118]
- Read more about other view integrations such as Angular and Vue[119]
- Invest a few minutes of your time and take the quiz[120]

---

[118]https://github.com/the-road-to-graphql/node-apollo-boost-github-graphql-api/tree/fd067ec045861e9832cc0b202b25f8d8efd651c9
[119]https://www.apollographql.com/docs/react/integrations.html
[120]https://www.surveymonkey.com/r/5T3W9BB

Apollo Client and a GraphQL Query

Now you are going to send your first query to GitHub's GraphQL API using Apollo Client. Import the following utility from Apollo Boost to define the query:

src/index.js

```
import 'cross-fetch/polyfill';
import ApolloClient, { gql } from 'apollo-boost';
```

Define your query with JavaScript template literals:

src/index.js

```
...

const GET_ORGANIZATION = gql`
  {
    organization(login: "the-road-to-learn-react") {
      name
      url
    }
  }
`;
```

Use the Apollo Client imperatively to send the query to GitHub's GraphQL API. Since the Apollo Client is promise-based, the query() method returns a promise that you can eventually resolve. Since the application runs in the command line, it's sufficient to console log the result there.

src/index.js

```
...

client
  .query({
    query: GET_ORGANIZATION,
  })
  .then(console.log);
```

That's all there is to sending a query with the Apollo Client. As noted, Apollo Client uses HTTP under the hood to send the defined query as payload in a POST method. The result on the command line after starting the application with npm start should look similar to the following:

Command Line

```
{
  data: {
    organization: {
      name: 'The Road to learn React',
      url: 'https://github.com/the-road-to-learn-react',
      __typename: 'Organization'
    }
  },
  loading: false,
  networkStatus: 7,
  stale: false
}
```

The requested information from the GraphQL query can be found in the `data` object. There, you will find the `organization` object with its `name` and `url` fields. The Apollo Client automatically requests the GraphQL meta field[121] `__typename`. The meta field can be used by the Apollo Client as an identifier, to allow caching and optimistic UI updates.

More meta information about the request can be found next to the `data` object. It shows whether the data is still loading, as well as specific details about the network status[122], and see whether the requested data is stale on the server-side.

Exercises:

- Confirm your source code for the last section[123]
- Explore GitHub's GraphQL API
    - Get comfortable navigating through their documentation
    - Add other fields for the `organization` field
- Read more about why you should use Apollo Client[124]
- Read more about the networkStatus property and its possible values[125]
- Invest 3 minutes of your time and take the quiz[126]

---

[121]http://graphql.org/learn/queries/#meta-fields
[122]https://github.com/apollographql/apollo-client/blob/master/packages/apollo-client/src/core/networkStatus.ts
[123]https://github.com/the-road-to-graphql/node-apollo-boost-github-graphql-api/tree/7a800c78e0e09f84b47f4e714abac1d23f5e599e
[124]https://www.apollographql.com/docs/react/why-apollo.html
[125]https://github.com/apollographql/apollo-client/blob/master/packages/apollo-client/src/core/networkStatus.ts
[126]https://www.surveymonkey.com/r/5MF35H5

Apollo Client with Pagination, Variables, Nested Objects and List Fields

You learned about GraphQL pagination and other GraphQL features in previous sections when you built the React with GraphQL application without Apollo. This section will introduce a couple of these features, like GraphQL variables. The login argument for the organization field in the previous query can be substituted with such a variable. First, you have to introduce the variable in your GraphQL query:

src/index.js

```
const GET_ORGANIZATION = gql`
  query($organization: String!) {
    organization(login: $organization) {
      name
      url
    }
  }
`;
```

And second, define it in a variables object in your query object:

src/index.js

```
client
  .query({
    query: GET_ORGANIZATION,
    variables: {
      organization: 'the-road-to-learn-react',
    },
  })
  .then(console.log);
```

That's how you pass variables to the query using an instance of the Apollo Client in your application. Next, add the nested repositories list field to your organization. There, you can request all GitHub repositories in an organization. You may want to rename the query variable as well, but remember to change it when you use the Apollo Client.

src/index.js

```
const GET_REPOSITORIES_OF_ORGANIZATION = gql`
  query($organization: String!) {
    organization(login: $organization) {
      name
      url
      repositories(first: 5) {
        edges {
          node {
            name
            url
          }
        }
      }
    }
  }
`;

client
  .query({
    query: GET_REPOSITORIES_OF_ORGANIZATION,
    variables: {
      organization: 'the-road-to-learn-react',
    },
  })
  .then(console.log);
```

You have seen a similar query structure in the application we created earlier, so this section has a couple of exercises for you to test the GraphQL skills you've learned. Solving the exercises will fortify your GraphQL skills you can focus on connecting the Apollo Client to your React application. You will find all the solutions to the exercises in a GitHub repository for this application at the end of the exercises, but you should consider working it out on your own first.

Exercises:

- Confirm your source code for the last section[127]
- Explore GitHub's GraphQL API
  - Extend the repositories list field by querying an ordered list of repositories which is ordered by the number of stargazers
- Extract the content of a repository node to a GraphQL a reusable fragment

---

[127]https://github.com/the-road-to-graphql/node-apollo-boost-github-graphql-api/tree/a5b1ce61a3dae3ead1b9795f5bf6e0d090c5d24f

- Read more about pagination in GraphQL[128]
- Add the pagination feature for list of repositories
    - Add the `pageInfo` field with its `endCursor` and `hasNextPage` fields in the query
    - Add the `after` argument and introduce a new `$cursor` variable for it
    - Perform the first query without a `cursor` argument
    - Perform a second query with the `endCursor` of the previous query result as `cursor` argument
- Take the three-minute quiz[129]

---

[128]https://graphql.org/learn/pagination
[129]https://www.surveymonkey.com/r/SWL9NJ7

Apollo Client and a GraphQL Mutation

Previously, you learned how to query data from GitHub's GraphQL API using the Apollo Client. Once the client is set up with a configuration, you can use its query() method to send a GraphQL query with optional variables. As you have learned, reading data with GraphQL is not everything, because there are mutations for writing data as well. In this section, you are going to define a mutation to star a repository on GitHub. The Apollo Client instance sends the mutation, but first you have to define it.

src/index.js

```
const ADD_STAR = gql`
  mutation AddStar($repositoryId: ID!) {
    addStar(input: { starrableId: $repositoryId }) {
      starrable {
        id
        viewerHasStarred
      }
    }
  }
`;
```

The identifier for the repository is required, or GitHub's GraphQL server wouldn't know which repository you want to star. In the next code snippet, the Apollo Client is used to star a specific GitHub repository with a given identifier. The identifier can be retrieved by adding the id field to your repository node field in the query. Use the mutate() method on the Apollo Client to send the mutation in a mutation and variables payload. Anything can be done with the result to fit your application, but In this case, the result it is simply logged in the command line.

src/index.js

```
client
  .mutate({
    mutation: ADD_STAR,
    variables: {
      repositoryId: 'MDEwOlJlcG9zaXRvcnk2MzM1Mjkw Nw==',
    },
  })
  .then(console.log);
```

The result should be encapsulated in a addStar object (the name of the mutation), which should reflect exactly the objects and fields that you have defined in the mutation: starrable, id and viewerHasStarred.

You've completed another learning step by using only Apollo Client without any view-layer library. This is to avoid confusing the features of Apollo Client and React Apollo.

Remember, Apollo Client can be used as a standalone GraphQL client without connecting it to a view-layer like React, though it may seem a bit dull to see the data only on the command line. We'll see how Apollo connects the data-layer to a React view-layer in the next section.

Exercises:

- Confirm your source code for the last section[130]
- Implement the removeStar mutation next to the addStar mutation
- Invest three minutes of your time and take the quiz[131]

You have seen how Apollo Client can be used standalone in a Node.js project. Before this, you have used React with GraphQL standalone without Apollo. In the next chapter, you will combine both worlds. Be excited for your first full-fledged React client application with Apollo Client and GraphQL.

[130]https://github.com/the-road-to-graphql/node-apollo-boost-github-graphql-api/tree/ed3363c9981c552223117e5e775bb8c535f79ff5
[131]https://www.surveymonkey.com/r/5XMNFSY

React with GraphQL and Apollo Client

In this tutorial, you will learn how to combine React with GraphQL in your application using Apollo. The Apollo toolset can be used to create a GraphQL client, GraphQL server, and other complementary applications, but you will use the Apollo Client for your React client-side application. Along the way, you will build a simplified GitHub client that consumes GitHub's GraphQL API[132] using Apollo instead of plain HTTP requests like the previous application. Apollo Client can be used to perform queries and mutations, and to read and write data. By the end, you should be able to showcase a React application using GraphQL and Apollo that can be used by other developers as a learning tool. You can find the final project as repository on GitHub[133].

---

[132]https://developer.github.com/v4/
[133]https://github.com/rwieruch/react-graphql-github-apollo

Writing your first React with GraphQL and Apollo Client

Now we'll focus on using Apollo Client in React by building another client application. Basically, you will learn how to connect the data-layer to the view-layer. We'll cover how to send queries and mutations from the view-layer, and how to update the view-layer to reflect the result. Further, you will learn to use GraphQL features like pagination, optimistic UI, caching, local state management, and prefetching with Apollo Client in React.

For this application, no elaborate React setup is needed. Simply use create-react-app[134] to create your React application. If you want to have an elaborate React setup instead, see this setup guide for using Webpack with React[135]. To get started, the following steps have to be performed:

- Create a new React application with create-react-app
- Create a folder/file structure for your project (recommendation below)

You can create your own folder and file structure for your components in the *src/* folder; the following top level structure is only a recommendation. If you adjust it to your own needs, keep in mind that the JavaScript import statements with their paths will need to be adjusted to match. If you don't want to create everything, you can clone this GitHub repository[136] instead and follow its installation instructions.

- App/
    - index.js
- Button/
- Error/
- FetchMore/
- Input/
- Issue/
    - IssueList/
    - IssueItem/
    - index.js
- Link/
- Loading/
- Organization/
- Profile/
- Repository/
    - RepositoryList/

---

[134]https://github.com/facebook/create-react-app
[135]https://www.robinwieruch.de/minimal-react-webpack-babel-setup/
[136]https://github.com/the-road-to-graphql/react-graphql-github-apollo-starter-kit

- – RepositoryItem/
  - – index.js
- TextArea/
- constants/
  - – routes.js
- index.js
- serviceWorker.js
- style.css

The folders primarily represent React components. Some components will be reusable UI components such as the Input and Link components, while other components like Repository and Profile components are domain specific for the GitHub client application. Only the top level folders are specified for now, though more can be introduced later if you choose. Moreover, the *constants* folder has only one file to specify the application's routes, which will be introduced later. You may want to navigate from a page that shows repositories of an organization (Organization component) to a page which shows repositories of yourself (Profile component).

This application will use plain CSS classes and CSS files. By following the plain CSS classes, you can avoid difficulties that may occur with other tools. You will find all the CSS files and their content in the appendix section for this application. The components will use their class names without explaining them. The next sections should be purely dedicated to JavaScript, React, and GraphQL.

Exercises:

- If you are not familiar with React, read up *The Road to learn React*
- Set up the recommended folder/file structure (if you are not going with your own structure and didn't clone the repository)
  - – Create the CSS *style.css* files in their specified folders from the CSS appendix section
  - – Create the *index.js* files for the components
  - – Create further folders on your own for non top level components (e.g. Navigation) when conducting the following sections
- Run the application with `npm start`
  - – Make sure there are no errors
  - – Render only a basic App component with *src/App/index.js* in the *src/index.js* file
- Invest 3 minutes of your time and take the quiz[137]

---

[137]https://www.surveymonkey.com/r/5N9W2WR

Configure Apollo Client for React and GitHub's GraphQL API

In this section, you will set up a Apollo Client instance like we did previously. However, this time you will use Apollo Client directly without the zero-configuration package Apollo Boost, meaning you'll need to configure the Apollo Client yourself without sensible defaults. While it's best to use a tool with sensible defaults for learning, configuring Apollo yourself exposes the composable ecosystem of Apollo Client, how to use it for an initial setup, and how to advance this setup later.

The Apollo Client setup can be completed in the top-level *src/index.js* file, where the React to HTML entry point exists as well. First, install the Apollo Client in your project folder using the command line:

Command Line

```
npm install apollo-client --save
```

Two utility packages are required for two mandatory configurations used to create the Apollo Client. The apollo-cache-inmemory[138] is a recommended cache (read also as: store or state) for your Apollo Client to manage the data, while apollo-link-http is used to configure the URI and additional network information once for an Apollo Client instance.

Command Line

```
npm install apollo-cache-inmemory apollo-link-http --save
```

As you can see, nothing has been mentioned about React, only the Apollo Client plus two packages for its configuration. There are two additional packages required for Apollo Client to work with GraphQL, to be used as internal dependencies by Apollo. The latter is also used to define queries and mutations. Previously, these utilities came directly from Apollo Boost.

Command Line

```
npm install graphql graphql-tag --save
```

That's it for package installation, so now we enter the Apollo Client setup and configuration. In your top level *src/index.js* file, where all the Apollo Client setup will be done in this section, import the necessary classes for the Apollo Client setup from the previously installed packages.

---

[138]https://github.com/apollographql/apollo-client/tree/master/packages/apollo-cache-inmemory

src/index.js

```
import React from 'react';
import ReactDOM from 'react-dom';
import { ApolloClient } from 'apollo-client';
import { HttpLink } from 'apollo-link-http';
import { InMemoryCache } from 'apollo-cache-inmemory';

import './style.css';
import App from './App';

...
```

The `ApolloClient` class is used to create the client instance, and the `HttpLink` and `InMemoryCache` are used for its mandatory configurations. First, you can create a configured `HttpLink` instance, which will be fed to the Apollo Client creation.

src/index.js

```
const GITHUB_BASE_URL = 'https://api.github.com/graphql';

const httpLink = new HttpLink({
  uri: GITHUB_BASE_URL,
  headers: {
    authorization: `Bearer ${
      process.env.REACT_APP_GITHUB_PERSONAL_ACCESS_TOKEN
    }`,
  },
});
```

You may recall the mandatory configuration from previous applications. The `uri` is a mandatory value to define the only GraphQL API endpoint used by the Apollo Client. In this case, Github's GraphQL endpoint is passed as value. When consuming the GitHub GraphQL API, you have to authorize yourself with your personal access token. You should have already created the token in a previous section, which you can now define in a *.env* file in your project folder. Afterward, it should be accessible with `process.env`. Keep in mind that you have to use the REACT_APP prefix when using create-react-app, because that's how it is required by create-react-app. Otherwise, you would be free to choose your own naming for it.

Second, create the cache as the place where the data is managed in Apollo Client. The cache normalizes your data, caches requests to avoid duplicates, and makes it possible to read and write data to the cache. You will use it multiple times while developing this application. The cache instantiation is straight forward, as it doesn't require you to pass any arguments to it. Check the API to explore further configurations.

src/index.js

```
const cache = new InMemoryCache();
```

Finally, you can use both instantiated configurations, the link and the cache, to create the instance of the Apollo Client in the *src/index.js* file.

src/index.js

```
const client = new ApolloClient({
  link: httpLink,
  cache,
});
```

To initialize Apollo Client, you must specify link and cache properties on the config object. Once you start your application again, there should be no errors. If it doesn't, check whether you have implemented a basic App component in your *src/App/index.js* file because the ReactDOM API needs to hook this component into the HTML.

Exercises:

- Confirm your source code for the last section[139]
- Read more about the network layer configuration in Apollo Client[140]
- Invest 3 minutes of your time and take the quiz[141]

---

[139]https://github.com/the-road-to-graphql/react-graphql-github-apollo/tree/c7454c9f6b5f7cdf9d65722ccae7ae38f648aef3
[140]https://www.apollographql.com/docs/react/advanced/network-layer.html
[141]https://www.surveymonkey.com/r/5FYZT8T

Connect Data-Layer to View-Layer: Introducing React Apollo

All we've done thus far has been the framework agnostic part of Apollo Client. However, without connecting React to it, you'd have a hard time making effective use of GraphQL. That's why there is an official library to connect both worlds: react-apollo[142]. The great thing about those connecting libraries is that there are solutions for other view-layer solutions like Angular and Vue, too, so you can use the Apollo Client in a framework agnostic way. In the following, it needs two steps to connect the Apollo Client with React. First, install the library in the command line in your project folder:

Command Line

```
npm install react-apollo --save
```

Second, import its ApolloProvider component, and use it as a composing component around your App component in the *src/index.js* file. Under the hood, it uses React's Context API[143] to pass the Apollo Client through your application.

src/index.js

```
import React from 'react';
import ReactDOM from 'react-dom';
import { ApolloProvider } from 'react-apollo';
import { ApolloClient } from 'apollo-client';
import { HttpLink } from 'apollo-link-http';
import { InMemoryCache } from 'apollo-cache-inmemory';

...

ReactDOM.render(
  <ApolloProvider client={client}>
    <App />
  </ApolloProvider>,
  document.getElementById('root')
);
```

Now you have implicit access to the Apollo Client in your React view-layer. It says implicit because most often you will not use the client explicitly. You will see in the next section what this means.

---

[142]https://github.com/apollographql/react-apollo
[143]https://www.robinwieruch.de/react-context-api/

Exercises:

- Confirm your source code for the last section[144]
- Read more about configuring and connecting Apollo Client to React[145]
- Invest 3 minutes of your time and take the quiz[146]

---

[144]https://github.com/the-road-to-graphql/react-graphql-github-apollo/tree/8377cbc55de3c860df0150d8946e261938a67db5
[145]https://www.apollographql.com/docs/react/essentials/get-started.html
[146]https://www.surveymonkey.com/r/5FHMHW8

GraphQL Query with Apollo Client in React

In this section, you will implement your first GraphQL query using Apollo Client in React. You've seen how different entities, such as the current user (viewer) or repositories, can be queried from GitHub's GraphQL API. This time you will do it in React. A Profile component might be the best place to render the current user and its associated repositories. Start by using the not-yet-implemented Profile component in your App component in the *src/App/index.js* file, which we'll take care of next. It makes sense to extract the Profile component now, because the App component will be the static frame around the application later. Components like Navigation and Footer are static, and components such as Profile and Organization are dynamically rendered based on routing (URLs).

src/App/index.js

```
import React, { Component } from 'react';

import Profile from '../Profile';

class App extends Component {
  render() {
    return <Profile />;
  }
}

export default App;
```

In your *src/Profile/index.js* file, add a simple functional stateless component. In the next step you will extend it with a GraphQL query.

src/Profile/index.js

```
import React from 'react';

const Profile = () =>
  <div>Profile</div>

export default Profile;
```

Now we'll learn to query data with GraphQL and Apollo Client. The Apollo Client was provided in a previous section with React's Context API in a top level component. You have implicit access to it, but never use it directly for standard queries and mutations. It says "standard" here, because there will be situations where you use the Apollo Client instance directly while implementing this application.

The React Apollo package grants access to a Query component, which takes a query as prop and executes it when its rendered. That's the important part: it executes the query when it is rendered. It uses React's render props[147] pattern, using a child as a function implementation where you can access the result of the query as an argument.

src/Profile/index.js

```
import React from 'react';
import { Query } from 'react-apollo';

const Profile = () => (
  <Query query={}>
    {() => <div>My Profile</div>}
  </Query>
);

export default Profile;
```

This is a function that returns only JSX, but you have access to additional information in the function arguments. First, define the GraphQL query to request your authorizations. You can use a previously installed utility package to define the query.

src/Profile/index.js

```
import React from 'react';
import gql from 'graphql-tag';
import { Query } from 'react-apollo';

const GET_CURRENT_USER = gql`
  {
    viewer {
      login
      name
    }
  }
`;

const Profile = () => (
  <Query query={GET_CURRENT_USER}>
    {() => <div>My Profile</div>}
  </Query>
);

export default Profile;
```

---

[147]https://www.robinwieruch.de/react-render-props-pattern/

Use the children as a function pattern to retrieve the query result as a data object, and render the information in your JSX.

src/Profile/index.js

```
import React from 'react';
import gql from 'graphql-tag';
import { Query } from 'react-apollo';

const GET_CURRENT_USER = gql`
  {
    viewer {
      login
      name
    }
  }
`;

const Profile = () => (
  <Query query={GET_CURRENT_USER}>
    {({ data }) => {
      const { viewer } = data;

      return (
        <div>
          {viewer.name} {viewer.login}
        </div>
      );
    }}
  </Query>
);

export default Profile;
```

Make sure to give some type of visual feedback until your view-layer can be rendered with actual data.:

src/Profile/index.js

```
const Profile = () => (
  <Query query={GET_CURRENT_USER}>
    {({ data }) => {
      const { viewer } = data;

      if (!viewer) {
        return null;
      }

      return (
        <div>
          {viewer.name} {viewer.login}
        </div>
      );
    }}
  </Query>
);
```

That's how you define a GraphQL query in a declarative way in React. Once the Query component renders, the request is executed. The Apollo Client is used, provided in a top level component, to perform the query. The render props pattern makes it possible to access the result of the query in the child function. You can try it in your browser to verify that it actually works for you.

There is more information found in the render prop function. Check the official React Apollo API for additional information beyond the examples in this application. Next, let's show a loading indicator when a query is pending:

src/Profile/index.js

```
const Profile = () => (
  <Query query={GET_CURRENT_USER}>
    {({ data, loading }) => {
      const { viewer } = data;

      if (loading || !viewer) {
        return <div>Loading ...</div>;
      }

      return (
        <div>
          {viewer.name} {viewer.login}
        </div>
      );
```

```
    }}
  </Query>
);
```

The application now shows a loading indicator when there is no `viewer` object or the `loading` boolean is set to true. As you can assume that the request will be pending when there is no `viewer`, you can show the loading indicator from the beginning. At this point, it's best to extract the loading indicator as its own component because you will have to reuse it later for other queries. You created a Loading folder for it before, which will house the *src/Loading/index.js* file. Then, use it in your Profile component.

src/Loading/index.js

```
import React from 'react';

const Loading = () =>
  <div>Loading ...</div>

export default Loading;
```

Next, extend the query with a nested list field for querying your own GitHub repositories. You have done it a few times before, so the query structure shouldn't be any different now. The following query requests a lot of information you will use in this application:

src/Profile/index.js

```
const GET_REPOSITORIES_OF_CURRENT_USER = gql`
  {
    viewer {
      repositories(
        first: 5
        orderBy: { direction: DESC, field: STARGAZERS }
      ) {
        edges {
          node {
            id
            name
            url
            descriptionHTML
            primaryLanguage {
              name
            }
            owner {
              login
```

```
            url
          }
          stargazers {
            totalCount
          }
          viewerHasStarred
          watchers {
            totalCount
          }
          viewerSubscription
        }
      }
    }
  }
`;
```

Use this extended and renamed query in your Query component to request additional information about repositories. Pass these repositories from the query result to a new RepositoryList component which should do all the rendering for you. It's not the responsibility of the Profile component, and you may want to render a list of repositories somewhere else.

src/Profile/index.js

```
...

import RepositoryList from '../Repository';
import Loading from '../Loading';


...

const Profile = () => (
  <Query query={GET_REPOSITORIES_OF_CURRENT_USER}>
    {(({ data, loading }) => {
      const { viewer } = data;

      if (loading || !viewer) {
        return <Loading />;
      }

      return <RepositoryList repositories={viewer.repositories} />;
    }}
  </Query>
);
```

In your *src/Repository/index.js* file, create your first import/export statements for the RepositoryList component from a dedicated file in this folder. The *index.js* file is used as your entry point to this Repository module. Everything used from this module should be accessible by importing it from this *index.js* file.

src/Repository/index.js

```
import RepositoryList from './RepositoryList';

export default RepositoryList;
```

Next, define the RepositoryList component in your *src/Repository/RepositoryList/index.js* file. The component only takes the array of repositories as props, which will be retrieved by the GraphQL query to render a list of RepositoryItem components. The identifier of each repository can be passed as key attribute to the rendered list. Otherwise, all props from one repository node are passed to the RepositoryItem using the JavaScript spread operator.

src/Repository/RepositoryList/index.js

```
import React from 'react';

import RepositoryItem from '../RepositoryItem';

import '../style.css';

const RepositoryList = ({ repositories }) =>
  repositories.edges.map(({ node }) => (
    <div key={node.id} className="RepositoryItem">
      <RepositoryItem {...node} />
    </div>
  ));

export default RepositoryList;
```

Finally, define the RepositoryItem component in the *src/Repository/RepositoryItem/index.js* file to render all the queried information about each repository. The file already uses a couple of stylings which you may have defined in a CSS file as suggested before. Otherwise, the component renders only static information for now.

src/Repository/RepositoryItem/index.js

```
import React from 'react';

import Link from '../../Link';

import '../style.css';

const RepositoryItem = ({
  name,
  url,
  descriptionHTML,
  primaryLanguage,
  owner,
  stargazers,
  watchers,
  viewerSubscription,
  viewerHasStarred,
}) => (
  <div>
    <div className="RepositoryItem-title">
      <h2>
        <Link href={url}>{name}</Link>
      </h2>

      <div className="RepositoryItem-title-action">
        {stargazers.totalCount} Stars
      </div>
    </div>

    <div className="RepositoryItem-description">
      <div
        className="RepositoryItem-description-info"
        dangerouslySetInnerHTML={{ __html: descriptionHTML }}
      />
      <div className="RepositoryItem-description-details">
        <div>
          {primaryLanguage && (
            <span>Language: {primaryLanguage.name}</span>
          )}
        </div>
        <div>
          {owner && (
            <span>
```

```
        Owner: <a href={owner.url}>{owner.login}</a>
      </span>
    )}
  </div>
 </div>
 </div>
 </div>
);
```

```
export default RepositoryItem;
```

The anchor element to link to the repository is already extracted as a Link component. The Link component in the *src/Link/index.js* file could look like the following, to make it possible to open those URLs in an extra browser tab:

src/Link/index.js
```
import React from 'react';

const Link = ({ children, ...props }) => (
  <a {...props} target="_blank" rel="noopener noreferrer">
    {children}
  </a>
);
```

```
export default Link;
```

Once you restart your application, you should see a styled list of repositories with a name, url, description, star count, owner, and the project's implementation language. If you can't see any repositories, check to see if your GitHub account has any public repositories. If it doesn't, then it's normal that nothing showed up. I recommend you make yourself comfortable with GitHub by creating a couple of repositories, both for the sake of learning about GitHub and to use this data to practice with this tutorial. Another way to create repositories for your own account is forking repositories from other people.

What you have done in the last steps of this section were pure React implementation, but this is only one opinionated way on how to structure components. The most important part from this section though happens in the Profile component. There, you introduced a Query component that takes a query as prop. Once the Query component renders, it executes the GraphQL query. The result of the query is made accessible as an argument within React's render props pattern.

Exercises:

- Confirm your source code for the last section[148]

---

[148]https://github.com/the-road-to-graphql/react-graphql-github-apollo/tree/44ceb0482442eb07e56d134e6e1da8abefd68afe

- Read more about queries with Apollo Client in React[149]
- Invest 3 minutes of your time and take the quiz[150]

---

[149]https://www.apollographql.com/docs/react/essentials/queries.html
[150]https://www.surveymonkey.com/r/53Q6K3V

Apollo Client Error Handling in React

Before diving into GraphQL mutations in React with Apollo Client, this section should clarify error handling with Apollo in React. The error handling happens on two levels: the application level and the query/mutation level. Both can be implemented with the two cases that follow. On a query level, in your Profile component, you have access to the query `data` and `loading` properties. Apart from these, you can also access the `error` object, which can be used to show a conditional error message.

src/Profile/index.js

```
...

import RepositoryList from '../Repository';
import Loading from '../Loading';
import ErrorMessage from '../Error';

...

const Profile = () => (
  <Query query={GET_REPOSITORIES_OF_CURRENT_USER}>
    {(({ data, loading, error }) => {
      if (error) {
        return <ErrorMessage error={error} />;
      }

      const { viewer } = data;

      if (loading || !viewer) {
        return <Loading />;
      }

      return <RepositoryList repositories={viewer.repositories} />;
    }}
  </Query>
);

export default Profile;
```

Whereas the ErrorMessage component from the *src/Error/index.js* could look like the following:

src/Error/index.js

```
import React from 'react';

import './style.css';

const ErrorMessage = ({ error }) => (
  <div className="ErrorMessage">
    <small>{error.toString()}</small>
  </div>
);

export default ErrorMessage;
```

Try to change the name of a field in your query to something not offered by GitHub's GraphQL API, and observe what's rendered in the browser. You should see something like this: *Error: GraphQL error: Field 'viewers' doesn't exist on type 'Query'*. Or, if you simulate offline functionality, you'll see: *Error: Network error: Failed to fetch*. That's how errors can be separated into GraphQL errors and network errors. You can handle errors on a component or query level, but it will also help with mutations later. To implement error handling on an application level, install another Apollo package:

Command Line

```
npm install apollo-link-error --save
```

You can import it in your *src/index.js* file and create such an error link:

src/index.js

```
import React from 'react';
import ReactDOM from 'react-dom';
import { ApolloProvider } from 'react-apollo';
import { ApolloClient } from 'apollo-client';
import { HttpLink } from 'apollo-link-http';
import { onError } from 'apollo-link-error';
import { InMemoryCache } from 'apollo-cache-inmemory';

...

const errorLink = onError(({ graphQLErrors, networkError }) => {
  if (graphQLErrors) {
    // do something with graphql error
  }
```

```
  if (networkError) {
    // do something with network error
  }
});
```

You could differentiate the error handling at the application level into development and production mode. During development, it might be sufficient to console log the errors to a developer console in the browser. In production mode, you can setup a error tracking service like Sentry[151]. It will teach you to identify bugs in a web dashboard more efficient

Now you have two links in your application: `httpLink` and `errorLink`. To combing them for use with the Apollo Client instance, we'll download yet another useful package in the Apollo ecosystem that makes link compositions possible in the command line:

Command Line

```
npm install apollo-link --save
```

And second, use it to combine your two links in the *src/index.js* file:

src/index.js

```
...
import { ApolloClient } from 'apollo-client';
import { ApolloLink } from 'apollo-link';
import { HttpLink } from 'apollo-link-http';
import { onError } from 'apollo-link-error';
import { InMemoryCache } from 'apollo-cache-inmemory';


...

const httpLink = ...

const errorLink = ...

const link = ApolloLink.from([errorLink, httpLink]);

const cache = new InMemoryCache();

const client = new ApolloClient({
  link,
  cache,
});
```

---
[151]https://sentry.io

That's how two or multiple links can be composed for creating a Apollo Client instance. There are several links developed by the community and Apollo maintainers that extend the Apollo Client with advanced functionality. Remember, it's important to understand that links can be used to access and modify the GraphQL control flow. When doing so, be careful to chain the control flow in the correct order. The `apollo-link-http` is called a **terminating link** because it turns an operation into a result that usually occurs from a network request. On the other side, the `apollo-link-error` is a **non-terminating link**. It only enhances your terminating link with features, since a terminating link has to be last entity in the control flow chain.

Exercises:

- Confirm your source code for the last section[152]
- Read more about different Apollo Error types and error policies[153]
- Read more about Apollo Links[154]
- Read more about composable Apollo Links[155]
- Implement the apollo-link-retry[156] in case a network request fails
- Invest 3 minutes of your time and take the quiz[157]

---

[152]https://github.com/the-road-to-graphql/react-graphql-github-apollo/tree/fa06945db4a933fe4a29c41f46fdc7034bceeb6e
[153]https://www.apollographql.com/docs/react/features/error-handling.html
[154]https://www.apollographql.com/docs/link/
[155]https://www.apollographql.com/docs/link/composition.html
[156]https://www.apollographql.com/docs/link/links/retry.html
[157]https://www.surveymonkey.com/r/53HLLFX

GraphQL Mutation with Apollo Client in React

The previous sections have taught you how to query data with React Apollo and the Apollo Client. In this section, you will learn about mutations. As in other applications before, you will implement starring a repository with GitHub's exposed `addStar` mutation.

The mutation starts out with a variable to identify the repository to be starred. We haven't used a variable in Query component yet, but the following mutation works the same way, which can be defined in the *src/Repository/RepositoryItem/index.js* file.

src/Repository/RepositoryItem/index.js

```
import React from 'react';
import gql from 'graphql-tag';

...

const STAR_REPOSITORY = gql`
  mutation($id: ID!) {
    addStar(input: { starrableId: $id }) {
      starrable {
        id
        viewerHasStarred
      }
    }
  }
`;

...
```

The mutation definition takes the `id` variable as input for the `addStar` mutation. As before, you can decide what should be returned in case of a successful mutation. Now, you can use a Mutation component that represents the previously used Query component, but this time for mutations. You have to pass the mutation prop, but also a variable prop for passing the identifier for the repository.

src/Repository/RepositoryItem/index.js

```
import React from 'react';
import gql from 'graphql-tag';
import { Mutation } from 'react-apollo';

...

const RepositoryItem = ({
  id,
  name,
  url,
  descriptionHTML,
  primaryLanguage,
  owner,
  stargazers,
  watchers,
  viewerSubscription,
  viewerHasStarred,
}) => (
  <div>
    <div className="RepositoryItem-title">
      <h2>
        ...
      </h2>

      <div>
        <Mutation mutation={STAR_REPOSITORY} variables={{ id }}>
          {addStar => <div>{stargazers.totalCount} Star</div>}
        </Mutation>
      </div>
    </div>

    <div className="RepositoryItem-description">
      ...
    </div>
  </div>
);
```

Note: The div element surrounding the Mutation component is there for other mutations you will implement in this section.

The `id` for each repository should be available due to previous query result. It has to be used as a variable for the mutation to identify the repository. The Mutation component is used like the

Query component, because it implements the render prop pattern as well. The first argument is different, though, as it is the mutation itself instead of the mutation result. Use this function to trigger the mutation before expecting a result. Later, you will see how to retrieve the mutation result; for now, the mutating function can be used in a button element. In this case, it is already in a Button component:

src/Repository/RepositoryItem/index.js

```
...

import Link from '../../Link';
import Button from '../../Button';

...

const RepositoryItem = ({ ... }) => (
  <div>
    <div className="RepositoryItem-title">
      ...

    <div>
      <Mutation mutation={STAR_REPOSITORY} variables={{ id }}>
        {(addStar) => (
          <Button
            className={'RepositoryItem-title-action'}
            onClick={addStar}
          >
            {stargazers.totalCount} Star
          </Button>
        )}
      </Mutation>
    </div>
  </div>

    ...
  </div>
);
```

The styled Button component could be implemented in the *src/Button/index.js* file. It's already extracted, because you will use it in this application later.

src/Button/index.js

```
import React from 'react';

import './style.css';

const Button = ({
  children,
  className,
  color = 'black',
  type = 'button',
  ...props
}) => (
  <button
    className={`${className} Button Button_${color}`}
    type={type}
    {...props}
  >
    {children}
  </button>
);

export default Button;
```

Let's get to the mutation result which was left out before. Access it as a second argument in your child function of the render prop.

src/Repository/RepositoryItem/index.js

```
const RepositoryItem = ({ ... }) => (
  <div>
    <div className="RepositoryItem-title">

      ...

    <div>
      <Mutation mutation={STAR_REPOSITORY} variables={{ id }}>
        {(addStar, { data, loading, error }) => (
          <Button
            className={'RepositoryItem-title-action'}
            onClick={addStar}
          >
            {stargazers.totalCount} Star
          </Button>
        )}
```

```
        </Mutation>
      </div>
    </div>


    ...
  </div>
);
```

A mutation works like a query when using React Apollo. It uses the render prop pattern to access the mutation and the result of the mutation. The mutation can be used as a function in the UI. It has access to the variables that are passed in the Mutation component, but it can also override the variables when you pass them in a configuration object to the function (e.g. `addStar({ variables: { id } })`). That's a general pattern in React Apollo: You can specify information like variables in the Mutation component, or when you call the mutating function to override it.

Note that if you use the `viewerHasStarred` boolean from the query result to show either a "Star" or "Unstar" button, you can do it with a conditional rendering:

src/Repository/RepositoryItem/index.js

```
const RepositoryItem = ({ ... }) => (
  <div>
    <div className="RepositoryItem-title">

      ...


    <div>
      {!viewerHasStarred ? (
        <Mutation mutation={STAR_REPOSITORY} variables={{ id }}>
          {(addStar, { data, loading, error }) => (
            <Button
              className={'RepositoryItem-title-action'}
              onClick={addStar}
            >
              {stargazers.totalCount} Star
            </Button>
          )}
        </Mutation>
      ) : (
        <span>{/* Here comes your removeStar mutation */}</span>
      )}


      {/* Here comes your updateSubscription mutation */}
    </div>
  </div>
```

```
    . . .
  </div>
);
```

When you star a repository as above, the "Star" button disappears. This is what we want, because it means the `viewerHasStarred` boolean has been updated in Apollo Client's cache for the identified repository. Apollo Client was able to match the mutation result with the repository identifier to the repository entity in Apollo Client's cache, the props were updated, and the UI re-rendered. Yet, on the other side, the count of stargazers who have starred the repository isn't updated because it cannot be retrieved from GitHub's API. The count must be updated the count in Apollo Client's cache. You will find out more about this topic in one of the following sections.

Exercises:

- Confirm your source code for the last section[158]
- Read more about mutations with Apollo Client in React[159]
- Implement other mutations in the RepositoryItem component
    - Implement the `removeStar` mutation when the `viewerHasStarred` boolean is true
    - Show a button with the watchers count which should be used to watch/unwatch a repository
        * Implement the `updateSubscription` mutation from GitHub's GraphQL API to watch/unwatch a repository based on the `viewerSubscription` status
- Invest three minutes of your time and take the quiz[160]

---

[158]https://github.com/the-road-to-graphql/react-graphql-github-apollo/tree/feb2b794392f9c5b1d2566ed39ad4ca5f650f194
[159]https://www.apollographql.com/docs/react/essentials/mutations.html
[160]https://www.surveymonkey.com/r/5GJQWXC

GraphQL Query/Mutation with Higher-Order Components in React

We've done Query and Mutation components from React Apollo to connect a data-layer (Apollo Client) with a view-layer (React). The Query component executes the query when it is rendered, whereas the Mutation component gives access to a function that triggers the mutation. Both components use the render props pattern to make the results accessible in their child functions.

Higher-Order Components (HOC)[161] is a widely accepted alternative to React's render prop pattern. The React Apollo package implements a Higher-Order Component for queries and mutations as well, though the team behind Apollo doesn't advertise it, and even spoke in favor of render props as their first choice. Nonetheless, this section shows you the alternative, using a Higher-Order Component instead of a Render Prop, though this application will continue to use the render prop pattern afterward. If you already have access to the query result in the Profile component's arguments, there is no Query component needed in the component itself:

src/Profile/index.js

```
const Profile = ({ data, loading, error }) => {
  if (error) {
    return <ErrorMessage error={error} />;
  }

  const { viewer } = data;

  if (loading || !viewer) {
    return <Loading />;
  }

  return <RepositoryList repositories={viewer.repositories} />;
};
```

There is no GraphQL involved here, because all you see is the pure view-layer. Instead, the data-layer logic is extracted into a Higher-Order Component. We import the graphql HOC from the React Apollo package in order to apply it on the Profile component, which takes the query definition as argument.

---

[161]https://www.robinwieruch.de/gentle-introduction-higher-order-components/

src/Profile/index.js

```
import React from 'react';
import gql from 'graphql-tag';
import { graphql } from 'react-apollo';

...

const GET_REPOSITORIES_OF_CURRENT_USER = gql`
  {
    viewer {
      ...
    }
  }
`;

const Profile = ({ data, loading, error }) => {
  ...
};

export default graphql(GET_REPOSITORIES_OF_CURRENT_USER)(Profile);
```

I find the HOC approach cleaner than the render props, because it co-locates both the data-layer and view-layer instead of inserting the one into the other. However, the team behind Apollo made the decision to favor render props instead. While I find the HOC approach more concise, the render prop pattern comes with its own advantages for mutating and querying data. For instance, imagine a query depends on a prop used as variable. It would be cumbersome to access the incoming prop in a statically-defined Higher-Order Component, but it can be dynamically used in a render prop because it is used within the Profile component where the props are naturally accessible. Another advantage is the power of composition for render props, which is useful when one query depends on the result of another. It can be achieved with HOCs as well, but again, it is more cumbersome. It boils down to seemingly never ending "Higher-Order Components vs Render Props" discussions.

Exercises:

- Confirm your source code for the last section[162]
- Come up with your own opinion about the advantages and disadvantages of using a Higher-Order Component or Render Prop
- Try to implement one of your mutations with a Higher-Order Component
- Invest 3 minutes of your time and take the quiz[163]

---

[162]https://github.com/the-road-to-graphql/react-graphql-github-apollo/tree/694cc4ec8f0d3546c13e0a32cd1f18ba9a990713
[163]https://www.surveymonkey.com/r/5G6QPLY

Local State Management with Apollo Client in React

Let's get back to the Repository component. You have experienced that the `viewerHasStarred` boolean updates in the Apollo Client's cache after a mutation was successful. That's great, because Apollo Client handles this for you, based on the mutation result. If you have followed the exercises of the mutation section, you should probably see something like a toggling "Star" and "Unstar" label for the button. All of this happens because you returned the `viewerHasStarred` boolean in your mutation result. Apollo Client is clever enough to update the repository entity, which is normalized accessible in the cache. That's powerful default behavior, isn't it? You don't need to handle the local state management yourself, since Apollo Client figures it out for you as long as you provide useful information in the mutation's result.

Apollo Client doesn't update the count of stars after the mutation, though. Normally, it is assumed that the count of stars increments by one when it is starred, with the opposite for unstarring. Since we don't return a count of stargazers in the mutation result, you have to handle the update in Apollo Client's cache yourself. Using Apollo Client's `refetchQueries` option is the naive approach for a mutation call, or a Mutation component to trigger a refetch for all queries, where the query result might be affected by the mutation. But that's not the best way to deal with this problem. It costs another query request to keep the data consistent after a mutation. In a growing application, this approach will eventually become problematic. Fortunately, the Apollo Client offers other functionalities to read/write manually from/to the cache locally without more network requests. The Mutation component offers a prop where you can insert update functionality that has access to the Apollo Client instance for the update mechanism.

Before implementing the update functionality for the local state management, let's refactor another piece of code that will be useful for a local state update mechanism. The query definition next to your Profile component has grown to several fields with multiple object nestings. Previously, you learned about GraphQL fragments, and how they can be used to split parts of a query to reuse later. Next, we will split all the field information you used for the repository's node. You can define this fragment in the *src/Repository/fragments.js* file to keep it reusable for other components.

src/Repository/fragments.js

```
import gql from 'graphql-tag';

const REPOSITORY_FRAGMENT = gql`
  fragment repository on Repository {
    id
    name
    url
    descriptionHTML
    primaryLanguage {
      name
    }
```

```
    owner {
      login
      url
    }
    stargazers {
      totalCount
    }
    viewerHasStarred
    watchers {
      totalCount
    }
    viewerSubscription
  }
`;

export default REPOSITORY_FRAGMENT;
```

You split this partial query (fragment), because it is used more often in this application in the next sections for a local state update mechanism, hence the previous refactoring.

The fragment shouldn't be imported directly from the *src/Repository/fragments.js* path to your Profile component, because the *src/Repository/index.js* file is the preferred entry point to this module.

src/Repository/index.js

```
import RepositoryList from './RepositoryList';
import REPOSITORY_FRAGMENT from './fragments';

export { REPOSITORY_FRAGMENT };

export default RepositoryList;
```

Finally, import the fragment in the Profile component's file to use it again.

src/Profile/index.js

```
...

import RepositoryList, { REPOSITORY_FRAGMENT } from '../Repository';
import Loading from '../Loading';
import ErrorMessage from '../Error';

const GET_REPOSITORIES_OF_CURRENT_USER = gql`
  {
```

```
    viewer {
      repositories(
        first: 5
        orderBy: { direction: DESC, field: STARGAZERS }
      ) {
        edges {
          node {
            ...repository
          }
        }
      }
    }
  }

  ${REPOSITORY_FRAGMENT}
`;
```

```
...
```

The refactoring is done. Your query is now more concise, and the fragment in its natural repository module can be reused for other places and functionalities. Next, use Mutation component's update prop to pass a function which will update the local cache eventually.

src/Repository/RepositoryItem/index.js

```
...

const updateAddStar = (client, mutationResult) => {
  ...
};

const RepositoryItem = ({ ... }) => (
  <div>
    <div className="RepositoryItem-title">
      ...

    <div>
      {viewerHasStarred ? (
        ...
      ) : (
        <Mutation
          mutation={STAR_REPOSITORY}
          variables={{ id }}
          update={updateAddStar}
```

```
        >
            . . .
        </Mutation>
      )}
    </div>
  </div>

  . . .
  </div>
);


export default RepositoryItem;
```

The function is extracted as its own JavaScript variable, otherwise ends up too verbose in the RepositoryItem component when keeping it inlined in the Mutation component. The function has access to the Apollo Client and the mutation result in its argument, and you need both to update data so you can destructure the mutation result in the function signature. If you don't know how the mutation result looks like, check the STAR_REPOSITORY mutation definition again, where you defined all fields that should appear in the mutation result. For now, the id of the to be updated repository is the important part.

src/Repository/RepositoryItem/index.js

```
const updateAddStar = (
  client,
  { data: { addStar: { starrable: { id } } } },
) => {
  . . .
};
```

You could have passed the id of the repository to the updateAddStar() function, which was a higher-order function in the Mutation component's render prop child function. You already have access to the repository's identifier in the Repository component.

Now comes the most exciting part of this section. You can use the Apollo Client to read data from the cache, but also to write data to it. The goal is to read the starred repository from the cache, which is why we need the id to increment its stargazers count by one and write the updated repository back to the cache. You got the repository by its id from the cache by extracting the repository fragment. You can use it along with the repository identifier to retrieve the actual repository from Apollo Client's cache without querying all the data with a naive query implementation.

src/Repository/RepositoryItem/index.js

```
...

import REPOSITORY_FRAGMENT from '../fragments';
import Link from '../../Link';
import Button from '../../Button';

...

const updateAddStar = (
  client,
  { data: { addStar: { starrable: { id } } } },
) => {
  const repository = client.readFragment({
    id: `Repository:${id}`,
    fragment: REPOSITORY_FRAGMENT,
  });

  // update count of stargazers of repository

  // write repository back to cache
};
```

The Apollo Client's cache that you set up to initialize the Apollo Client normalizes and stores queried data. Otherwise, the repository would be a deeply nested entity in a list of repositories for the query structure used in the Profile component. Normalization of a data structure makes it possible to retrieve entities by their identifier and their GraphQL __typename meta field. The combination of both is the default key, which is called a composite key[164], to read or write an entity from or to the cache. You may find out more about changing this default composite key in the exercises of this section.

Furthermore, the resulting entity has all properties specified in the fragment. If there is a field in the fragment not found on the entity in the cache, you may see the following error message: *Can't find field __typename on object ....* That's why we use the identical fragment to read from the local cache to query the GraphQL API.

After you have retrieved the repository entity with a fragment and its composite key, you can update the count of stargazers and write back the data to your cache. In this case, increment the number of stargazers.

---

[164]https://en.wikipedia.org/wiki/Compound_key

src/Repository/RepositoryItem/index.js

```
const updateAddStar = (
  client,
  { data: { addStar: { starrable: { id } } } },
) => {
  const repository = client.readFragment({
    id: `Repository:${id}`,
    fragment: REPOSITORY_FRAGMENT,
  });

  const totalCount = repository.stargazers.totalCount + 1;

  client.writeFragment({
    id: `Repository:${id}`,
    fragment: REPOSITORY_FRAGMENT,
    data: {
      ...repository,
      stargazers: {
        ...repository.stargazers,
        totalCount,
      },
    },
  });
};
```

Let's recap all three steps here. First, you have retrieved (read) the repository entity from the Apollo Client using an identifier and the fragment; second, you updated the information of the entity; and third, you wrote back the data with updated information, but kept all remaining information intact using the JavaScript spread operator. This is a manual update mechanism that can be used when a mutation is missing data.

It is a good practice to use an identical fragment for all three parts: the initial query, the `readFragment()`, and `writeFragment()` cache method. Your data structure for the entity stays consistent in your cache. For instance, if you forget to include a property defined by the fragment's fields in data object of the `writeFragment()` method, you get a warning: *Missing field __typename in ....*

On an implementation level, you learned about extracting fragments from a query or mutation. Fragments allow you to define your shared entities by GraphQL types. You can reuse those in your queries, mutations or local state management methods to update the cache. On a higher level, you learned that Apollo Client's cache normalizes your data, so you can retrieve entities that were fetched with a deeply nested query using their type and identifier as composite key. Without it, you'd have to perform normalizations for all the fetched data before putting it in your store/state.

Exercises:

- Confirm your source code for the last section[165]
- Read more about Local State Management in Apollo Client[166]
- Read more about Fragments in Apollo Client[167]
- Implement local cache updates for all the other mutations from the previous exercises
  - Implement the identical local cache update, but with decreasing the count of stargazers, for your `removeStar` mutation
  - Implement the local cache update for the `updateSubscription` mutation
  - You will see in the next section a working solution for it
- Read more about Caching in Apollo Client and the composite key to identify entities[168]
- Invest 3 minutes of your time and take the quiz[169]

---

[165]https://github.com/the-road-to-graphql/react-graphql-github-apollo/tree/24bb647ac94f1af1c52b61e41cebba6a6fd95f4f
[166]https://www.apollographql.com/docs/react/essentials/local-state.html
[167]https://www.apollographql.com/docs/react/advanced/fragments.html
[168]https://www.apollographql.com/docs/react/advanced/caching.html
[169]https://www.surveymonkey.com/r/5BSDXF7

Apollo Client Optimistic UI in React

We've covered the basics, so now it's time for the advanced topics. One of those topics is the optimistic UI with React Apollo, which makes everything onscreen more synchronous. For instance, when liking a post on Twitter, the like appears immediately. As developers, we know there is a request that sends the information for the like to the Twitter backend. This request is asynchronous and doesn't resolve immediately with a result. The optimistic UI immediately assumes a successful request and mimics the result of such request for the frontend so it can update its UI immediately, before the real response arrives later. With a failed request, the optimistic UI performs a rollback and updates itself accordingly. Optimistic UI improves the user experience by omitting inconvenient feedback (e.g. loading indicators) for the user. The good thing is that React Apollo comes with this feature out of the box.

In this section, you will implement an optimistic UI for when a user clicks the watch/unwatch mutation you implemented in a previous exercise. If you haven't, it's time to implement it now, or you can substitute it with the star or unstar mutation. Either way, completing the optimistic UI behavior for all three mutations is the next exercise. For completeness, this is a possible implementation of the watch mutation as a button next to the "Star"/"Unstar" buttons. First, the mutation:

src/Repository/RepositoryItem/index.js

```
const WATCH_REPOSITORY = gql`
  mutation ($id: ID!, $viewerSubscription: SubscriptionState!) {
    updateSubscription(
      input: { state: $viewerSubscription, subscribableId: $id }
    ) {
      subscribable {
        id
        viewerSubscription
      }
    }
  }
`;
```

Second, the usage of the mutation with a Mutation render prop component:

src/Repository/RepositoryItem/index.js

```
const VIEWER_SUBSCRIPTIONS = {
  SUBSCRIBED: 'SUBSCRIBED',
  UNSUBSCRIBED: 'UNSUBSCRIBED',
};

const isWatch = viewerSubscription =>
  viewerSubscription === VIEWER_SUBSCRIPTIONS.SUBSCRIBED;

const updateWatch = () => {
  ...
};

const RepositoryItem = ({ ... }) => (
  <div>
    <div className="RepositoryItem-title">
      ...

      <div>
        ...

        <Mutation
          mutation={WATCH_REPOSITORY}
          variables={{
            id,
            viewerSubscription: isWatch(viewerSubscription)
              ? VIEWER_SUBSCRIPTIONS.UNSUBSCRIBED
              : VIEWER_SUBSCRIPTIONS.SUBSCRIBED,
          }}
          update={updateWatch}
        >
          {(updateSubscription, { data, loading, error }) => (
            <Button
              className="RepositoryItem-title-action"
              onClick={updateSubscription}
            >
              {watchers.totalCount}{' '}
              {isWatch(viewerSubscription) ? 'Unwatch' : 'Watch'}
            </Button>
          )}
        </Mutation>

        ...
```

```
      </div>
    </div>

    ...
  </div>
);
```

And third, the missing update function that is passed to the Mutation component:

src/Repository/RepositoryItem/index.js

```
const updateWatch = (
  client,
  {
    data: {
      updateSubscription: {
        subscribable: { id, viewerSubscription },
      },
    },
  },
) => {
  const repository = client.readFragment({
    id: `Repository:${id}`,
    fragment: REPOSITORY_FRAGMENT,
  });

  let { totalCount } = repository.watchers;
  totalCount =
    viewerSubscription === VIEWER_SUBSCRIPTIONS.SUBSCRIBED
      ? totalCount + 1
      : totalCount - 1;

  client.writeFragment({
    id: `Repository:${id}`,
    fragment: REPOSITORY_FRAGMENT,
    data: {
      ...repository,
      watchers: {
        ...repository.watchers,
        totalCount,
      },
    },
  });
};
```

Now let's get to the optimistic UI feature. Fortunately, the Mutation component offers a prop for the optimistic UI strategy called `optimisticResponse`. It returns the same result, which is accessed as argument in the function passed to the `update` prop of the Mutation component. With a watch mutation, only the `viewerSubscription` status changes to subscribed or unsubscribed. This is an optimistic UI.

src/Repository/RepositoryItem/index.js

```
const RepositoryItem = ({ ... }) => (
  <div>
    <div className="RepositoryItem-title">
      ...

    <div>
      ...

      <Mutation
        mutation={WATCH_REPOSITORY}
        variables={{
          id,
          viewerSubscription: isWatch(viewerSubscription)
            ? VIEWER_SUBSCRIPTIONS.UNSUBSCRIBED
            : VIEWER_SUBSCRIPTIONS.SUBSCRIBED,
        }}
        optimisticResponse={{
          updateSubscription: {
            __typename: 'Mutation',
            subscribable: {
              __typename: 'Repository',
              id,
              viewerSubscription: isWatch(viewerSubscription)
                ? VIEWER_SUBSCRIPTIONS.UNSUBSCRIBED
                : VIEWER_SUBSCRIPTIONS.SUBSCRIBED,
            },
          },
        }}
        update={updateWatch}
      >
        ...
      </Mutation>

      ...
```

```
      </div>
    </div>

    ...

  </div>
);
```

When you start your application and watch a repository, the "Watch" and "Unwatch" label of the button changes immediately after clicking it. This is because the optimistic response arrives synchronously, while the real response is pending and resolves later. Since the `__typename` meta field comes with every Apollo request, include those as well.

An additional benefit of the optimistic response is that it makes the count of watchers updates optimistic, too. The function used in the `update` prop is called twice now, the first time with the optimistic response, and the second with a response from GitHub's GraphQL API. It makes sense to capture identical information in the optimistic response expected as a mutation result in the function passed to the `update` prop of the Mutation component. For instance, if you don't pass the `id` property in the `optimisticResponse` object, the function passed to the `update` prop throws an error, because it can't retrieve the repository from the cache without an identifier.

At this point, it becomes debatable whether or not the Mutation component becomes too verbose. Using the Render Props pattern co-locates the data layer even more to the view-layer than Higher-Order Components. One could argue it doesn't co-locate the data-layer, but inserts it into the view-layer. When optimizations like the `update` and `optimisticResponse` props are put into the Render Prop Component, it can become too verbose for a scaling application. I advise using techniques you've learned as well as your own strategies to keep your source code concise. I see four different ways to solve this issue:

- Keep the declarations inlined (see: `optimisticUpdate`)
- Extracting the inlined declarations as variable (see: `update`).
- Perform a combination of 1 and 2 whereas only the most verbose parts are extracted
- Use Higher-Order Components instead of Render Props to co-locate data-layer, instead of inserting it in the view-layer

The first three are about **inserting** a data-layer into the view-layer, while the last is about **co-locating** it. Each comes with drawbacks. Following the second way, you might yourself declaring functions instead of objects, or higher-order functions instead of functions because you need to pass arguments to them. With the fourth, you could encounter the same challenge in keeping HOCs concise. There, you could use the other three ways too, but this time in a HOC rather than a Render Prop.

Exercises:

- Confirm your source code for the last section[170]

---

[170]https://github.com/the-road-to-graphql/react-graphql-github-apollo/tree/2fd3f5bad7668655feebe876db7bc9247905c475

- Throttle your internet connection (often browsers offers such functionality) and experience how the `optimisticResponse` takes the `update` function into account even though the request is slow
- Try different ways of co-locating or inserting your data-layer with render props and higher-order components
- Implement the optimistic UIs for the star and unstar mutations
- Read more about Apollo Optimistic UI in React with GraphQL[171]
- Invest 3 minutes of your time and take the quiz[172]

---

[171]https://www.apollographql.com/docs/react/features/optimistic-ui.html
[172]https://www.surveymonkey.com/r/5B6D8BX

GraphQL Pagination with Apollo Client in React

Finally, you are going to implement another advanced feature when using a GraphQL API called **pagination**. In this section, you implement a button that allows successive pages of repositories to be queries, a simple "More" button rendered below the list of repositories in the RepositoryList component. When is clicked, another page of repositories is fetched and merged with the previous list as one state into Apollo Client's cache.

First, extend the query next for your Profile component with the necessary information to allow pagination for the list of repositories:

src/Profile/index.js

```
const GET_REPOSITORIES_OF_CURRENT_USER = gql`
  query($cursor: String) {
    viewer {
      repositories(
        first: 5
        orderBy: { direction: DESC, field: STARGAZERS }
        after: $cursor
      ) {
        edges {
          node {
            ...repository
          }
        }
        pageInfo {
          endCursor
          hasNextPage
        }
      }
    }
  }
  ${REPOSITORY_FRAGMENT}
`;
```

The endCursor can be used as $cursor variable when fetching the next page of repositories, but the hasNextPage can disable the functionality (e.g. not showing the "More" button) to fetch another page. The initial request to fetch the first page of repositories will have a $cursor variable of undefined, though. GitHub's GraphQL API will handle this case gracefully and return the first items from the list of repositories without considering the after argument. Every other request to fetch more items from the list will send a defined after argument with the cursor, which is the endCursor from the query.

Now we have all information to fetch more pages of repositories from GitHub's GraphQL API. The Query component exposes a function to retrieve them in its child function. Since the button to fetch more repositories fits best in the the RepositoryList component, you can pass this function as prop to it.

src/Profile/index.js

```
const Profile = () => (
  <Query query={GET_REPOSITORIES_OF_CURRENT_USER}>
    {({ data, loading, error, fetchMore }) => {
      ...

      return (
        <RepositoryList
          repositories={viewer.repositories}
          fetchMore={fetchMore}
        />
      );
    }}
  </Query>
);
```

Next, use the function in the RepositoryList component, and add a button to fetch successive pages of repositories that appears when another page is available.

src/Repository/RepositoryList/index.js

```
import React, { Fragment } from 'react';

...

const RepositoryList = ({ repositories, fetchMore }) => (
  <Fragment>
    {repositories.edges.map(({ node }) => (
      ...
    ))}

    {repositories.pageInfo.hasNextPage && (
      <button
        type="button"
        onClick={() =>
          fetchMore({
            /* configuration object */
          })
        }
```

```
    >
      More Repositories
    </button>
  )}
</Fragment>
);


export default RepositoryList;
```

The `fetchMore()` function performs the query from the initial request, and takes a configuration object, which can be used to override variables. With pagination, this means you pass the `endCursor` of the previous query result to use it for the query as `after` argument. Otherwise, you would perform the initial request again because no variables are specified.

src/Repository/RepositoryList/index.js

```
const RepositoryList = ({ repositories, fetchMore }) => (
  <Fragment>

    ...

    {repositories.pageInfo.hasNextPage && (
      <button
        type="button"
        onClick={() =>
          fetchMore({
            variables: {
              cursor: repositories.pageInfo.endCursor,
            },
          })
        }
      >
        More Repositories
      </button>
    )}
  </Fragment>
);
```

If you attempt to click the button, you should get the following error message: *Error: updateQuery option is required.*. The `updateQuery` function is needed to tell Apollo Client how to merge the previous result with a new one. Define the function outside of the button, because it would become too verbose otherwise.

src/Repository/RepositoryList/index.js

```
const updateQuery = (previousResult, { fetchMoreResult }) => {
  ...
};

const RepositoryList = ({ repositories, fetchMore }) => (
  <Fragment>
    ...

    {repositories.pageInfo.hasNextPage && (
      <button
        type="button"
        onClick={() =>
          fetchMore({
            variables: {
              cursor: repositories.pageInfo.endCursor,
            },
            updateQuery,
          })
        }
      >
        More Repositories
      </button>
    )}
  </Fragment>
);
```

The function has access to the previous query result, and to the next result that resolves after the button click:

src/Repository/RepositoryList/index.js

```
const updateQuery = (previousResult, { fetchMoreResult }) => {
  if (!fetchMoreResult) {
    return previousResult;
  }

  return {
    ...previousResult,
    viewer: {
      ...previousResult.viewer,
      repositories: {
        ...previousResult.viewer.repositories,
```

```
          ...fetchMoreResult.viewer.repositories,
          edges: [
            ...previousResult.viewer.repositories.edges,
            ...fetchMoreResult.viewer.repositories.edges,
          ],
        },
      },
    };
};
```

In this function, you can merge both results with the JavaScript spread operator. If there is no new result, return the previous result. The important part is merging the edges of both repositories objects to have a merge list of items. The fetchMoreResult takes precedence over the previousResult in the repositories object because it contains the new pageInfo, with its endCursor and hasNextPage properties from the last paginated result. You need to have those when clicking the button another time to have the correct cursor as an argument. If you want to checkout an alternative to the verbose JavaScript spread operator when dealing with deeply nested data, checkout the changes in this GitHub Pull Request[173] that uses Lenses from Ramda.js.

To add one more small improvement for user friendliness, add a loading indicator when more pages are fetched. So far, the loading boolean in the Query component of the Profile component is only true for the initial request, but not for the following requests. Change this behavior with a prop that is passed to the Query component, and the loading boolean will be updated accordingly.

src/Profile/index.js

```
const Profile = () => (
  <Query
    query={GET_REPOSITORIES_OF_CURRENT_USER}
    notifyOnNetworkStatusChange={true}
  >
    {(({ data, loading, error, fetchMore }) => {
      ...
    }}
  </Query>
);
```

When you run your application again and try the "More" button, you should see odd behavior. Every time you load another page of repositories, the loading indicator is shown, but the list of repositories disappears entirely, and the merged list is rendered as assumed. Since the loading boolean becomes true with the initial and successive requests, the conditional rendering in the Profile component will always show the loading indicator. It returns from the Profile function early, never reaching the code

---

[173]https://github.com/the-road-to-graphql/react-graphql-github-apollo/pull/14

to render the RepositoryList. A quick change from || to && of the condition will allow it to show the loading indicator for the initial request only. Every request after that, where the `viewer` object is available, is beyond this condition, so it renders the RepositoryList component.

src/Profile/index.js

```
const Profile = () => (
  <Query
    query={GET_REPOSITORIES_OF_CURRENT_USER}
    notifyOnNetworkStatusChange={true}
  >
    {({ data, loading, error, fetchMore }) => {
      ...

      const { viewer } = data;

      if (loading && !viewer) {
        return <Loading />;
      }

      return (
        <RepositoryList
          loading={loading}
          repositories={viewer.repositories}
          fetchMore={fetchMore}
        />
      );
    }}
  </Query>
);
```

The boolean can be passed down to the RepositoryList component. There it can be used to show a loading indicator instead of the "More" button. Since the boolean never reaches the RepositoryList component for the initial request, you can be sure that the "More" button only changes to the loading indicator when there is a successive request pending.

src/Repository/RepositoryList/index.js

```
import React, { Fragment } from 'react';

import Loading from '../../Loading';
import RepositoryItem from '../RepositoryItem';

...

const RepositoryList = ({ repositories, loading, fetchMore }) => (
  <Fragment>
    ...

    {loading ? (
      <Loading />
    ) : (
      repositories.pageInfo.hasNextPage && (
        <button
          ...
        >
          More Repositories
        </button>
      )
    )}
  </Fragment>
);
```

The pagination feature is complete now, and you are fetching successive pages of an initial page, then merging the results in Apollo Client's cache. In addition, you show your user feedback about pending requests for either the initial request or further page requests.

Now we'll take it a step further, making the button used to fetch more repositories reusable. Let me explain why this would be a neat abstraction. In an upcoming section, you have another list field that could potentially implement the pagination feature. There, you have to introduce the More button, which could be nearly identical to the More button you have in the RepositoryList component. Having only one button in a UI would be a satisfying abstraction, but this abstraction wouldn't work in a real-world coding scenario. You would have to introduce a second list field first, implement the pagination feature for it, and then consider an abstraction for the More button. For the sake of the tutorial, we implement this abstraction for the pagination feature only in this section, though you should be aware this is a premature optimization put in place for you to learn it.

For another way, imagine you wanted to extract the functionality of the More button into a FetchMore component. The most important thing you would need is the fetchMore() function from the query result. The fetchMore() function takes an object to pass in the necessary variables and updateQuery information as a configuration. While the former is used to define the next page by its cursor, the latter is used to define how the results should be merged in the local state. These are the three essential parts: fetchMore, variables, and updateQuery. You may also want to shield away the conditional renderings in the FetchMore component, which happens because of the loading or hasNextPage booleans. Et voilÃ ! That's how you get the interface to your FetchMore abstraction component.

src/Repository/RepositoryList/index.js

```
import React, { Fragment } from 'react';

import FetchMore from '../../FetchMore';
import RepositoryItem from '../RepositoryItem';

...

const RepositoryList = ({ repositories, loading, fetchMore }) => (
  <Fragment>
    {repositories.edges.map(({ node }) => (
      <div key={node.id} className="RepositoryItem">
        <RepositoryItem {...node} />
      </div>
    ))}

    <FetchMore
      loading={loading}
      hasNextPage={repositories.pageInfo.hasNextPage}
      variables={{
        cursor: repositories.pageInfo.endCursor,
      }}
      updateQuery={updateQuery}
      fetchMore={fetchMore}
    >
      Repositories
    </FetchMore>
  </Fragment>
);

export default RepositoryList;
```

Now this FetchMore component can be used by other paginated lists as well, because every part that can be dynamic is passed as props to it. Implementing a FetchMore component in the *src/FetchMore/index.js* is the next step. First, the main part of the component:

src/FetchMore/index.js

```
import React from 'react';

import './style.css';

const FetchMore = ({
  variables,
  updateQuery,
  fetchMore,
  children,
}) => (
  <div className="FetchMore">
    <button
      type="button"
      className="FetchMore-button"
      onClick={() => fetchMore({ variables, updateQuery })}
    >
      More {children}
    </button>
  </div>
);

export default FetchMore;
```

Here, you can see how the `variables` and `updateQuery` are taken as configuration object for the `fetchMore()` function when it's invoked. The button can be made cleaner using the Button component you defined in a previous section. To add a different style, let's define a specialized ButtonUnobtrusive component next to the Button component in the *src/Button/index.js* file:

src/Button/index.js

```
import React from 'react';

import './style.css';

const Button = ({ ... }) => ...

const ButtonUnobtrusive = ({
  children,
  className,
  type = 'button',
  ...props
}) => (
```

```
  <button
    className={`${className} Button_unobtrusive`}
    type={type}
    {...props}
  >
    {children}
  </button>
);


export { ButtonUnobtrusive };


export default Button;
```

Now the ButtonUnobtrusive component is used as button instead of the button element in the FetchMore component. In addition, the two booleans `loading` and `hasNextPage` can be used for the conditional rendering, to show the Loading component or nothing, because there is no next page which can be fetched.

src/FetchMore/index.js

```
import React from 'react';

import Loading from '../Loading';
import { ButtonUnobtrusive } from '../Button';

import './style.css';

const FetchMore = ({
  loading,
  hasNextPage,
  variables,
  updateQuery,
  fetchMore,
  children,
}) => (
  <div className="FetchMore">
    {loading ? (
      <Loading />
    ) : (
      hasNextPage && (
        <ButtonUnobtrusive
          className="FetchMore-button"
          onClick={() => fetchMore({ variables, updateQuery })}
        >
```

```
        More {children}
      </ButtonUnobtrusive>
    )
  )}
  </div>
);


export default FetchMore;
```

That's it for the abstraction of the FetchMore button for paginated lists with Apollo Client. Basically, you pass in everything needed by the `fetchMore()` function, including the function itself. You can also pass all booleans used for conditional renderings. You end up with a reusable FetchMore button that can be used for every paginated list.

Exercises:

- Confirm your source code for the last section[174]
- Read more about pagination with Apollo Client in React[175]
- Invest 3 minutes of your time and take the quiz[176]

---

[174]https://github.com/the-road-to-graphql/react-graphql-github-apollo/tree/65cb143d605b1c7e9c080f36b5f64805f02aba29
[175]https://www.apollographql.com/docs/react/features/pagination.html
[176]https://www.surveymonkey.com/r/5HYMGN7

GraphQL Caching of Queries with Apollo Client in React

In this section, you introduce React Router[177] to show two separate pages for your application. At the moment, you are only showing one page with a Profile component that displays all your repositories. We want to add another Organization component that shows repositories by an organization, and there could be a search field as well, to lookup individual organizations with their repositories on that page. Let's do this by introducing React Router to your application. If you haven't used React Router before, make sure to conduct the exercises of this section to learn more about it.

Command Line

```
npm install react-router-dom --save
```

In your *src/constants/routes.js* file, you can specify both routes you want to make accessible by React Router. The ORGANIZATION route points to the base URL, while the PROFILE route points to a more specific URL.

src/constants/routes.js

```
export const ORGANIZATION = '/';
export const PROFILE = '/profile';
```

Next, map both routes to their components. The App component is the perfect place to do it because the two routes will exchange the Organization and Profile components based on the URL there.

src/App/index.js

```
import React, { Component } from 'react';
import { BrowserRouter as Router, Route } from 'react-router-dom';

import Profile from '../Profile';
import Organization from '../Organization';

import * as routes from '../constants/routes';

import './style.css';

class App extends Component {
  render() {
    return (
      <Router>
        <div className="App">
```

---

[177]https://github.com/ReactTraining/react-router

```
              <div className="App-main">
                <Route
                  exact
                  path={routes.ORGANIZATION}
                  component={() => (
                    <div className="App-content_large-header">
                      <Organization />
                    </div>
                  )}
                />
                <Route
                  exact
                  path={routes.PROFILE}
                  component={() => (
                    <div className="App-content_small-header">
                      <Profile />
                    </div>
                  )}
                />
              </div>
            </div>
          </Router>
        );
      }
    }


    export default App;
```

The Organization component wasn't implemented yet, but you can start with a functional stateless component in the *src/Organization/index.js* file, that acts as a placeholder to keep the application working for now.

src/Organization/index.js

```
import React from 'react';

const Organization = () => <div>Organization</div>;

export default Organization;
```

Since you mapped both routes to their respective components, so you want to implement navigation from one route to another. For this, introduce a **Navigation** component in the App component.

src/App/index.js

```
...

import Navigation from './Navigation';
import Profile from '../Profile';
import Organization from '../Organization';

...

class App extends Component {
  render() {
    return (
      <Router>
        <div className="App">
          <Navigation />

          <div className="App-main">
            ...
          </div>
        </div>
      </Router>
    );
  }
}

export default App;
```

Next, we'll implement the Navigation component, which is responsible for displaying the two links to navigate between your routes using React Router's Link component.

src/App/Navigation/index.js

```
import React from 'react';
import { Link } from 'react-router-dom';

import * as routes from '../../constants/routes';

import './style.css';

const Navigation = () => (
  <header className="Navigation">
    <div className="Navigation-link">
      <Link to={routes.PROFILE}>Profile</Link>
```

```
    </div>
    <div className="Navigation-link">
      <Link to={routes.ORGANIZATION}>Organization</Link>
    </div>
  </header>
);


export default Navigation;
```

The Profile page works as before, but the Organization page is empty. In the last step, you defined the two routes as constants, used them in the App component to map to their respective components, and introduced Link components to navigate to them in the Navigation component.

Another great feature of the Apollo Client is that it caches query requests. When navigating from the Profile page to the Organization page and back to the Profile page, the results appear immediately because the Apollo Client checks its cache before making the query to the remote GraphQL API. It's a pretty powerful tool.

The next part of this section is the Organization component. It is the same as the Profile component, except the query differs because it takes a variable for the organization name to identify the organization's repositories.

src/Organization/index.js

```
import React from 'react';
import gql from 'graphql-tag';
import { Query } from 'react-apollo';

import { REPOSITORY_FRAGMENT } from '../Repository';

const GET_REPOSITORIES_OF_ORGANIZATION = gql`
  query($organizationName: String!) {
    organization(login: $organizationName) {
      repositories(first: 5) {
        edges {
          node {
            ...repository
          }
        }
      }
    }
  }
  ${REPOSITORY_FRAGMENT}
`;
```

```
const Organization = ({ organizationName }) => (
  <Query
    query={GET_REPOSITORIES_OF_ORGANIZATION}
    variables={{
      organizationName,
    }}
    skip={organizationName === ''}
  >
    {({ data, loading, error }) => {
      ...
    }}
  </Query>
);


export default Organization;
```

The Query component in the Organization component takes a query tailored to the organization being the top level field of the query. It takes a variable to identify the organization, and it uses the newly introduced `skip` prop to skip executing the query if no organization identifier is provided. Later, you will pass an organization identifier from the App component. You may have noticed that the repository fragment you introduced earlier to update the local state in the cache can be reused here. It saves lines of code, and more importantly, ensures the returned list of repositories have identical structures to the list of repositories in the Profile component.

Next, extend the query to fit the requirements of the pagination feature. It requires the `cursor` argument to identify the next page of repositories. The `notifyOnNetworkStatusChange` prop is used to update the `loading` boolean for paginated requests as well.

src/Organization/index.js

```
...

const GET_REPOSITORIES_OF_ORGANIZATION = gql`
  query($organizationName: String!, $cursor: String) {
    organization(login: $organizationName) {
      repositories(first: 5, after: $cursor) {
        edges {
          node {
            ...repository
          }
        }
        pageInfo {
          endCursor
          hasNextPage
```

```
        }
      }
    }
  }
  ${REPOSITORY_FRAGMENT}
`;

const Organization = ({ organizationName }) => (
  <Query
    query={GET_REPOSITORIES_OF_ORGANIZATION}
    variables={{
      organizationName,
    }}
    skip={organizationName === ''}
    notifyOnNetworkStatusChange={true}
  >
    {({ data, loading, error, fetchMore }) => {
      ...
    }}
  </Query>
);

export default Organization;
```

Lastly, the render prop child function needs to be implemented. It doesn't differ much from the Query's content in the Profile component. Its purpose is to handle edge cases like loading and 'no data' errors, and eventually, to show a list of repositories. Because the RepositoryList component handles the pagination feature, this improvement is included in the newly implemented Organization component.

src/Organization/index.js

```
...

import RepositoryList, { REPOSITORY_FRAGMENT } from '../Repository';
import Loading from '../Loading';
import ErrorMessage from '../Error';

...

const Organization = ({ organizationName }) => (
  <Query ... >
    {({ data, loading, error, fetchMore }) => {
```

```
      if (error) {
        return <ErrorMessage error={error} />;
      }

      const { organization } = data;

      if (loading && !organization) {
        return <Loading />;
      }

      return (
        <RepositoryList
          loading={loading}
          repositories={organization.repositories}
          fetchMore={fetchMore}
        />
      );
    }}
  </Query>
);

export default Organization;
```

Provide a `organizationName` as prop when using the Organization in the App component, and leave it inlined for now. Later, you will make it dynamic with a search field.

src/App/index.js

```
class App extends Component {
  render() {
    return (
      <Router>
        <div className="App">
          <Navigation />

          <div className="App-main">
            <Route
              exact
              path={routes.ORGANIZATION}
              component={() => (
                <div className="App-content_large-header">
                  <Organization
                    organizationName={'the-road-to-learn-react'}
```

```
                    />
                </div>
              )}
            />
            ...
          </div>
        </div>
      </Router>
    );
  }
}
```

The Organization component should almost work now, as the More button is the only incomplete part. The remaining issue is the resolving block for the pagination feature in the updateQuery function. It assumes that the nested data structure always starts with a viewer object. It does for the Profile page, but not for the Organization page. There the top level object is the organization followed by the list of repositories. Only the top level object changes from page to page, where the underlying structure stays identical.

When the top level object changes from page to page, the ideal next step is to tell the RepositoryList component its top level object from the outside. With the Organization component, its the top-level object organization, which could be passed as a string and reused as a dynamic key later:

src/Organization/index.js

```
const Organization = ({ organizationName }) => (
  <Query ... >
    {(({ data, loading, error, fetchMore }) => {
      ...

      return (
        <RepositoryList
          loading={loading}
          repositories={organization.repositories}
          fetchMore={fetchMore}
          entry={'organization'}
        />
      );
    }}
  </Query>
);
```

With the Profile component, the viewer would be the top level object:

src/Profile/index.js

```
const Profile = () => (
  <Query ... >
    {({ data, loading, error, fetchMore }) => {
      ...

      return (
        <RepositoryList
          loading={loading}
          repositories={viewer.repositories}
          fetchMore={fetchMore}
          entry={'viewer'}
        />
      );
    }}
  </Query>
);
```

Now you can handle the new case in the RepositoryList component by passing the entry as computed property name[178] to the updateQuery function. Instead of passing the updateQuery function directly to the FetchMore component, it can be derived from a higher-order function needed to pass the new entry property.

src/Repository/RepositoryList/index.js

```
const RepositoryList = ({
  repositories,
  loading,
  fetchMore,
  entry,
}) => (
  <Fragment>
    ...

    <FetchMore
      loading={loading}
      hasNextPage={repositories.pageInfo.hasNextPage}
      variables={{
        cursor: repositories.pageInfo.endCursor,
      }}
      updateQuery={getUpdateQuery(entry)}
      fetchMore={fetchMore}
```

---

[178]https://developer.mozilla.org/my/docs/Web/JavaScript/Reference/Operators/Object_initializer#Computed_property_names

```
    >
      Repositories
    </FetchMore>
  </Fragment>
);
```

The higher-order function next to the RepositoryList component is completed as such:

src/Repository/RepositoryList/index.js

```
const getUpdateQuery = entry => (
  previousResult,
  { fetchMoreResult },
) => {
  if (!fetchMoreResult) {
    return previousResult;
  }

  return {
    ...previousResult,
    [entry]: {
      ...previousResult[entry],
      repositories: {
        ...previousResult[entry].repositories,
        ...fetchMoreResult[entry].repositories,
        edges: [
          ...previousResult[entry].repositories.edges,
          ...fetchMoreResult[entry].repositories.edges,
        ],
      },
    },
  };
};
```

That's how a deeply-nested object is updated with the fetchMoreResult, even though the top level component from the query result is not static. The pagination feature should work on both pages now. Take a moment to recap the last implementations again and why these were necessary.

Next, we'll implement the search function I mentioned earlier. The best place to add the search field would be the Navigation component, but only when the Organization page is active. React Router comes with a useful higher-order component to access to the current URL, which can be used to show a search field.

src/App/Navigation/index.js

```
import React from 'react';
import { Link, withRouter } from 'react-router-dom';

import * as routes from '../../constants/routes';

import './style.css';

const Navigation = ({
  location: { pathname },
}) => (
  <header className="Navigation">
    <div className="Navigation-link">
      <Link to={routes.PROFILE}>Profile</Link>
    </div>
    <div className="Navigation-link">
      <Link to={routes.ORGANIZATION}>Organization</Link>
    </div>

    {pathname === routes.ORGANIZATION && (
      <OrganizationSearch />
    )}
  </header>
);

export default withRouter(Navigation);
```

The OrganizationSearch component is implemented next to the Navigation component in the next steps. Before that can work, there needs to be some kind of initial state for the OrganizationSearch, as well as a callback function to update the initial state in the Navigation component. To accommodate this, the Navigation component becomes a class component.

src/App/Navigation/index.js

```
...

class Navigation extends React.Component {
  state = {
    organizationName: 'the-road-to-learn-react',
  };

  onOrganizationSearch = value => {
    this.setState({ organizationName: value });
```

```
  };

  render() {
    const { location: { pathname } } = this.props;

    return (
      <header className="Navigation">
        <div className="Navigation-link">
          <Link to={routes.PROFILE}>Profile</Link>
        </div>
        <div className="Navigation-link">
          <Link to={routes.ORGANIZATION}>Organization</Link>
        </div>

        {pathname === routes.ORGANIZATION && (
          <OrganizationSearch
            organizationName={this.state.organizationName}
            onOrganizationSearch={this.onOrganizationSearch}
          />
        )}
      </header>
    );
  }
}

export default withRouter(Navigation);
```

The OrganizationSearch component implemented in the same file would also work with the following implementation. It handles its own local state, the value that shows up in the input field, but uses it as an initial value from the parent component. It also receives a callback handler, which can be used in the onSubmit() class method to propagate the search fields value on a submit interaction up the component tree.

src/App/Navigation/index.js

```
...

import Button from '../../Button';
import Input from '../../Input';

import './style.css';

const Navigation = ({ ... }) => ...
```

```
class OrganizationSearch extends React.Component {
  state = {
    value: this.props.organizationName,
  };

  onChange = event => {
    this.setState({ value: event.target.value });
  };

  onSubmit = event => {
    this.props.onOrganizationSearch(this.state.value);

    event.preventDefault();
  };

  render() {
    const { value } = this.state;

    return (
      <div className="Navigation-search">
        <form onSubmit={this.onSubmit}>
          <Input
            color={'white'}
            type="text"
            value={value}
            onChange={this.onChange}
          />{' '}
          <Button color={'white'} type="submit">
            Search
          </Button>
        </form>
      </div>
    );
  }
}

export default withRouter(Navigation);
```

The Input component is a slightly styled input element that is defined in *src/Input/index.js* as its own component.

src/Input/index.js

```
import React from 'react';

import './style.css';

const Input = ({ children, color = 'black', ...props }) => (
  <input className={`Input Input_${color}`} {...props}>
    {children}
  </input>
);

export default Input;
```

While the search field works in the Navigation component, it doesn't help the rest of the application. It only updates the state in the Navigation component when a search request is submitted. However, the value of the search request is needed in the Organization component as a GraphQL variable for the query, so the local state needs to be lifted up from the Navigation component to the App component. The Navigation component becomes a stateless functional component again.

src/App/Navigation/index.js

```
const Navigation = ({
  location: { pathname },
  organizationName,
  onOrganizationSearch,
}) => (
  <header className="Navigation">
    <div className="Navigation-link">
      <Link to={routes.PROFILE}>Profile</Link>
    </div>
    <div className="Navigation-link">
      <Link to={routes.ORGANIZATION}>Organization</Link>
    </div>

    {pathname === routes.ORGANIZATION && (
      <OrganizationSearch
        organizationName={organizationName}
        onOrganizationSearch={onOrganizationSearch}
      />
    )}
  </header>
);
```

The App component takes over the responsibility from the Navigation component, managing the local state, passing the initial state and a callback function to update the state to the Navigation component, and passing the state itself to the Organization component to perform the query:

src/App/index.js

```
...

class App extends Component {
  state = {
    organizationName: 'the-road-to-learn-react',
  };

  onOrganizationSearch = value => {
    this.setState({ organizationName: value });
  };

  render() {
    const { organizationName } = this.state;

    return (
      <Router>
        <div className="App">
          <Navigation
            organizationName={organizationName}
            onOrganizationSearch={this.onOrganizationSearch}
          />

          <div className="App-main">
            <Route
              exact
              path={routes.ORGANIZATION}
              component={() => (
                <div className="App-content_large-header">
                  <Organization organizationName={organizationName} />
                </div>
              )}
            />
            ...
          </div>
        </div>
      </Router>
    );
  }
}
```

```
}

export default App;
```

You have implemented a dynamic GraphQL query with a search field. Once a new `organizationName` is passed to the Organization component from a local state change, the Query component triggers another request due to a re-render. The request is not always made to the remote GraphQL API, though. The Apollo Client cache is used when an organization is searched twice. Also, you have used the well-known technique called lifting state in React to share the state across components.

Exercises:

- Confirm your source code for the last section[179]
- If you are not familiar with React Router, try it out in this pragmatic tutorial[180]
- Invest 3 minutes of your time and take the quiz[181]

---

[179]https://github.com/the-road-to-graphql/react-graphql-github-apollo/tree/3ab9c752ec0ec8c3e5f7a1ead4519ea3a626785b
[180]https://www.robinwieruch.de/complete-firebase-authentication-react-tutorial/
[181]https://www.surveymonkey.com/r/5HFQ3TD

Implementing the Issues Feature: Setup

In the previous sections you have implemented most of the common Apollo Client features in your React application. Now you can start implementing extensions for the application on your own. This section showcases how a full-fledged feature can be implemented with Apollo Client in React.

So far, you have dealt with GitHub repositories from organizations and your account. This will take that one step further, fetching GitHub issues that are made available using a list field associated to a repository in a GraphQL query. However, this section doesn't only show you how to render a nested list field in your React application.

The foundation will be rendering the list of issues. You will implement client-side filtering with plain React to show opened, closed, or no issue. Finally, you will refactor the filtering to a server-side filtering using GraphQL queries. We will only fetch the issues by their state from the server rather than filtering the issue's state on the client-side. Implementing pagination for the issues will be your exercise.

First, render a new component called 'Issues' in your RepositoryList component. This component takes two props that are used later in a GraphQL query to identify the repository from which you want to fetch the issues.

src/Repository/RepositoryList/index.js

```
...

import FetchMore from '../../FetchMore';
import RepositoryItem from '../RepositoryItem';
import Issues from '../../Issue';

...

const RepositoryList = ({
  repositories,
  loading,
  fetchMore,
  entry,
}) => (
  <Fragment>
    {repositories.edges.map(({ node }) => (
      <div key={node.id} className="RepositoryItem">
        <RepositoryItem {...node} />

        <Issues
          repositoryName={node.name}
          repositoryOwner={node.owner.login}
```

```
      />
    </div>
  ))}


  ...
  </Fragment>
);


export default RepositoryList;
```

In the *src/Issue/index.js* file, import and export the Issues component. Since the issue feature can be kept in a module on its own, it has this *index.js* file again. That's how you can tell other developers to access only this feature module, using the *index.js* file as its interface. Everything else is kept private.

src/Issue/index.js

```
import Issues from './IssueList';


export default Issues;
```

Note how the component is named Issues, not IssueList. The naming convention is used to break down the rendering of a list of items: Issues, IssueList and IssueItem. Issues is the container component, where you query the data and filter the issues, and the IssueList and IssueItem are only there as presentational components for rendering. In contrast, the Repository feature module hasn't a Repositories component, because there was no need for it. The list of repositories already came from the Organization and Profile components and the Repository module's components are mainly only there for the rendering. This is only one opinionated approach of naming the components, however.

Let's start implementing Issues and IssueList components in the *src/Issue/IssueList/index.js* file. You could argue to split both components up into their own files, but for the sake of this tutorial, they are kept together in one file.

First, there needs to be a new query for the issues. You might wonder: Why do we need a new query here? It would be simpler to include the issues list field in the query at the top next to the Organization and Profile components. That's true, but it comes with a cost. Adding more nested (list) fields to a query often results into performance issues on the server-side. There you may have to make multiple roundtrips to retrieve all the entities from the database.

- Roundtrip 1: get organization by name
- Roundtrip 2: get repositories of organization by organization identifier
- Roundtrip 3: get issues of repository by repository identifier

It is simple to conclude that nesting queries in a naive way solves all of our problems. Whereas it solves the problem of only requesting the data once and not with multiple network request (similar roundtrips as shown for the database), GraphQL doesn't solve the problem of retrieving all the data from the database for you. That's not the responsibility of GraphQL after all. So by having a dedicated query in the Issues component, you can decide **when** to trigger this query. In the next steps, you will just trigger it on render because the Query component is used. But when adding the client-side filter later on, it will only be triggered when the "Filter" button is toggled. Otherwise the issues should be hidden. Finally, that's how all the initial data loading can be delayed to a point when the user actually wants to see the data.

First, define the Issues component which has access to the props which were passed in the RepositoryList component. It doesn't render much yet.

src/Issue/IssueList/index.js

```
import React from 'react';

import './style.css';

const Issues = ({ repositoryOwner, repositoryName }) =>
  <div className="Issues">
  </div>


export default Issues;
```

Second, define the query in the *src/Issue/IssueList/index.js* file to retrieve issues of a repository. The repository is identified by its owner and name. Also, add the state field as one of the fields for the query result. This is used for client-side filtering, for showing issues with an open or closed state.

src/Issue/IssueList/index.js

```
import React from 'react';
import gql from 'graphql-tag';

import './style.css';

const GET_ISSUES_OF_REPOSITORY = gql`
  query($repositoryOwner: String!, $repositoryName: String!) {
    repository(name: $repositoryName, owner: $repositoryOwner) {
      issues(first: 5) {
        edges {
          node {
            id
            number
            state
```

```
          title
          url
          bodyHTML
        }
      }
    }
  }
}
`;
```

...

Third, introduce the Query component and pass it the previously defined query and the necessary variables. Use its render prop child function to access the data, to cover all edge cases and to render a IssueList component eventually.

src/Issue/IssueList/index.js

```
import React from 'react';
import { Query } from 'react-apollo';
import gql from 'graphql-tag';

import IssueItem from '../IssueItem';
import Loading from '../../Loading';
import ErrorMessage from '../../Error';

import './style.css';

const Issues = ({ repositoryOwner, repositoryName }) => (
  <div className="Issues">
    <Query
      query={GET_ISSUES_OF_REPOSITORY}
      variables={{
        repositoryOwner,
        repositoryName,
      }}
    >
      {({ data, loading, error }) => {
        if (error) {
          return <ErrorMessage error={error} />;
        }

        const { repository } = data;
```

```
        if (loading && !repository) {
          return <Loading />;
        }

        if (!repository.issues.edges.length) {
          return <div className="IssueList">No issues ...</div>;
        }

        return <IssueList issues={repository.issues} />;
      }}
    </Query>
  </div>
);

const IssueList = ({ issues }) => (
  <div className="IssueList">
    {issues.edges.map(({ node }) => (
      <IssueItem key={node.id} issue={node} />
    ))}
  </div>
);

export default Issues;
```

Finally, implement a basic IssueItem component in the *src/Issue/IssueItem/index.js* file. The snippet below shows a placeholder where you can implement the Commenting feature, which we'll cover later.

src/Issue/IssueItem/index.js

```
import React from 'react';

import Link from '../../Link';

import './style.css';

const IssueItem = ({ issue }) => (
  <div className="IssueItem">
    {/* placeholder to add a show/hide comment button later */}

    <div className="IssueItem-content">
      <h3>
        <Link href={issue.url}>{issue.title}</Link>
      </h3>
```

```
      <div dangerouslySetInnerHTML={{ __html: issue.bodyHTML }} />

      {/* placeholder to render a list of comments later */}
    </div>
  </div>
);

export default IssueItem;
```

Once you start your application again, you should see the initial page of paginated issues rendered below each repository. That's a performance bottleneck. Worse, the GraphQL requests are not bundled in one request, as with the issues list field in the Organization and Profile components. In the next steps you are implementing client-side filtering. The default is to show no issues, but it can toggle between states of showing none, open issues, and closed issues using a button, so the issues will not be queried before toggling one of the issue states.

Exercises:

- Confirm your source code for the last section[182]
- Read more about the rate limit when using a (or in this case GitHub's) GraphQL API[183]

---

[182]https://github.com/the-road-to-graphql/react-graphql-github-apollo/tree/6781b487d6799e55a4deea48dfe706253b373f0a
[183]https://developer.github.com/v4/guides/resource-limitations/

Implementing the Issues Feature: Client-Side Filter

In this section, we enhance the Issue feature with client-side filtering. It prevents the initial issue querying because it happens with a button, and it lets the user filter between closed and open issues.

First, let's introduce our three states as enumeration next to the Issues component. The NONE state is used to show no issues; otherwise, the other states are used to show open or closed issues.

src/Issue/IssueList/index.js

```
const ISSUE_STATES = {
  NONE: 'NONE',
  OPEN: 'OPEN',
  CLOSED: 'CLOSED',
};
```

Second, let's implement a short function that decides whether it is a state to show the issues or not. This function can be defined in the same file.

src/Issue/IssueList/index.js

```
const isShow = issueState => issueState !== ISSUE_STATES.NONE;
```

Third, the function can be used for conditional rendering, to either query the issues and show the IssueList, or to do nothing. It's not clear yet where the issueState property comes from.

src/Issue/IssueList/index.js

```
const Issues = ({ repositoryOwner, repositoryName }) => (
  <div className="Issues">
    {isShow(issueState) && (
      <Query ... >
        ...
      </Query>
    )}
  </div>
);
```

The issueState property must come from the local state to toggle it via a button in the component, so the Issues component must be refactored to a class component to manage this state.

src/Issue/IssueList/index.js

```
class Issues extends React.Component {
  state = {
    issueState: ISSUE_STATES.NONE,
  };

  render() {
    const { issueState } = this.state;
    const { repositoryOwner, repositoryName } = this.props;

    return (
      <div className="Issues">
        {isShow(issueState) && (
          <Query ... >
            ...
          </Query>
        )}
      </div>
    );
  }
}
```

The application should be error-free now, because the initial state is set to NONE and the conditional rendering prevents the query and the rendering of a result. However, the client-side filtering is not done yet, as you still need to toggle the issueState property with React's local state. The ButtonUnobtrusive component has the appropriate style, so we can reuse it to implement this toggling behavior to transition between the three available states.

src/Issue/IssueList/index.js

```
...

import IssueItem from '../IssueItem';
import Loading from '../../Loading';
import ErrorMessage from '../../Error';
import { ButtonUnobtrusive } from '../../Button';

class Issues extends React.Component {
  state = {
    issueState: ISSUE_STATES.NONE,
  };

  onChangeIssueState = nextIssueState => {
```

```
    this.setState({ issueState: nextIssueState });
  };

  render() {
    const { issueState } = this.state;
    const { repositoryOwner, repositoryName } = this.props;

    return (
      <div className="Issues">
        <ButtonUnobtrusive
          onClick={() =>
            this.onChangeIssueState(TRANSITION_STATE[issueState])
          }
        >
          {TRANSITION_LABELS[issueState]}
        </ButtonUnobtrusive>

        {isShow(issueState) && (
          <Query ... >
            ...
          </Query>
        )}
      </div>
    );
  }
}
```

In the last step, you introduced the button to toggle between the three states. You used two enumerations, TRANSITION_LABELS and TRANSITION_STATE, to show an appropriate button label and to define the next state after a state transition. These enumerations can be defined next to the ISSUE_STATES enumeration.

src/Issue/IssueList/index.js

```
const TRANSITION_LABELS = {
  [ISSUE_STATES.NONE]: 'Show Open Issues',
  [ISSUE_STATES.OPEN]: 'Show Closed Issues',
  [ISSUE_STATES.CLOSED]: 'Hide Issues',
};

const TRANSITION_STATE = {
  [ISSUE_STATES.NONE]: ISSUE_STATES.OPEN,
  [ISSUE_STATES.OPEN]: ISSUE_STATES.CLOSED,
```

```
[ISSUE_STATES.CLOSED]: ISSUE_STATES.NONE,
};
```

As you can see, whereas the former enumeration only matches a label to a given state, the latter enumeration matches the next state to a given state. That's how the toggling to a next state can be made simple. Last but not least, the issueState from the local state has to be used to filter the list of issues after they have been queried and should be rendered.

src/Issue/IssueList/index.js

```
class Issues extends React.Component {
  ...

  render() {
    ...

    return (
      <div className="Issues">

        ...

        {isShow(issueState) && (
          <Query ... >
            {(({ data, loading, error }) => {
              if (error) {
                return <ErrorMessage error={error} />;
              }

              const { repository } = data;

              if (loading && !repository) {
                return <Loading />;
              }

              const filteredRepository = {
                issues: {
                  edges: repository.issues.edges.filter(
                    issue => issue.node.state === issueState,
                  ),
                },
              };

              if (!filteredRepository.issues.edges.length) {
                return <div className="IssueList">No issues ...</div>;
              }
```

```
        return (
          <IssueList issues={filteredRepository.issues} />
        );
      }}
    </Query>
  )}
  </div>
  );
  }
}
```

You have implemented client-side filtering. The button is used to toggle between the three states managed in the local state of the component. The issues are only queried in filtered and rendered states. In the next step, the existing client-side filtering should be advanced to a server-side filtering, which means the filtered issues are already requested from the server and not filtered afterward on the client.

Exercises:

- Confirm your source code for the last section[184]
- Install the recompose[185] library which implements many higher-order components
- Refactor the Issues component from class component to functional stateless component
- Use the `withState` HOC for the Issues component to manage the `issueState`

---

[184]https://github.com/the-road-to-graphql/react-graphql-github-apollo/tree/0f261b13696046832ad65f1909266957d6275d6c
[185]https://github.com/acdlite/recompose

Implementing the Issues Feature: Server-Side Filter

Before starting with the server-side filtering, let's recap the last exercise in case you had difficulties with it. Basically you can perform the refactoring in three steps. First, install recompose as package for your application on the command line:

Command Line

```
npm install recompose --save
```

Second, import the `withState` higher-order component in the *src/Issue/IssueList/index.js* file and use it to wrap your exported Issues component, where the first argument is the property name in the local state, the second argument is the handler to change the property in the local state, and the third argument is the initial state for that property.

src/Issue/IssueList/index.js

```
import React from 'react';
import { Query } from 'react-apollo';
import gql from 'graphql-tag';
import { withState } from 'recompose';

...

export default withState(
  'issueState',
  'onChangeIssueState',
  ISSUE_STATES.NONE,
)(Issues);
```

Finally, refactor the Issues component from a class component to a functional stateless component. It accesses the `issueState` and `onChangeIssueState()` function in its props now. Remember to change the usage of the `onChangeIssueState` prop to being a function and not a class method anymore.

src/Issue/IssueList/index.js

```
...

const Issues = ({
  repositoryOwner,
  repositoryName,
  issueState,
  onChangeIssueState,
}) => (
  <div className="Issues">
    <ButtonUnobtrusive
      onClick={() => onChangeIssueState(TRANSITION_STATE[issueState])}
    >
      {TRANSITION_LABELS[issueState]}
    </ButtonUnobtrusive>

    ...
  </div>
);


...
```

The previous section makes writing stateful components, where the state is much more convenient. Next, advance the filtering from client-side to server-side. We use the defined GraphQL query and its arguments to make a more exact query by requesting only open or closed issues. In the *src/Issue/IssueList/index.js* file, extend the query with a variable to specify the issue state:

src/Issue/IssueList/index.js

```
const GET_ISSUES_OF_REPOSITORY = gql`
  query(
    $repositoryOwner: String!
    $repositoryName: String!
    $issueState: IssueState!
  ) {
    repository(name: $repositoryName, owner: $repositoryOwner) {
      issues(first: 5, states: [$issueState]) {
        edges {
          node {
            id
            number
            state
            title
```

```
                url
                bodyHTML
            }
          }
        }
      }
    }
  }
`;
```

Next, you can use the `issueState` property as variable for your Query component. In addition, remove the client-side filter logic from the Query component's render prop function.

src/Issue/IssueList/index.js

```
const Issues = ({
  repositoryOwner,
  repositoryName,
  issueState,
  onChangeIssueState,
}) => (
  <div className="Issues">
    ...

    {isShow(issueState) && (
      <Query
        query={GET_ISSUES_OF_REPOSITORY}
        variables={{
          repositoryOwner,
          repositoryName,
          issueState,
        }}
      >
        {({ data, loading, error }) => {
          if (error) {
            return <ErrorMessage error={error} />;
          }

          const { repository } = data;

          if (loading && !repository) {
            return <Loading />;
          }

          return <IssueList issues={repository.issues} />;
```

```
        }}
      </Query>
    )}
  </div>
);
```

You are only querying open or closed issues. Your query became more exact, and the filtering is no longer handled by the client.

Exercises:

- Confirm your source code for the last section[186]
- Implement the pagination feature for the Issue feature
  - Add the pageInfo information to the query
  - Add the additional cursor variable and argument to the query
  - Add the FetchMore component to the IssueList component

---

[186]https://github.com/the-road-to-graphql/react-graphql-github-apollo/tree/df737276a4bc8d2d889d182937b77ba9e474e70c

Apollo Client Prefetching in React

This section is all about prefetching data, though the user doesn't need it immediately. It is another UX technique that can be deployed to the optimistic UI technique you used earlier. You will implement the prefetching data feature for the list of issues, but feel free to implement it for other data fetching later as your exercise.

When your application renders for the first time, there no issues fetched, so no issues are rendered. The user has to toggle the filter button to fetch open issues, and do it again to fetch closed issues. The third click will hide the list of issues again. The goal of this section is to prefetch the next bulk of issues when the user hovers the filter button. For instance, when the issues are still hidden and the user hovers the filter button, the issues with the open state are prefetched in the background. When the user clicks the button, there is no waiting time, because the issues with the open state are already there. The same scenario applies for the transition from open to closed issues. To prepare this behavior, split out the filter button as its own component in the *src/Issue/IssueList/index.js* file:

src/Issue/IssueList/index.js

```
const Issues = ({
  repositoryOwner,
  repositoryName,
  issueState,
  onChangeIssueState,
}) => (
  <div className="Issues">
    <IssueFilter
      issueState={issueState}
      onChangeIssueState={onChangeIssueState}
    />

    {isShow(issueState) && (
      ...
    )}
  </div>
);

const IssueFilter = ({ issueState, onChangeIssueState }) => (
  <ButtonUnobtrusive
    onClick={() => onChangeIssueState(TRANSITION_STATE[issueState])}
  >
    {TRANSITION_LABELS[issueState]}
  </ButtonUnobtrusive>
);
```

Now it is easier to focus on the IssueFilter component where most of the logic for data prefetching is implemented. Like before, the prefetching should happen when the user hovers over the button. There needs to be a prop for it, and a callback function which is executed when the user hovers over it. There is such a prop (attribute) for a button (element). We are dealing with HTML elements here.

src/Issue/IssueList/index.js

```
const prefetchIssues = () => {};


...


const IssueFilter = ({ issueState, onChangeIssueState }) => (
  <ButtonUnobtrusive
    onClick={() => onChangeIssueState(TRANSITION_STATE[issueState])}
    onMouseOver={prefetchIssues}
  >
    {TRANSITION_LABELS[issueState]}
  </ButtonUnobtrusive>
);
```

The prefetchIssue() function has to execute the identical GraphQL query executed by the Query component in the Issues component, but this time it is done in an imperative way instead of declarative. Rather than using the Query component for it, use the the Apollo Client instance directly to execute a query. Remember, the Apollo Client instance is hidden in the component tree, because you used React's Context API to provide the Apollo Client instance the component tree's top level. The Query and Mutation components have access to the Apollo Client, even though you have never used it yourself directly. However, this time you use it to query the prefetched data. Use the ApolloConsumer component from the React Apollo package to expose the Apollo Client instance in your component tree. You have used the ApolloProvider somewhere to provide the client instance, and you can use the ApolloConsumer to retrieve it now. In the *src/Issue/IssueList/index.js* file, import the ApolloConsumer component and use it in the IssueFilter component. It gives you access to the Apollo Client instance via its render props child function.

src/Issue/IssueList/index.js

```
import React from 'react';
import { Query, ApolloConsumer } from 'react-apollo';
import gql from 'graphql-tag';
import { withState } from 'recompose';


...


const IssueFilter = ({ issueState, onChangeIssueState }) => (
  <ApolloConsumer>
    {client => (
```

```
      <ButtonUnobtrusive
        onClick={() =>
          onChangeIssueState(TRANSITION_STATE[issueState])
        }
        onMouseOver={() => prefetchIssues(client)}
      >
        {TRANSITION_LABELS[issueState]}
      </ButtonUnobtrusive>
    )}
  </ApolloConsumer>
);
```

Now you have access to the Apollo Client instance to perform queries and mutations, which will enable you to query GitHub's GraphQL API imperatively. The variables needed to perform the prefetching of issues are the same ones used in the Query component. You need to pass those to the IssueFilter component, and then to the prefetchIssues() function.

src/Issue/IssueList/index.js

```
...

const Issues = ({
  repositoryOwner,
  repositoryName,
  issueState,
  onChangeIssueState,
}) => (
  <div className="Issues">
    <IssueFilter
      repositoryOwner={repositoryOwner}
      repositoryName={repositoryName}
      issueState={issueState}
      onChangeIssueState={onChangeIssueState}
    />

    {isShow(issueState) && (
      ...
    )}
  </div>
);

const IssueFilter = ({
  repositoryOwner,
  repositoryName,
```

```
  issueState,
  onChangeIssueState,
}) => (
  <ApolloConsumer>
    {client => (
      <ButtonUnobtrusive
        onClick={() =>
          onChangeIssueState(TRANSITION_STATE[issueState])
        }
        onMouseOver={() =>
          prefetchIssues(
            client,
            repositoryOwner,
            repositoryName,
            issueState,
          )
        }
      >
        {TRANSITION_LABELS[issueState]}
      </ButtonUnobtrusive>
    )}
  </ApolloConsumer>
);
```

...

Use this information to perform the prefetching data query. The Apollo Client instance exposes a query() method for this. Make sure to retrieve the next issueState, because when prefetching open issues, the current issueState should be NONE.

src/Issue/IssueList/index.js

```
const prefetchIssues = (
  client,
  repositoryOwner,
  repositoryName,
  issueState,
) => {
  const nextIssueState = TRANSITION_STATE[issueState];

  if (isShow(nextIssueState)) {
    client.query({
      query: GET_ISSUES_OF_REPOSITORY,
      variables: {
```

```
        repositoryOwner,
        repositoryName,
        issueState: nextIssueState,
      },
    });
  }
};
```

That's it. Once the button is hovered, it should prefetch the issues for the next `issueState`. The Apollo Client makes sure that the new data is updated in the cache like it would do for the Query component. There shouldn't be any visible loading indicator in between except when the network request takes too long and you click the button right after hovering it. You can verify that the request is happening in your network tab in the developer development tools of your browser. In the end, you have learned about two UX improvements that can be achieved with ease when using Apollo Client: optimistic UI and prefetching data.

Exercises:

- Confirm your source code for the last section[187]
- Read more about Apollo Prefetching and Query Splitting in React[188]
- Invest 3 minutes of your time and take the quiz[189]

---

[187]https://github.com/the-road-to-graphql/react-graphql-github-apollo/tree/87dc6eee7948dad6e1eb4c15078063337eff94db
[188]https://www.apollographql.com/docs/react/features/performance.html
[189]https://www.surveymonkey.com/r/5PLMBR3

Exercise: Commenting Feature

This last section is for hands-on experience with the application and implementing features yourself. I encourage you to continue implementing features for the application and improving it. There are a couple of guiding points to help you implementing the Commenting feature. In the end it should be possible to show a list of paginated comments per issue on demand. Finally, a user should be able to leave a comment. The source code of the implemented feature can be found here[190].

- Introduce components for fetching a list of comments (e.g. Comments), rendering a list of comments (e.g. CommentList), and rendering a single comment (e.g. CommentItem). They can render sample data for now.
- Use the top level comments component (e.g. Comments), which will be your container component that is responsible to query the list of comments, in the *src/Issue/IssueItem/index.js* file. In addition, add a toggle to either show or hide comments. The IssueItem component has to become a class component or needs to make use of the withState HOC from the recompose library.
- Use the Query component from React Apollo in your container Comments component to fetch a list of comments. It should be similar to the query that fetches the list of issues. You only need to identify the issue for which the comments should be fetched.
- Handle all edge cases in the Comments to show loading indicator, no data, or error messages. Render the list of comments in the CommentList component and a single comment in the CommentItem component.
- Implement the pagination feature for comments. Add the necessary fields in the query, the additional props and variables to the Query component, and the reusable FetchMore component. Handle the merging of the state in the updateQuery prop.
- Enable prefetching of the comments when hovering the "Show/Hide Comments" button.
- Implement an AddComment component that shows a textarea and a submit button to enable user comments. Use the addComment mutation from GitHub's GraphQL API and the Mutation component from React Apollo to execute the mutation with the submit button.
- Improve the AddComment component with the optimistic UI feature (perhaps read again the Apollo documentation about the optimistic UI with a list of items[191]). A comment should show up in the list of comments, even if the request is pending.

I hope this section, building your own feature in the application with all the learned tools and techniques, matched your skills and challenged you to implement React applications with Apollo and GraphQL. I would recommend working to improve and extend the existing application. If you haven't implemented a GraphQL server yet, find other third-party APIs that offer a GraphQL API and build your own React with Apollo application by consuming it. Keep yourself challenged to grow your skills as a developer.

---

[190]https://github.com/the-road-to-graphql/react-graphql-github-apollo/tree/c689a90d43272bbcb64c05f85fbc84ad4fe4308d
[191]https://www.apollographql.com/docs/react/features/optimistic-ui.html

Appendix: CSS Files and Styles

This section has all the CSS files as well as their content and locations, to give your React with GraphQL and Apollo Client application a nice touch. It even makes it responsive for mobile and tablet devices. These are only recommendations, though; you can experiment with them, or come up with your own styles.

src/style.css

```css
#root,
html,
body {
  height: 100%;
}

body {
  margin: 0;
  padding: 0;
  font-family: 'Source Sans Pro', sans-serif;
  font-weight: 200;
  text-rendering: optimizeLegibility;
}

h2 {
  font-size: 24px;
  font-weight: 600;
  line-height: 34px;
  margin: 5px 0;
}

h3 {
  font-size: 20px;
  font-weight: 400;
  line-height: 27px;
  margin: 5px 0;
}

ul,
li {
  list-style: none;
  padding-left: 0;
}
```

```css
a {
  text-decoration: none;
  color: #000;
  opacity: 1;
  transition: opacity 0.25s ease-in-out;
}

a:hover {
  opacity: 0.35;
  text-decoration: none;
}

a:active {
  text-decoration: none;
}

pre {
  white-space: pre-wrap;
}
```

src/App/style.css

```css
.App {
  min-height: 100%;
  display: flex;
  flex-direction: column;
}

.App-main {
  flex: 1;
}

.App-content_large-header,
.App-content_small-header {
  margin-top: 54px;
}

@media only screen and (max-device-width: 480px) {
  .App-content_large-header {
    margin-top: 123px;
  }

  .App-content_small-header {
```

```
      margin-top: 68px;
  }
}
```

src/App/Navigation/style.css

```css
.Navigation {
  overflow: hidden;
  position: fixed;
  top: 0;
  width: 100%;
  z-index: 1;
  background-color: #24292e;
  display: flex;
  align-items: baseline;
}

@media only screen and (max-device-width: 480px) {
  .Navigation {
    flex-direction: column;
    justify-content: center;
    align-items: center;
  }
}

.Navigation-link {
  font-size: 12px;
  letter-spacing: 3.5px;
  font-weight: 500;
  text-transform: uppercase;
  padding: 20px;
  text-decoration: none;
}

.Navigation-link a {
  color: #ffffff;
}

.Navigation-search {
  padding: 0 10px;
}

@media only screen and (max-device-width: 480px) {
```

```css
  .Navigation-link {
    padding: 10px;
  }

  .Navigation-search {
    padding: 10px 10px;
  }
}
```

src/Button/style.css

```css
.Button {
  padding: 10px;
  background: none;
  cursor: pointer;
  transition: color 0.25s ease-in-out;
  transition: background 0.25s ease-in-out;
}

.Button_white {
  border: 1px solid #fff;
  color: #fff;
}

.Button_white:hover {
  color: #000;
  background: #fff;
}

.Button_black {
  border: 1px solid #000;
  color: #000;
}

.Button_black:hover {
  color: #fff;
  background: #000;
}

.Button_unobtrusive {
  padding: 0;
  color: #000;
  background: none;
```

```
  border: none;
  cursor: pointer;
  opacity: 1;
  transition: opacity 0.25s ease-in-out;
  outline: none;
}

.Button_unobtrusive:hover {
  opacity: 0.35;
}

.Button_unobtrusive:focus {
  outline: none;
}
```

src/Error/style.css

```
.ErrorMessage {
  margin: 20px;
  display: flex;
  justify-content: center;
}
```

src/FetchMore/style.css

```
.FetchMore {
  display: flex;
  flex-direction: column;
  align-items: center;
}

.FetchMore-button {
  margin: 20px 0;
}
```

src/Input/style.css

```css
.Input {
  border: none;
  padding: 10px;
  background: none;
  outline: none;
}

.Input:focus {
  outline: none;
}

.Input_white {
  border-bottom: 1px solid #fff;
  color: #fff;
}

.Input_black {
  border-bottom: 1px solid #000;
  color: #000;
}
```

src/Issue/IssueItem/style.css

```css
.IssueItem {
  margin-bottom: 10px;
  display: flex;
  align-items: baseline;
}

.IssueItem-content {
  margin-left: 10px;
  padding-left: 10px;
  border-left: 1px solid #000;
}
```

src/Issue/IssueList/style.css

```css
.Issues {
  display: flex;
  flex-direction: column;
  align-items: center;
  margin: 0 20px;
}

.Issues-content {
  margin-top: 20px;
  display: flex;
  flex-direction: column;
}

.IssueList {
  margin: 20px 0;
}

@media only screen and (max-device-width: 480px) {
  .Issues-content {
    align-items: center;
  }
}
```

src/Loading/style.css

```css
.LoadingIndicator {
  display: flex;
  flex-direction: column;
  align-items: center;
  margin: 20px 0;
}

.LoadingIndicator_center {
  margin-top: 30%;
}
```

src/Repository/style.css

```css
.RepositoryItem {
  padding: 20px;
  border-bottom: 1px solid #000;
}


.RepositoryItem-title {
  display: flex;
  justify-content: space-between;
  align-items: baseline;
}


@media only screen and (max-device-width: 480px) {
  .RepositoryItem-title {
    flex-direction: column;
    align-items: center;
  }
}


.RepositoryItem-title-action {
  margin-left: 10px;
}


.RepositoryItem-description {
  margin: 10px 0;
  display: flex;
  justify-content: space-between;
}


@media only screen and (max-device-width: 480px) {
  .RepositoryItem-description {
    flex-direction: column;
    align-items: center;
  }
}


.RepositoryItem-description-info {
  margin-right: 20px;
}


@media only screen and (max-device-width: 480px) {
  .RepositoryItem-description-info {
    text-align: center;
```

```
    margin: 20px 0;
  }
}


.RepositoryItem-description-details {
  text-align: right;
  white-space: nowrap;
}

@media only screen and (max-device-width: 480px) {
  .RepositoryItem-description-details {
    text-align: center;
  }
}
```

You can find the final repository on GitHub[192] that showcases most of the exercise tasks. The application is not feature-complete and it doesn't cover all edge cases, but it should give insight into using GraphQL with Apollo in React applications. If you want to dive more deeply into different topics like testing and state management with GraphQL on the client-side, you can start here: A minimal Apollo Client in React Example[193]. Try to apply what you've learned in this application (e.g. testing, state management). Otherwise, I encourage you to try to build your own GraphQL client library, which helps you understand more of the GraphQL internals: How to build a GraphQL client library for React[194]. Whichever you decide, keep tinkering on this application, or start with another GraphQL client application to fortify your skill set. You have finished all the GraphQL client chapters now.

---

[192]https://github.com/rwieruch/react-graphql-github-apollo
[193]https://www.robinwieruch.de/react-apollo-client-example
[194]https://www.robinwieruch.de/react-graphql-client-library

Node.js with GraphQL and Apollo Server

In this chapter, you will implement server-side architecture using GraphQL and Apollo Server. The GraphQL query language is implemented as a reference implementation in JavaScript by Facebook, while Apollo Server builds on it to simplify building GraphQL servers in JavaScript. Since GraphQL is a query language, its transport layer and data format is not set in stone. GraphQL isn't opinionated about it, but it is used as alternative to the popular REST architecture for client-server communication over HTTP with JSON.

In the end, you should have a fully working GraphQL server boilerplate project that implements authentication, authorization, a data access layer with a database, domain specific entities such as users and messages, different pagination strategies, and real-time abilities due to subscriptions. You can find a working solution of it, as well as a working client-side application in React, in this GitHub repository: Full-stack Apollo with React and Express Boilerplate Project[195]. I consider it an ideal starter project to realize your own idea.

While building this application with me in the following sections, I recommend to verify your implementations with the built-in GraphQL client application (e.g. GraphQL Playground). Once you have your database setup done, you can verify your stored data over there as well. In addition, if you feel comfortable with it, you can implement a client application (in React or something else) which consumes the GraphQL API of this server. So let's get started!

---

[195]https://github.com/rwieruch/fullstack-apollo-react-express-boilerplate-project

Apollo Server Setup with Express

There are two ways to start out with this application. You can follow my guidance in this minimal Node.js setup guide step by step[196] or you can find a starter project in this GitHub repository[197] and follow its installation instructions.

Apollo Server can be used with several popular libraries for Node.js like Express, Koa, Hapi. It is kept library agnostic, so it's possible to connect it with many different third-party libraries in client and server applications. In this application, you will use Express[198], because it is the most popular and common middleware library for Node.js.

Install these two dependencies to the *package.json* file and *node_modules* folder:

Command Line

```
npm install apollo-server apollo-server-express --save
```

As you can see by the library names, you can use any other middleware solution (e.g. Koa, Hapi) to complement your standalone Apollo Server. Apart from these libraries for Apollo Server, you need the core libraries for Express and GraphQL:

Command Line

```
npm install express graphql --save
```

Now every library is set to get started with the source code in the *src/index.js* file. First, you have to import the necessary parts for getting started with Apollo Server in Express:

src/index.js

```
import express from 'express';
import { ApolloServer } from 'apollo-server-express';
```

Second, use both imports for initializing your Apollo Server with Express:

---

[196]https://www.robinwieruch.de/minimal-node-js-babel-setup
[197]https://github.com/rwieruch/node-babel-server
[198]https://expressjs.com/

src/index.js

```
import express from 'express';
import { ApolloServer } from 'apollo-server-express';

const app = express();

const schema = ...
const resolvers = ...

const server = new ApolloServer({
  typeDefs: schema,
  resolvers,
});

server.applyMiddleware({ app, path: '/graphql' });

app.listen({ port: 8000 }, () => {
  console.log('Apollo Server on http://localhost:8000/graphql');
});
```

Using Apollo Server's applyMiddleware() method, you can opt-in any middleware, which in this case is Express. Also, you can specify the path for your GraphQL API endpoint. Beyond this, you can see how the Express application gets initialized. The only missing items are the definition for the schema and resolvers for creating the Apollo Server instance. We'll implement them first and learn about them after:

src/index.js

```
import express from 'express';
import { ApolloServer, gql } from 'apollo-server-express';

const app = express();

const schema = gql`
  type Query {
    me: User
  }

  type User {
    username: String!
  }
`;
```

```
const resolvers = {
  Query: {
    me: () => {
      return {
        username: 'Robin Wieruch',
      };
    },
  },
};
```

. . .

The **GraphQL schema** provided to the Apollo Server is all the available data for reading and writing data via GraphQL. It can happen from any client who consumes the GraphQL API. The schema consists of **type definitions**, starting with a mandatory top level **Query type** for reading data, followed by **fields** and **nested fields**. In the schema from the Apollo Server setup, you have defined a me field, which is of the **object type** User. In this case, a User type has only a username field, a **scalar type**. There are various scalar types in the GraphQL specification for defining strings (String), booleans (Boolean), integers (Int), and more. At some point, the schema has to end at its leaf nodes with scalar types to resolve everything properly. Think about it as similar to a JavaScript object with objects or arrays inside, except it requires primitives like strings, booleans, or integers at some point.

Code Playground

```
const data = {
  me: {
    username: 'Robin Wieruch',
  },
};
```

In the GraphQL schema for setting up an Apollo Server, **resolvers** are used to return data for fields from the schema. The data source doesn't matter, because the data can be hardcoded, can come from a database, or from another (RESTful) API endpoint. You will learn more about potential data sources later. For now, it only matters that the resolvers are agnostic according to where the data comes from, which separates GraphQL from your typical database query language. Resolvers are functions that resolve data for your GraphQL fields in the schema. In the previous example, only a user object with the username "Robin Wieruch" gets resolved from the me field.

Your GraphQL API with Apollo Server and Express should be working now. On the command line, you can always start your application with the npm start script to verify it works after you make changes. To verify it without a client application, Apollo Server comes with GraphQL Playground, a built-in client for consuming GraphQL APIs. It is found by using a GraphQL API endpoint in a browser at http://localhost:8000/graphql. In the application, define your first GraphQL query to see its result:

GraphQL Playground

```
{
  me {
    username
  }
}
```

The result for the query should this or your defined sample data:

GraphQL Playground

```
{
  "data": {
    "me": {
      "username": "Robin Wieruch"
    }
  }
}
```

I might not mention GraphQL Playground as much moving forward, but I leave it to you to verify your GraphQL API with it after you make changes. It is useful tool to experiment and explore your own API. Optionally, you can also add CORS[199] to your Express middleware. First, install CORS on the command line:

Command Line

```
npm install cors --save
```

Second, use it in your Express middleware:

src/index.js

```
import cors from 'cors';
import express from 'express';
import { ApolloServer, gql } from 'apollo-server-express';

const app = express();


app.use(cors());


...
```

CORS is needed to perform HTTP requests from another domain than your server domain to your server. Otherwise you may run into cross-origin resource sharing errors for your GraphQL server.

---

[199]https://developer.mozilla.org/en-US/docs/Web/HTTP/CORS

Exercises:

- Confirm your source code for the last section[200]
- Read more about GraphQL[201]
- Experiment with the schema and the resolver
  - Add more fields to the user type
  - Fulfill the requirements in the resolver
  - Query your fields in the GraphQL Playground
- Read more about Apollo Server Standalone[202]
- Read more about Apollo Server in Express Setup[203]

---

[200]https://github.com/the-road-to-graphql/fullstack-apollo-react-express-boilerplate-project/tree/b6468a84ad77018bf940d951016b7e2c1e07404f
[201]https://graphql.org/learn
[202]https://www.apollographql.com/docs/apollo-server/v2/getting-started.html
[203]https://www.apollographql.com/docs/apollo-server/v2/essentials/server.html

Apollo Server: Type Definitions

This section is all about GraphQL type definitions and how they are used to define the overall GraphQL schema. A GraphQL schema is defined by its types, the relationships between the types, and their structure. Therefore GraphQL uses a **Schema Definition Language (SDL)**. However, the schema doesn't define where the data comes from. This responsibility is handled by resolvers outside of the SDL. When you used Apollo Server before, you used a User object type within the schema and defined a resolver which returned a user for the corresponding me field.

Note the exclamation point for the username field in the User object type. It means that the username is a **non-nullable** field. Whenever a field of type User with a username is returned from the GraphQL schema, the user has to have a username. It cannot be undefined or null. However, there isn't an exclamation point for the user type on the me field. Does it mean that the result of the me field can be null? That is the case for this particular scenario. There shouldn't be always a user returned for the me field, because a server has to know what the field contains before it can respond. Later, you will implement an authentication mechanism (sign up, sign in, sign out) with your GraphQL server. The me field is populated with a user object like account details only when a user is authenticated with the server. Otherwise, it remains null. When you define GraphQL type definitions, there must be conscious decisions about the types, relationships, structure and (non-null) fields.

We extend the schema by extending or adding more type definitions to it, and use **GraphQL arguments** to handle user fields:

src/index.js

```
const schema = gql`
  type Query {
    me: User
    user(id: ID!): User
  }

  type User {
    username: String!
  }
`;
```

GraphQL arguments can be used to make more fine-grained queries because you can provide them to the GraphQL query. Arguments can be used on a per-field level with parentheses. You must also define the type, which in this case is a non-nullable identifier to retrieve a user from a data source. The query returns the User type, which can be null because a user entity might not be found in the data source when providing a non identifiable id for it. Now you can see how two queries share the same GraphQL type, so when adding fields to the it, a client can use them implicitly for both queries id field:

src/index.js

```
const schema = gql`
  type Query {
    me: User
    user(id: ID!): User
  }

  type User {
    id: ID!
    username: String!
  }
`;
```

You may be wondering about the ID scalar type. The ID denotes an identifier used internally for advanced features like caching or refetching. It is a superior string scalar type. All that's missing from the new GraphQL query is the resolver, so we'll add it to the map of resolvers with sample data:

src/index.js

```
const resolvers = {
  Query: {
    me: () => {
      return {
        username: 'Robin Wieruch',
      };
    },
    user: () => {
      return {
        username: 'Dave Davids',
      };
    },
  },
};
```

Second, make use of the incoming id argument from the GraphQL query to decide which user to return. All the arguments can be found in the second argument in the resolver function's signature:

src/index.js

```
const resolvers = {
  Query: {
    me: () => {
      return {
        username: 'Robin Wieruch',
      };
    },
    user: (parent, args) => {
      return {
        username: 'Dave Davids',
      };
    },
  },
};
```

The first argument is called parent as well, but you shouldn't worry about it for now. Later, it will be showcased where it can be used in your resolvers. Now, to make the example more realistic, extract a map of sample users and return a user based on the id used as a key in the extracted map:

src/index.js

```
let users = {
  1: {
    id: '1',
    username: 'Robin Wieruch',
  },
  2: {
    id: '2',
    username: 'Dave Davids',
  },
};

const me = users[1];

const resolvers = {
  Query: {
    user: (parent, { id }) => {
      return users[id];
    },
    me: () => {
      return me;
    },
```

```
  },
};
```

Now try out your queries in GraphQL Playground:

GraphQL Playground

```
{
  user(id: "2") {
    username
  }
  me {
    username
  }
}
```

It should return this result:

GraphQL Playground

```
{
  "data": {
    "user": {
      "username": "Dave Davids"
    },
    "me": {
      "username": "Robin Wieruch"
    }
  }
}
```

Querying a list of of users will be our third query. First, add the query to the schema again:

src/index.js

```
const schema = gql`
  type Query {
    users: [User!]
    user(id: ID!): User
    me: User
  }

  type User {
    id: ID!
```

```
    username: String!
  }
`;
```

In this case, the users field returns a list of users of type User, which is denoted with the square brackets. Within the list, no user is allowed to be null, but the list itself can be null in case there are no users (otherwise, it could be also [User!]!). Once you add a new query to your schema, you are obligated to define it in your resolvers within the Query object:

src/index.js

```
const resolvers = {
  Query: {
    users: () => {
      return Object.values(users);
    },
    user: (parent, { id }) => {
      return users[id];
    },
    me: () => {
      return me;
    },
  },
};
```

You have three queries that can be used in your GraphQL client (e.g. GraphQL Playground) applications. All of them operate on the same User type to fulfil the data requirements in the resolvers, so each query has to have a matching resolver. All queries are grouped under one unique, mandatory Query type, which lists all available GraphQL queries exposed to your clients as your GraphQL API for reading data. Later, you will learn about the Mutation type, for grouping a GraphQL API for writing data.

Exercises:

- Confirm your source code for the last section[204]
- Read more about the GraphQL schema with Apollo Server[205]
- Read more about the GraphQL mindset: Thinking in Graphs[206]
- Read more about nullability in GraphQL[207]

---

[204]https://github.com/the-road-to-graphql/fullstack-apollo-react-express-boilerplate-project/tree/469080f810a0049442f02393fae746cebc391cc0
[205]https://www.apollographql.com/docs/apollo-server/v2/essentials/schema.html
[206]https://graphql.github.io/learn/thinking-in-graphs/
[207]https://blog.apollographql.com/using-nullability-in-graphql-2254f84c4ed7

Apollo Server: Resolvers

This section continuous with the GraphQL schema in Apollo Server, but transitions more to the resolver side of the subject. In your GraphQL type definitions you have defined types, their relations and their structure. But there is nothing about how to get the data. That's where the GraphQL resolvers come into play.

In JavaScript, the resolvers are grouped in a JavaScript object, often called a **resolver map**. Each top level query in your Query type has to have a resolver. Now, we'll resolve things on a per-field level.

src/index.js

```
const resolvers = {
  Query: {
    users: () => {
      return Object.values(users);
    },
    user: (parent, { id }) => {
      return users[id];
    },
    me: () => {
      return me;
    },
  },

  User: {
    username: () => 'Hans',
  },
};
```

Once you start your application again and query for a list of users, every user should have an identical username.

GraphQL Playground

```
// query
{
  users {
    username
    id
  }
}

// query result
```

```
{
  "data": {
    "users": [
      {
        "username": "Hans",
        "id": "1"
      },
      {
        "username": "Hans",
        "id": "2"
      }
    ]
  }
}
```

The GraphQL resolvers can operate more specifically on a per-field level. You can override the username of every User type by resolving a username field. Otherwise, the default username property of the user entity is taken for it. Generally this applies to every field. Either you decide specifically what the field should return in a resolver function or GraphQL tries to fallback for the field by retrieving the property automatically from the JavaScript entity.

Let's evolve this a bit by diving into the function signatures of resolver functions. Previously, you have seen that the second argument of the resolver function is the incoming arguments of a query. That's how you were able to retrieve the id argument for the user from the Query. The first argument is called the parent or root argument, and always returns the previously resolved field. Let's check this for the new username resolver function.

src/index.js

```
const resolvers = {
  Query: {
    users: () => {
      return Object.values(users);
    },
    user: (parent, { id }) => {
      return users[id];
    },
    me: () => {
      return me;
    },
  },

  User: {
    username: parent => {
```

```
      return parent.username;
    }
  },
};
```

When you query your list of users again in a running application, all usernames should complete correctly. That's because GraphQL first resolves all users in the users resolver, and then goes through the User's username resolver for each user. Each user is accessible as the first argument in the resolver function, so they can be used to access more properties on the entity. You can rename your parent argument to make it more explicit:

src/index.js

```
const resolvers = {
  Query: {
    ...
  },

  User: {
    username: user => {
      return user.username;
    }
  },
};
```

In this case, the username resolver function is redundant, because it only mimics the default behavior of a GraphQL resolver. If you leave it out, the username would still resolves with its correct property. However, this fine control over the resolved fields opens up powerful possibilities. It gives you the flexibility to add data mapping without worrying about the data sources behind the GraphQL layer. Here, we expose the full username of a user, a combination of its first and last name by using template literals:

src/index.js

```
const resolvers = {
  ...

  User: {
    username: user => `${user.firstname} ${user.lastname}`,
  },
};
```

For now, we are going to leave out the username resolver, because it only mimics the default behavior with Apollo Server. These are called **default resolvers**, because they work without explicit definitions. Next, look to the other arguments in the function signature of a GraphQL resolver:

Code Playground

```
(parent, args, context, info) => { ... }
```

The context argument is the third argument in the resolver function used to inject dependencies from the outside to the resolver function. Assume the signed-in user is known to the outside world of your GraphQL layer because a request to your GraphQL server is made and the authenticated user is retrieved from elsewhere. You might decide to inject this signed in user to your resolvers for application functionality, which is done with with the me user for the me field. Remove the declaration of the me user (let me = ...) and pass it in the context object when Apollo Server gets initialized instead:

src/index.js

```
const server = new ApolloServer({
  typeDefs: schema,
  resolvers,
  context: {
    me: users[1],
  },
});
```

Next, access it in the resolver's function signature as a third argument, which gets destructured into the me property from the context object.

src/index.js

```
const resolvers = {
  Query: {
    users: () => {
      return Object.values(users);
    },
    user: (parent, { id }) => {
      return users[id];
    },
    me: (parent, args, { me }) => {
      return me;
    },
  },
};
```

The context should be the same for all resolvers now. Every resolver that needs to access the context, or in this case the me user, can do so using the third argument of the resolver function.

The fourth argument in a resolver function, the info argument, isn't used very often, because it only gives you internal information about the GraphQL request. It can be used for debugging, error handling, advanced monitoring, and tracking. You don't need to worry about it for now.

A couple of words about the a resolver's return values: a resolver can return arrays, objects and scalar types, but it has to be defined in the matching type definitions. The type definition has to define an array or non-nullable field to have the resolvers working appropriately. What about JavaScript promises? Often, you will make a request to a data source (database, RESTful API) in a resolver, returning a JavaScript promise in the resolver. GraphQL can deal with it, and waits for the promise to resolve. That's why you don't need to worry about asynchronous requests to your data source later.

Exercises:

- Confirm your source code for the last section[208]
- Read more about GraphQL resolvers in Apollo[209]

---

[208]https://github.com/the-road-to-graphql/fullstack-apollo-react-express-boilerplate-project/tree/5d8ebc22260455ac6803af20838cbc1f2636be8f
[209]https://www.apollographql.com/docs/apollo-server/v2/essentials/data.html

Apollo Server: Type Relationships

You started to evolve your GraphQL schema by defining queries, mutations, and type definitions. In this section, let's add a second GraphQL type called Message and see how it behaves with your User type. In this application, a user can have messages. Basically, you could write a simple chat application with both types. First, add two new top level queries and the new Message type to your GraphQL schema:

src/index.js

```
const schema = gql`
  type Query {
    users: [User!]
    user(id: ID!): User
    me: User

    messages: [Message!]!
    message(id: ID!): Message!
  }

  type User {
    id: ID!
    username: String!
  }

  type Message {
    id: ID!
    text: String!
  }
`;
```

Second, you have to add two resolvers for Apollo Server to match the two new top level queries:

src/index.js

```
let messages = {
  1: {
    id: '1',
    text: 'Hello World',
  },
  2: {
    id: '2',
    text: 'By World',
  },
```

```js
};

const resolvers = {
  Query: {
    users: () => {
      return Object.values(users);
    },
    user: (parent, { id }) => {
      return users[id];
    },
    me: (parent, args, { me }) => {
      return me;
    },
    messages: () => {
      return Object.values(messages);
    },
    message: (parent, { id }) => {
      return messages[id];
    },
  },
};
```

Once you run your application again, your new GraphQL queries should work in GraphQL playground. Now we'll add relationships to both GraphQL types. Historically, it was common with REST to add an identifier to each entity to resolve its relationship.

src/index.js

```js
const schema = gql`
  type Query {
    users: [User!]
    user(id: ID!): User
    me: User

    messages: [Message!]!
    message(id: ID!): Message!
  }

  type User {
    id: ID!
    username: String!
  }

  type Message {
```

```
      id: ID!
      text: String!
      userId: ID!
    }
`;
```

With GraphQL, Instead of using an identifier and resolving the entities with multiple waterfall requests, you can use the User entity within the message entity directly:

src/index.js

```
const schema = gql`
  ...

  type Message {
    id: ID!
    text: String!
    user: User!
  }
`;
```

Since a message doesn't have a user entity in your model, the default resolver doesn't work. You need to set up an explicit resolver for it.

src/index.js

```
const resolvers = {
  Query: {
    users: () => {
      return Object.values(users);
    },
    user: (parent, { id }) => {
      return users[id];
    },
    me: (parent, args, { me }) => {
      return me;
    },
    messages: () => {
      return Object.values(messages);
    },
    message: (parent, { id }) => {
      return messages[id];
    },
  },
```

```
  Message: {
    user: (parent, args, { me }) => {
      return me;
    },
  },
};
```

In this case, every message is written by the authenticated me user. If you query the following about messages, you will get this result:

GraphQL Playground

```
// query
{
  message(id: "1") {
    id
    text
    user {
      id
      username
    }
  }
}

// query result
{
  "data": {
    "message": {
      "id": "1",
      "text": "Hello World",
      "user": {
        "id": "1",
        "username": "Robin Wieruch"
      }
    }
  }
}
```

Let's make the behavior more like in a real world application. Your sample data needs keys to reference entities to each other, so the message passes a userId property:

src/index.js

```
let messages = {
  1: {
    id: '1',
    text: 'Hello World',
    userId: '1',
  },
  2: {
    id: '2',
    text: 'By World',
    userId: '2',
  },
};
```

The parent argument in your resolver function can be used to get a message's userId, which can then be used to retrieve the appropriate user.

src/index.js

```
const resolvers = {
  ...

  Message: {
    user: message => {
      return users[message.userId];
    },
  },
};
```

Now every message has its own dedicated user. The last steps were crucial for understanding GraphQL. Even though you have default resolver functions or this fine-grained control over the fields by defining your own resolver functions, it is up to you to retrieve the data from a data source. The developer makes sure every field can be resolved. GraphQL lets you group those fields into one GraphQL query, regardless of the data source.

Let's recap this implementation detail again with another relationship that involves user messages. In this case, the relationships go in the other direction.

src/index.js

```
let users = {
  1: {
    id: '1',
    username: 'Robin Wieruch',
    messageIds: [1],
  },
  2: {
    id: '2',
    username: 'Dave Davids',
    messageIds: [2],
  },
};
```

This sample data could come from any data source. The important part is that it has a key that defines a relationship to another entity. All of this is independent from GraphQL, so let's define the relationship from users to their messages in GraphQL.

src/index.js

```
const schema = gql`
  type Query {
    users: [User!]
    user(id: ID!): User
    me: User

    messages: [Message!]!
    message(id: ID!): Message!
  }

  type User {
    id: ID!
    username: String!
    messages: [Message!]
  }

  type Message {
    id: ID!
    text: String!
    user: User!
  }
`;
```

Since a user entity doesn't have messages, but message identifiers, you can write a custom resolver for the messages of a user again. In this case, the resolver retrieves all messages from the user from the list of sample messages.

src/index.js

```
const resolvers = {
  ...

  User: {
    messages: user => {
      return Object.values(messages).filter(
        message => message.userId === user.id,
      );
    },
  },

  Message: {
    user: message => {
      return users[message.userId];
    },
  },
};
```

This section has shown you how to expose relationships in your GraphQL schema. If the default resolvers don't work, you have to define your own custom resolvers on a per field level for resolving the data from different data sources.

Exercises:

- Confirm your source code for the last section[210]
- Query a list of users with their messages
- Query a list of messages their user
- Read more about the GraphQL schema[211]

---

[210]https://github.com/the-road-to-graphql/fullstack-apollo-react-express-boilerplate-project/tree/491d93a90f4ee3413d9226e0a18c10b7407949ef
[211]https://graphql.github.io/learn/schema/

Apollo Server: Queries and Mutations

So far, you have only defined queries in your GraphQL schema using two related GraphQL types for reading data. These should work in GraphQL Playground, because you have given them equivalent resolvers. Now we'll cover GraphQL mutations for writing data. In the following, you create two mutations: one to create a message, and one to delete it. Let's start with creating a message as the currently signed in user (the me user).

src/index.js

```
const schema = gql`
  type Query {
    users: [User!]
    user(id: ID!): User
    me: User

    messages: [Message!]!
    message(id: ID!): Message!
  }

  type Mutation {
    createMessage(text: String!): Message!
  }

  ...
`;
```

Apart from the Query type, there are also Mutation and Subscription types. There, you can group all your GraphQL operations for writing data instead of reading it. In this case, the createMessage mutation accepts a non-nullable text input as an argument, and returns the created message. Again, you have to implement the resolver as counterpart for the mutation the same as with the previous queries, which happens in the mutation part of the resolver map:

src/index.js

```
const resolvers = {
  Query: {
    ...
  },

  Mutation: {
    createMessage: (parent, { text }, { me }) => {
      const message = {
        text,
```

```
      userId: me.id,
    };

    return message;
  },
},


  ...
};
```

The mutation's resolver has access to the text in its second argument. It also has access to the signed-in user in the third argument, used to associate the created message with the user. The parent argument isn't used. The one thing missing to make the message complete is an identifier. To make sure a unique identifier is used, install this neat library in the command line:

Command Line

```
npm install uuid --save
```

And import it to your file:

src/index.js

```
import uuidv4 from 'uuid/v4';
```

Now you can give your message a unique identifier:

src/index.js

```
const resolvers = {
  Query: {
    ...
  },

  Mutation: {
    createMessage: (parent, { text }, { me }) => {
      const id = uuidv4();
      const message = {
        id,
        text,
        userId: me.id,
      };

      return message;
```

```
      },
    },

    ...
};
```

So far, the mutation creates a message object and returns it to the API. However, most mutations have side-effects, because they are writing data to your data source or performing another action. Most often, it will be a write operation to your database, but in this case, you only need to update your users and messages variables. The list of available messages needs to be updated, and the user's reference list of messageIds needs to have the new message id.

src/index.js

```
const resolvers = {
  Query: {
    ...
  },

  Mutation: {
    createMessage: (parent, { text }, { me }) => {
      const id = uuidv4();
      const message = {
        id,
        text,
        userId: me.id,
      };

      messages[id] = message;
      users[me.id].messageIds.push(id);

      return message;
    },
  },

  ...
};
```

That's it for the first mutation. You can try it right now in GraphQL Playground:

GraphQL Playground

```
mutation {
  createMessage (text: "Hello GraphQL!") {
    id
    text
  }
}
```

The last part is essentially your writing operation to a data source. In this case, you have only updated the sample data, but it would most likely be a database in practical use. Next, implement the mutation for deleting messages:

src/index.js

```
const schema = gql`
  type Query {
    users: [User!]
    user(id: ID!): User
    me: User

    messages: [Message!]!
    message(id: ID!): Message!
  }

  type Mutation {
    createMessage(text: String!): Message!
    deleteMessage(id: ID!): Boolean!
  }

  ...
`;
```

The mutation returns a boolean that tells if the deletion was successful or not, and it takes an identifier as input to identify the message. The counterpart of the GraphQL schema implementation is a resolver:

src/index.js

```
const resolvers = {
  Query: {
    ...
  },

  Mutation: {
    ...

    deleteMessage: (parent, { id }) => {
      const { [id]: message, ...otherMessages } = messages;

      if (!message) {
        return false;
      }

      messages = otherMessages;

      return true;
    },
  },

  ...
};
```

The resolver finds the message by id from the messages object using destructuring. If there is no message, the resolver returns false. If there is a message, the remaining messages without the deleted message are the updated versions of the messages object. Then, the resolver returns true. Otherwise, if no message is found, the resolver returns false. Mutations in GraphQL and Apollo Server aren't much different from GraphQL queries, except they write data.

There is only one GraphQL operation missing for making the messages features complete. It is possible to read, create, and delete messages, so the only operation left is updating them as an exercise.

Exercises:

- Confirm your source code for the last section[212]
- Create a message in GraphQL Playground with a mutation
  - Query all messages
  - Query the me user with messages

[212]https://github.com/the-road-to-graphql/fullstack-apollo-react-express-boilerplate-project/tree/a10c54ec1b82043d98fcff2a6395fcd8e405bfda

- Delete a message in GraphQL Playground with a mutation
    - Query all messages
    - Query the me user with messages
- Implement an `updateMessage` mutation for completing all CRUD operations for a message in GraphQL
- Read more about GraphQL queries and mutations[213]

---

[213]https://graphql.github.io/learn/queries/

GraphQL Schema Stitching with Apollo Server

Schema stitching is a powerful feature in GraphQL. It's about merging multiple GraphQL schemas into one schema, which may be consumed in a GraphQL client application. For now, you only have one schema in your application, but there may come a need for more complicated operations that use multiple schemas and schema stitching. For instance, assume you have a GraphQL schema you want to modularize based on domains (e.g. user, message). You may end up with two schemas, where each schema matches one type (e.g. User type, Message type). The operation requires merging both GraphQL schemas to make the entire GraphQL schema accessible with your GraphQL server's API. That's one of the basic motivations behind schema stitching.

But you can take this one step further: you may end up with microservices or third-party platforms that expose their dedicated GraphQL APIs, which then can be used to merge them into one GraphQL schema, where schema stitching becomes a single source of truth. Then again, a client can consume the entire schema, which is composed out of multiple domain-driven microservices.

In our case, let's start with a separation by technical concerns for the GraphQL schema and resolvers. Afterward, you will apply the separation by domains that are users and messages.

Technical Separation

Let's take the GraphQL schema from the application where you have a User type and Message type. In the same step, split out the resolvers to a dedicated place. The *src/index.js* file, where the schema and resolvers are needed for the Apollo Server instantiation, should only import both things. It becomes three things when outsourcing data, which in this case is the sample data, now called models.

src/index.js

```
import cors from 'cors';
import express from 'express';
import { ApolloServer } from 'apollo-server-express';

import schema from './schema';
import resolvers from './resolvers';
import models from './models';

const app = express();

app.use(cors());

const server = new ApolloServer({
  typeDefs: schema,
  resolvers,
```

```
  context: {
    models,
    me: models.users[1],
  },
});


server.applyMiddleware({ app, path: '/graphql' });

app.listen({ port: 8000 }, () => {
  console.log('Apollo Server on http://localhost:8000/graphql');
});
```

As an improvement, models are passed to the resolver function's as context. The models are your data access layer, which can be sample data, a database, or a third-party API. It's always good to pass those things from the outside to keep the resolver functions pure. Then, you don't need to import the models in each resolver file. In this case, the models are the sample data moved to the *src/models/index.js* file:

src/models/index.js

```
let users = {
  1: {
    id: '1',
    username: 'Robin Wieruch',
    messageIds: [1],
  },
  2: {
    id: '2',
    username: 'Dave Davids',
    messageIds: [2],
  },
};

let messages = {
  1: {
    id: '1',
    text: 'Hello World',
    userId: '1',
  },
  2: {
    id: '2',
    text: 'By World',
    userId: '2',
  },
```

```
};

export default {
  users,
  messages,
};
```

Since you have passed the models to your Apollo Server context, they are accessible in each resolver. Next, move the resolvers to the *src/resolvers/index.js* file, and adjust the resolver's function signature by adding the models when they are needed to read/write users or messages.

src/resolvers/index.js

```
import uuidv4 from 'uuid/v4';

export default {
  Query: {
    users: (parent, args, { models }) => {
      return Object.values(models.users);
    },
    user: (parent, { id }, { models }) => {
      return models.users[id];
    },
    me: (parent, args, { me }) => {
      return me;
    },
    messages: (parent, args, { models }) => {
      return Object.values(models.messages);
    },
    message: (parent, { id }, { models }) => {
      return models.messages[id];
    },
  },

  Mutation: {
    createMessage: (parent, { text }, { me, models }) => {
      const id = uuidv4();
      const message = {
        id,
        text,
        userId: me.id,
      };

      models.messages[id] = message;
```

```
        models.users[me.id].messageIds.push(id);

        return message;
    },

    deleteMessage: (parent, { id }, { models }) => {
      const { [id]: message, ...otherMessages } = models.messages;

        if (!message) {
          return false;
        }

        models.messages = otherMessages;

        return true;
    },
  },

  User: {
    messages: (user, args, { models }) => {
      return Object.values(models.messages).filter(
        message => message.userId === user.id,
      );
    },
  },

  Message: {
    user: (message, args, { models }) => {
      return models.users[message.userId];
    },
  },
};
```

The resolvers receive all sample data as models in the context argument rather than operating directly on the sample data as before. As mentioned, it keeps the resolver functions pure. Later, you will have an easier time testing resolver functions in isolation. Next, move your schema's type definitions in the *src/schema/index.js* file:

src/schema/index.js

```
import { gql } from 'apollo-server-express';

export default gql`
  type Query {
    users: [User!]
    user(id: ID!): User
    me: User

    messages: [Message!]!
    message(id: ID!): Message!
  }

  type Mutation {
    createMessage(text: String!): Message!
    deleteMessage(id: ID!): Boolean!
  }

  type User {
    id: ID!
    username: String!
    messages: [Message!]
  }

  type Message {
    id: ID!
    text: String!
    user: User!
  }
`;
```

The technical separation is complete, but the separation by domains, where schema stitching is needed, isn't done yet. So far, you have only outsourced the schema, resolvers and data (models) from your Apollo Server instantiation file. Everything is separated by technical concerns now. You also made a small improvement for passing the models through the context, rather than importing them in resolver files.

Domain Separation

In the next step, modularize the GraphQL schema by domains (user and message). First, separate the user-related entity in its own schema definition file called *src/schema/user.js*:

src/schema/user.js

```
import { gql } from 'apollo-server-express';

export default gql`
  extend type Query {
    users: [User!]
    user(id: ID!): User
    me: User
  }

  type User {
    id: ID!
    username: String!
    messages: [Message!]
  }
`;
```

The same applies for the message schema definition in *src/schema/message.js*:

src/schema/message.js

```
import { gql } from 'apollo-server-express';

export default gql`
  extend type Query {
    messages: [Message!]!
    message(id: ID!): Message!
  }

  extend type Mutation {
    createMessage(text: String!): Message!
    deleteMessage(id: ID!): Boolean!
  }

  type Message {
    id: ID!
    text: String!
    user: User!
  }
`;
```

Each file only describes its own entity, with a type and its relations. A relation can be a type from a different file, such as a Message type that still has the relation to a User type even though the User type is defined somewhere else. Note the extend statement on the Query and Mutation types. Since you have more than one of those types now, you need to extend the types. Next, define shared base types for them in the *src/schema/index.js*:

src/schema/index.js

```
import { gql } from 'apollo-server-express';

import userSchema from './user';
import messageSchema from './message';

const linkSchema = gql`
  type Query {
    _: Boolean
  }

  type Mutation {
    _: Boolean
  }

  type Subscription {
    _: Boolean
  }
`;

export default [linkSchema, userSchema, messageSchema];
```

In this file, both schemas are merged with the help of a utility called linkSchema. The linkSchema defines all types shared within the schemas. It already defines a Subscription type for GraphQL subscriptions, which may be implemented later. As a workaround, there is an empty underscore field with a Boolean type in the merging utility schema, because there is no official way of completing this action yet. The utility schema defines the shared base types, extended with the extend statement in the other domain-specific schemas.

This time, the application runs with a stitched schema instead of one global schema. What's missing are the domain separated resolver maps. Let's start with the user domain again in file in the *src/resolvers/user.js* file, whereas I leave out the implementation details for saving space here:

src/resolvers/user.js

```
export default {
  Query: {
    users: (parent, args, { models }) => {
      ...
    },
    user: (parent, { id }, { models }) => {
      ...
    },
    me: (parent, args, { me }) => {
      ...
    },
  },

  User: {
    messages: (user, args, { models }) => {
      ...
    },
  },
};
```

Next, add the message resolvers in the *src/resolvers/message.js* file:

src/resolvers/message.js

```
import uuidv4 from 'uuid/v4';

export default {
  Query: {
    messages: (parent, args, { models }) => {
      ...
    },
    message: (parent, { id }, { models }) => {
      ...
    },
  },

  Mutation: {
    createMessage: (parent, { text }, { me, models }) => {
      ...
    },

    deleteMessage: (parent, { id }, { models }) => {
```

```
      ...
    },
  },

  Message: {
    user: (message, args, { models }) => {
      ...
    },
  },
};
```

Since the Apollo Server accepts a list of resolver maps too, you can import all of your resolver maps in your *src/resolvers/index.js* file, and export them as a list of resolver maps again:

src/resolvers/index.js

```
import userResolvers from './user';
import messageResolvers from './message';

export default [userResolvers, messageResolvers];
```

Then, the Apollo Server can take the resolver list to be instantiated. Start your application again and verify that everything is working for you.

In the last section, you extracted schema and resolvers from your main file and separated both by domains. The sample data is placed in a *src/models* folder, where it can be migrated to a database-driven approach later. The folder structure should look similar to this:

- src/
  - models/
    * index.js
  - resolvers/
    * index.js
    * user.js
    * message.js
  - schema/
    * index.js
    * user.js
    * message.js
  - index.js

You now have a good starting point for a GraphQL server application with Node.js. The last implementations gave you a universally usable GraphQL boilerplate project to serve as a foundation for your own software development projects. As we continue, the focus becomes connecting GraphQL server to databases, authentication and authorization, and using powerful features like pagination.

Exercises:

- Confirm your source code for the last section[214]
- Read more about schema stitching with Apollo Server[215]
- Schema stitching is only a part of **schema delegation**
    - Read more about schema delegation[216]
    - Familiarize yourself with the motivation behind **remote schemas** and **schema transforms**

---

[214]https://github.com/the-road-to-graphql/fullstack-apollo-react-express-boilerplate-project/tree/953ef4b2ac8edc7c6338fb73ecdc1446e9cbdc4d
[215]https://www.apollographql.com/docs/graphql-tools/schema-stitching.html
[216]https://www.apollographql.com/docs/graphql-tools/schema-delegation.html

PostgreSQL with Sequelize for a GraphQL Server

To create a full-stack GraphQL application, you'll need to introduce a sophisticated data source. Sample data is fluctuant, while a database gives persistent data. In this section, you'll set up PostgreSQL with Sequelize (ORM[217]) for Apollo Server. PostgreSQL[218] is a SQL database whereas an alternative would be the popular NoSQL database called MongoDB[219] (with Mongoose as ORM). The choice of tech is always opinionated. You could choose MongoDB or any other SQL/NoSQL solution over PostgreSQL, but for the sake of this application, let's stick to PostgreSQL.

This setup guide[220] will walk you through the basic PostgreSQL setup, including installation, your first database, administrative database user setup, and essential commands. These are the things you should have accomplished after going through the instructions:

- A running installation of PostgreSQL
- A database super user with username and password
- A database created with `createdb` or `CREATE DATABASE`

You should be able to run and stop your database with the following commands:

- pg_ctl -D /usr/local/var/postgres start
- pg_ctl -D /usr/local/var/postgres stop

Use the `psql` command to connect to your database in the command line, where you can list databases and execute SQL statements against them. You should find a couple of these operations in the PostgreSQL setup guide, but this section will also show some of them. Consider performing these in the same way you've been completing GraphQL operations with GraphQL Playground. The `psql` command line interface and GraphQL Playground are effective tools for testing applications manually.

Once you have installed PostgreSQL on your local machine, you'll also want to acquire PostgreSQL for Node.js[221] and Sequelize (ORM)[222] for your project. I highly recommend you keep the Sequelize documentation open, as it will be useful for reference when you connect your GraphQL layer (resolvers) with your data access layer (Sequelize).

---

[217]https://en.wikipedia.org/wiki/Object-relational_mapping
[218]https://www.postgresql.org/
[219]https://www.mongodb.com/
[220]https://www.robinwieruch.de/postgres-express-setup-tutorial/
[221]https://github.com/brianc/node-postgres
[222]https://github.com/sequelize/sequelize

Command Line

```
npm install pg sequelize --save
```

Now you can create models for the user and message domains. Models are usually the data access layer in applications. Then, set up your models with Sequelize to make read and write operations to your PostgreSQL database. The models can then be used in GraphQL resolvers by passing them through the context object to each resolver. These are the essential steps:

- Creating a model for the user domain
- Creating a model for the message domain
- Connecting the application to a database
    - Providing super user's username and password
    - Combining models for database use
- Synchronizing the database once application starts

First, implement the *src/models/user.js* model:

src/models/user.js

```
const user = (sequelize, DataTypes) => {
  const User = sequelize.define('user', {
    username: {
      type: DataTypes.STRING,
    },
  });

  User.associate = models => {
    User.hasMany(models.Message, { onDelete: 'CASCADE' });
  };

  return User;
};

export default user;
```

Next, implement the *src/models/message.js* model:

src/models/message.js

```
const message = (sequelize, DataTypes) => {
  const Message = sequelize.define('message', {
    text: {
      type: DataTypes.STRING,
    },
  });

  Message.associate = models => {
    Message.belongsTo(models.User);
  };

  return Message;
};


export default message;
```

Both models define the shapes of their entities. The message model has a database column with the name text of type string. You can add multiple database columns horizontally to your model. All columns of a model make up a table row in the database, and each row reflects a database entry, such as a message or user. The database table name is defined by an argument in the Sequelize model definition. The message domain has the table "message". You can define relationships between entities with Sequelize using associations. In this case, a message entity belongs to one user, and that user has many messages. That's a minimal database setup with two domains, but since we're focusing on server-side GraphQL, you should consider reading more about databases subjects outside of these applications to fully grasp the concept.

Next, connect to your database from within your application in the *src/models/index.js* file. We'll need the database name, a database super user, and the user's password. You may also want to define a database dialect, because Sequelize supports other databases as well.

src/models/index.js

```
import Sequelize from 'sequelize';

const sequelize = new Sequelize(
  process.env.DATABASE,
  process.env.DATABASE_USER,
  process.env.DATABASE_PASSWORD,
  {
    dialect: 'postgres',
  },
);
```

```
export { sequelize };
```

In the same file, you can physically associate all your models with each other to expose them to your application as data access layer (models) for the database.

src/models/index.js

```
import Sequelize from 'sequelize';

const sequelize = new Sequelize(
  process.env.DATABASE,
  process.env.DATABASE_USER,
  process.env.DATABASE_PASSWORD,
  {
    dialect: 'postgres',
  },
);

const models = {
  User: sequelize.import('./user'),
  Message: sequelize.import('./message'),
};

Object.keys(models).forEach(key => {
  if ('associate' in models[key]) {
    models[key].associate(models);
  }
});

export { sequelize };

export default models;
```

The database credentials–database name, database super user name, database super user password–can be stored as environment variables. In your *.env* file, add those credentials as key value pairs. My defaults for local development are:

.env

```
DATABASE=postgres
DATABASE_USER=postgres
DATABASE_PASSWORD=postgres
```

You set up environment variables when you started creating this application. If not, you can also leave credentials in the source code for now. Finally, the database needs to be migrated/synchronized once your Node.js application starts. To complete this operation in your *src/index.js* file:

src/index.js

```
import express from 'express';
import { ApolloServer } from 'apollo-server-express';

import schema from './schema';
import resolvers from './resolvers';
import models, { sequelize } from './models';

...

sequelize.sync().then(async () => {
  app.listen({ port: 8000 }, () => {
    console.log('Apollo Server on http://localhost:8000/graphql');
  });
});
```

We've completed the database setup for a GraphQL server. Next, you'll replace the business logic in your resolvers, because that is where Sequelize is used to access the database instead the sample data. The application isn't quite complete, because the resolvers don't use the new data access layer.

Exercises:

- Confirm your source code for the last section[223]
- Familiarize yourself with databases
  - Try the psql command-line interface to access a database
  - Check the Sequelize API by reading through their documentation
  - Look up any unfamiliar database jargon mentioned here.

---

[223]https://github.com/the-road-to-graphql/fullstack-apollo-react-express-boilerplate-project/tree/a1927fc375a62a9d7d8c514f8bf7f576587cca93

Connecting Resolvers and Database

Your PostgreSQL database is ready to connect to a GraphQL server on startup. Now, instead of using the sample data, you will use data access layer (models) in GraphQL resolvers for reading and writing data to and from a database. In the next section, we will cover the following:

- Use the new models in your GraphQL resolvers
- Seed your database with data when your application starts
- Add a user model method for retrieving a user by username
- Learn the essentials about psql for the command line

Let's start by refactoring the GraphQL resolvers. You passed the models via Apollo Server's context object to each GraphQL resolver earlier. We used sample data before, but the Sequelize API is necessary for our real-word database operations. In the *src/resolvers/user.js* file, change the following lines of code to use the Sequelize API:

src/resolvers/user.js

```
export default {
  Query: {
    users: async (parent, args, { models }) => {
      return await models.User.findAll();
    },
    user: async (parent, { id }, { models }) => {
      return await models.User.findById(id);
    },
    me: async (parent, args, { models, me }) => {
      return await models.User.findById(me.id);
    },
  },

  User: {
    messages: async (user, args, { models }) => {
      return await models.Message.findAll({
        where: {
          userId: user.id,
        },
      });
    },
  },
};
```

The `findAll()` and `findById()` are commonly used Sequelize methods for database operations. Finding all messages for a specific user is more specific, though. Here, you used the `where` clause to narrow down messages by the `userId` entry in the database. Accessing a database will add another layer of complexity to your application's architecture, so be sure to reference the Sequelize API documentation as much as needed going forward.

Next, return to the *src/resolvers/message.js* file and perform adjustments to use the Sequelize API:

src/resolvers/message.js

```
export default {
  Query: {
    messages: async (parent, args, { models }) => {
      return await models.Message.findAll();
    },
    message: async (parent, { id }, { models }) => {
      return await models.Message.findById(id);
    },
  },

  Mutation: {
    createMessage: async (parent, { text }, { me, models }) => {
      return await models.Message.create({
        text,
        userId: me.id,
      });
    },

    deleteMessage: async (parent, { id }, { models }) => {
      return await models.Message.destroy({ where: { id } });
    },
  },

  Message: {
    user: async (message, args, { models }) => {
      return await models.User.findById(message.userId);
    },
  },
};
```

Apart from the `findById()` and `findAll()` methods, you are creating and deleting a message in the mutations as well. Before, you had to generate your own identifier for the message, but now Sequelize takes care of adding a unique identifier to your message once it is created in the database.

There was one more crucial change in the two files: async/await[224]. Sequelize is a JavaScript promise-based ORM, so it always returns a JavaScript promise when operating on a database. That's where async/await can be used as a more readable version for asynchronous requests in JavaScript. You learned about the returned results of GraphQL resolvers in Apollo Server in a previous section. A result can be a JavaScript promise as well, because the resolvers are waiting for its actual result. In this case, you can also get rid of the async/await statements and your resolvers would still work. Sometimes it is better to be more explicit, however, especially when we add more business logic within the resolver's function body later, so we will keep the statements for now.

Now we'll shift to seeding the database with sample data when your applications starts with npm start. Once your database synchronizes before your server listens, you can create two user records manually with messages in your database. The following code for the *src/index.js* file shows how to perform these operations with async/await. Users will have a username with associated messages.

src/index.js

```
...

const eraseDatabaseOnSync = true;

sequelize.sync({ force: eraseDatabaseOnSync }).then(async () => {
  if (eraseDatabaseOnSync) {
    createUsersWithMessages();
  }

  app.listen({ port: 8000 }, () => {
    console.log('Apollo Server on http://localhost:8000/graphql');
  });
});

const createUsersWithMessages = async () => {
  await models.User.create(
    {
      username: 'rwieruch',
      messages: [
        {
          text: 'Published the Road to learn React',
        },
      ],
    },
    {
      include: [models.Message],
    },
```

---

[224]https://developer.mozilla.org/en-US/docs/Web/JavaScript/Reference/Statements/async_function

```
  );

  await models.User.create(
    {
      username: 'ddavids',
      messages: [
        {
          text: 'Happy to release ...',
        },
        {
          text: 'Published a complete ...',
        },
      ],
    },
    {
      include: [models.Message],
    },
  );
};
```

The `force` flag in your Sequelize `sync()` method can be used to seed the database on every application startup. You can either remove the flag or set it to `false` if you want to keep accumulated database changes over time. The flag should be removed for your production database at some point.

Next, we have to handle the `me` user. Before, you used one of the users from the sample data; now, the user will come from a database. It's a good opportunity to write a custom method for your user model in the *src/models/user.js* file:

src/models/user.js

```
const user = (sequelize, DataTypes) => {
  const User = sequelize.define('user', {
    username: {
      type: DataTypes.STRING,
    },
  });

  User.associate = models => {
    User.hasMany(models.Message, { onDelete: 'CASCADE' });
  };

  User.findByLogin = async login => {
    let user = await User.findOne({
      where: { username: login },
```

```
  });

  if (!user) {
    user = await User.findOne({
      where: { email: login },
    });
  }

  return user;
};

return User;
};


export default user;
```

The `findByLogin()` method on your user model retrieves a user by `username` or by `email` entry. You don't have an `email` entry on the user yet, but it will be added when the application has an authentication mechanism. The `login` argument is used for both `username` and `email`, for retrieving the user from the database, and you can see how it is used to sign in to an application with username or email.

You have introduced your first custom method on a database model. It is always worth considering where to put this business logic. When giving your model these access methods, you may end up with a concept called *fat models*. An alternative would be writing separate services like functions or classes for these data access layer functionalities.

The new model method can be used to retrieve the `me` user from the database. Then you can put it into the context object when the Apollo Server is instantiated in the *src/index.js* file:

src/index.js

```
const server = new ApolloServer({
  typeDefs: schema,
  resolvers,
  context: {
    models,
    me: models.User.findByLogin('rwieruch'),
  },
});
```

However, this cannot work yet, because the user is read asynchronously from the database, so `me` would be a JavaScript promise rather than the actual user; and because you may want to retrieve the `me` user on a per-request basis from the database. Otherwise, the `me` user has to stay the same after the Apollo Server is created. Instead, use a function that returns the context object rather than an object for the context in Apollo Server. This function uses the async/await statements. The function is invoked every time a request hits your GraphQL API, so the me user is retrieved from the database with every request.

src/index.js

```
const server = new ApolloServer({
  typeDefs: schema,
  resolvers,
  context: async () => ({
    models,
    me: await models.User.findByLogin('rwieruch'),
  }),
});
```

You should be able to start your application again. Try out different GraphQL queries and mutations in GraphQL Playground, and verify that everything is working for you. If there are any errors regarding the database, make sure that it is properly connected to your application and that the database is running on the command line too.

Since you have introduced a database now, GraphQL Playground is not the only manual testing tool anymore. Whereas GraphQL Playground can be used to test your GraphQL API, you may want to use the psql command line interface to query your database manually. For instance, you may want to check user message records in the database or whether a message exists there after it has been created with a GraphQL mutation. First, connect to your database on the command line:

Command Line

```
psql mydatabasename
```

And second, try the following SQL statements. It's the perfect opportunity to learn more about SQL itself:

psql

```
SELECT * from users;
SELECT text from messages;
```

Which leads to:

psql

```
mydatabase=# SELECT * from users;
 id | username |          createdAt          |          updatedAt
----+----------+-----------------------------+-----------------------------
  1 | rwieruch | 2018-08-21 21:15:38.758+08  | 2018-08-21 21:15:38.758+08
  2 | ddavids  | 2018-08-21 21:15:38.786+08  | 2018-08-21 21:15:38.786+08
(2 rows)


mydatabase=# SELECT text from messages;
              text
------------------------------------
 Published the Road to learn React
 Happy to release ...
 Published a complete ...
(3 rows)
```

Every time you perform GraphQL mutations, it is wise to check your database records with the `psql` command-line interface. It is a great way to learn about SQL[225], which is normally abstracted away by using an ORM such as Sequelize.

In this section, you have used a PostgreSQL database as data source for your GraphQL server, using Sequelize as the glue between your database and your GraphQL resolvers. However, this was only one possible solution. Since GraphQL is data source agnostic, you can opt-in any data source to your resolvers. It could be another database (e.g. MongoDB, Neo4j, Redis), multiple databases, or a (third-party) REST/GraphQL API endpoint. GraphQL only ensures all fields are validated, executed, and resolved when there is an incoming query or mutation, regardless of the data source.

Exercises:

- Confirm your source code for the last section[226]
- Experiment with psql and the seeding of your database
- Experiment with GraphQL playground and query data which comes from a database now
- Remove and add the async/await statements in your resolvers and see how they still work
  - Read more about GraphQL execution[227]

---

[225]https://en.wikipedia.org/wiki/SQL
[226]https://github.com/the-road-to-graphql/fullstack-apollo-react-express-boilerplate-project/tree/27a1372264760879e86be377e069da738270c4f3
[227]https://graphql.github.io/learn/execution/

Apollo Server: Validation and Errors

Validation, error, and edge case handling are not often verbalized in programming. This section should give you some insights into these topics for Apollo Server and GraphQL. With GraphQL, you are in charge of what returns from GraphQL resolvers. It isn't too difficult inserting business logic into your resolvers, for instance, before they read from your database.

src/resolvers/user.js

```
export default {
  Query: {
    users: async (parent, args, { models }) => {
      return await models.User.findAll();
    },
    user: async (parent, { id }, { models }) => {
      return await models.User.findById(id);
    },
    me: async (parent, args, { models, me }) => {
      if (!me) {
        return null;
      }

      return await models.User.findById(me.id);
    },
  },

  ...
};
```

It may be a good idea keeping the resolvers surface slim but adding business logic services on the side. Then it is always simple to reason about the resolvers. In this application, we keep the business logic in the resolvers to keep everything at one place and avoid scattering logic across the entire application.

Let's start with the validation, which will lead to error handling. GraphQL isn't directly concerned about validation, but it operates between tech stacks that are: the client application (e.g. showing validation messages) and the database (e.g. validation of entities before writing to the database).

Let's add some basic validation rules to your database models. This section gives an introduction to the topic, as it would become too verbose to cover all uses cases in this application. First, add validation to your user model in the *src/models/user.js* file:

src/models/user.js

```
const user = (sequelize, DataTypes) => {
  const User = sequelize.define('user', {
    username: {
      type: DataTypes.STRING,
      unique: true,
      allowNull: false,
      validate: {
        notEmpty: true,
      },
    },
  });

  ...

  return User;
};

export default user;
```

Next, add validation rules to your message model in the *src/models/message.js* file:

src/models/message.js

```
const message = (sequelize, DataTypes) => {
  const Message = sequelize.define('message', {
    text: {
      type: DataTypes.STRING,
      validate: { notEmpty: true },
    },
  });

  Message.associate = models => {
    Message.belongsTo(models.User);
  };

  return Message;
};

export default message;
```

Now, try to create a message with an empty text in GraphQL Playground. It still requires a non-empty text for your message in the database. The same applies to your user entities, which now require a unique username. GraphQL and Apollo Server can handle these cases. Let's try to create a message with an empty text. You should see a similar input and output:

GraphQL Playground

```
// mutation
mutation {
  createMessage(text: "") {
    id
  }
}

// mutation error result
{
  "data": null,
  "errors": [
    {
      "message": "Validation error: Validation notEmpty on text failed",
      "locations": [],
      "path": [
        "createMessage"
      ],
      "extensions": { ... }
    }
  ]
}
```

It seems like Apollo Server's resolvers make sure to transform JavaScript errors[228] into valid GraphQL output. It is already possible to use this common error format in your client application without any additional error handling.

If you want to add custom error handling to your resolver, you always can add the commonly try/catch block statements for async/await:

---

[228]https://developer.mozilla.org/en-US/docs/Web/JavaScript/Reference/Global_Objects/Error

src/resolvers/message.js

```
export default {
  Query: {
    ...
  },

  Mutation: {
    createMessage: async (parent, { text }, { me, models }) => {
      try {
        return await models.Message.create({
          text,
          userId: me.id,
        });
      } catch (error) {
        throw new Error(error);
      }
    },

    ...
  },

  ...
};
```

The error output for GraphQL should stay the same in GraphQL Playground, because you used the same error object to generate the Error instance. However, you could also use your custom message here with `throw new Error('My error message.');`.

Another way of adjusting your error message is in the database model definition. Each validation rule can have a custom validation message, which can be defined in the Sequelize model:

src/models/message.js

```
const message = (sequelize, DataTypes) => {
  const Message = sequelize.define('message', {
    text: {
      type: DataTypes.STRING,
      validate: {
        notEmpty: {
          args: true,
          msg: 'A message has to have a text.',
        },
      },
    },
```

```
  });

  Message.associate = models => {
    Message.belongsTo(models.User);
  };

  return Message;
};

export default message;
```

This would lead to the following error(s) when attempting to create a message with an empty text. Again, it is straightforward in your client application, because the error format stays the same:

GraphQL Playground

```
{
  "data": null,
  "errors": [
    {
      "message": "SequelizeValidationError: Validation error: A message has to have \
a text.",
      "locations": [],
      "path": [
        "createMessage"
      ],
      "extensions": { ... }
    }
  ]
}
```

That's one of the main benefits of using Apollo Server for GraphQL. Error handling is often free, because an error–be it from the database, a custom JavaScript error or another third-party–gets transformed into a valid GraphQL error result. On the client side, you don't need to worry about the error result's shape, because it comes in a common GraphQL error format where the data object is null but the errors are captured in an array. If you want to change your custom error, you can do it on a resolver per-resolver basis. Apollo Server comes with a solution for global error handling:

src/index.js

```
const server = new ApolloServer({
  typeDefs.: schema,
  resolvers,
  formatError: error => {
    // remove the internal sequelize error message
    // leave only the important validation error
    const message = error.message
      .replace('SequelizeValidationError: ', '')
      .replace('Validation error: ', '');

    return {
      ...error,
      message,
    };
  },
  context: async () => ({
    models,
    me: await models.User.findByLogin('rwieruch'),
  }),
});
```

These are the essentials for validation and error handling with GraphQL in Apollo Server. Validation can happen on a database (model) level or on a business logic level (resolvers). It can happen on a directive level too (see exercises). If there is an error, GraphQL and Apollo Server will format it to work with GraphQL clients. You can also format errors globally in Apollo Server.

Exercises:

- Confirm your source code for the last section[229]
- Add more validation rules to your database models
    - Read more about validation in the Sequelize documentation
- Read more about Error Handling with Apollo Server[230]
    - Get to know the different custom errors in Apollo Server
- Read more about GraphQL field level validation with custom directives[231]
    - Read more about custom schema directives[232]

---

[229]https://github.com/the-road-to-graphql/fullstack-apollo-react-express-boilerplate-project/tree/83b2a288ccd65c574ac3f2083c4ceee3197700e7
[230]https://www.apollographql.com/docs/apollo-server/v2/features/errors.html
[231]https://blog.apollographql.com/graphql-validation-using-directives-4908fd5c1055
[232]https://www.apollographql.com/docs/apollo-server/v2/features/directives.html

Apollo Server: Authentication

Authentication in GraphQL is a popular topic. There is no opinionated way of doing it, but many people need it for their applications. GraphQL itself isn't opinionated about authentication since it is only a query language. If you want authentication in GraphQL, consider using GraphQL mutations. In this section, we use a minimalistic approach to add authentication to your GraphQL server. Afterward, it should be possible to register (sign up) and login (sign in) a user to your application. The previously used me user will be the authenticated user.

In preparation for the authentication mechanism with GraphQL, extend the user model in the *src/models/user.js* file. The user needs an email address (as unique identifier) and a password. Both email address and username (another unique identifier) can be used to sign in to the application, which is why both properties were used for the user's findByLogin() method.

src/models/user.js

```
...

const user = (sequelize, DataTypes) => {
  const User = sequelize.define('user', {
    username: {
      type: DataTypes.STRING,
      unique: true,
      allowNull: false,
      validate: {
        notEmpty: true,
      },
    },
    email: {
      type: DataTypes.STRING,
      unique: true,
      allowNull: false,
      validate: {
        notEmpty: true,
        isEmail: true,
      },
    },
    password: {
      type: DataTypes.STRING,
      allowNull: false,
      validate: {
        notEmpty: true,
        len: [7, 42],
      },
```

```
    },
  });

  ...

  return User;
};

export default user;
```

The two new entries for the user model have their own validation rules, same as before. The password of a user should be between 7 and 42 characters, and the email should have a valid email format. If any of these validations fails during user creation, it generates a JavaScript error, transforms and transfers the error with GraphQL. The registration form in the client application could display the validation error then.

You may want to add the email, but not the password, to your GraphQL user schema in the *src/schema/user.js* file too:

src/schema/user.js

```
import { gql } from 'apollo-server-express';

export default gql`
  ...

  type User {
    id: ID!
    username: String!
    email: String!
    messages: [Message!]
  }
`;
```

Next, add the new properties to your seed data in the *src/index.js* file:

src/index.js

```
const createUsersWithMessages = async () => {
  await models.User.create(
    {
      username: 'rwieruch',
      email: 'hello@robin.com',
      password: 'rwieruch',
      messages: [ ... ],
    },
    {
      include: [models.Message],
    },
  );

  await models.User.create(
    {
      username: 'ddavids',
      email: 'hello@david.com',
      password: 'ddavids',
      messages: [ ... ],
    },
    {
      include: [models.Message],
    },
  );
};
```

That's the data migration of your database to get started with GraphQL authentication.

Registration (Sign Up) with GraphQL

Now, let's examine the details for GraphQL authentication. You will implement two GraphQL mutations: one to register a user, and one to log in to the application. Let's start with the sign up mutation in the *src/schema/user.js* file:

src/schema/user.js

```
import { gql } from 'apollo-server-express';

export default gql`
  extend type Query {
    users: [User!]
    user(id: ID!): User
    me: User
  }

  extend type Mutation {
    signUp(
      username: String!
      email: String!
      password: String!
    ): Token!
  }

  type Token {
    token: String!
  }

  type User {
    id: ID!
    username: String!
    messages: [Message!]
  }
`;
```

The signUp mutation takes three non-nullable arguments: username, email, and password. These are used to create a user in the database. The user should be able to take the username or email address combined with the password to enable a successful login.

Now we'll consider the return type of the signUp mutation. Since we are going to use a token-based authentication with GraphQL, it is sufficient to return a token that is nothing more than a string. However, to distinguish the token in the GraphQL schema, it has its own GraphQL type. You will learn more about tokens in the following, because the token is all about the authentication mechanism for this application.

First, add the counterpart for your new mutation in the GraphQL schema as a resolver function. In your *src/resolvers/user.js* file, add the following resolver function that creates a user in the database and returns an object with the token value as string.

src/resolvers/user.js

```
const createToken = async (user) => {
  ...
};

export default {
  Query: {
    ...
  },

  Mutation: {
    signUp: async (
      parent,
      { username, email, password },
      { models },
    ) => {
      const user = await models.User.create({
        username,
        email,
        password,
      });

      return { token: createToken(user) };
    },
  },

  ...
};
```

That's the GraphQL framework around a token-based registration. You created a GraphQL mutation and resolver for it, which creates a user in the database based on certain validations and its incoming resolver arguments. It creates a token for the registered user. For now, the set up is sufficient to create a new user with a GraphQL mutation.

Securing Passwords with Bcrypt

There is one major security flaw in this code: the user password is stored in plain text in the database, which makes it much easier for third parties to access it. To remedy this, we use add-ons like bcrypt[233] to hash passwords. First, install it on the command line:

[233]https://github.com/kelektiv/node.bcrypt.js

Command Line

```
npm install bcrypt --save
```

Note: If you run into any problems with bcrypt on Windows while installing it, you can try out a substitute called bcrypt.js[234]. It is slower, but people reported that it works on their machine.

Now it is possible to hash the password with bcrypt in the user's resolver function when it gets created on a signUp mutation. There is also an alternative way with Sequelize. In your user model, define a hook function that is executed every time a user entity is created:

src/models/user.js

```
const user = (sequelize, DataTypes) => {
  const User = sequelize.define('user', {
    ...
  });

  ...

  User.beforeCreate(user => {
    ...
  });

  return User;
};

export default user;
```

In this hook function, add the functionalities to alter your user entity's properties before they reach the database. Let's do it for the hashed password by using bcrypt.

src/models/user.js

```
import bcrypt from 'bcrypt';

const user = (sequelize, DataTypes) => {
  const User = sequelize.define('user', {
    ...
  });

  ...

  User.beforeCreate(async user => {
```

---
[234]https://github.com/dcodeIO/bcrypt.js

```
    user.password = await user.generatePasswordHash();
  });

  User.prototype.generatePasswordHash = async function() {
    const saltRounds = 10;
    return await bcrypt.hash(this.password, saltRounds);
  };

  return User;
};

export default user;
```

The bcrypt `hash()` method takes a string–the user's password–and an integer called salt rounds. Each salt round makes it more costly to hash the password, which makes it more costly for attackers to decrypt the hash value. A common value for salt rounds nowadays ranged from 10 to 12, as increasing the number of salt rounds might cause performance issues both ways.

In this implementation, the `generatePasswordHash()` function is added to the user's prototype chain. That's why it is possible to execute the function as method on each user instance, so you have the user itself available within the method as `this`. You can also take the user instance with its password as an argument, which I prefer, though using JavaScript's prototypal inheritance a good tool for any web developer. For now, the password is hashed with bcrypt before it gets stored every time a user is created in the database,.

Token based Authentication in GraphQL

We still need to implement the token based authentication. So far, there is only a placeholder in your application for creating the token that is returned on a sign up and sign in mutation. A signed in user can be identified with this token, and is allowed to read and write data from the database. Since a registration will automatically lead to a login, the token is generated in both phases.

Next are the implementation details for the token-based authentication in GraphQL. Regardless of GraphQL, you are going to use a JSON web token (JWT)[235] to identify your user. The definition for a JWT from the official website says: *JSON Web Tokens are an open, industry standard RFC 7519 method for representing claims securely between two parties.* In other words, a JWT is a secure way to handle the communication between two parties (e.g. a client and a server application). If you haven't worked on security related applications before, the following section will guide you through the process, and you'll see the token is just a secured JavaScript object with user information.

To create JWT in this application, we'll use the popular jsonwebtoken[236] node package. Install it on the command line:

---

[235]https://jwt.io/
[236]https://github.com/auth0/node-jsonwebtoken

Command Line

```
npm install jsonwebtoken --save
```

Now, import it in your *src/resolvers/user.js* file and use it to create the token:

src/resolvers/user.js

```
import jwt from 'jsonwebtoken';

const createToken = async user => {
  const { id, email, username } = user;
  return await jwt.sign({ id, email, username });
};

...
```

The first argument to "sign" a token can be any user information except sensitive data like passwords, because the token will land on the client side of your application stack. Signing a token means putting data into it, which you've done, and securing it, which you haven't done yet. To secure your token, pass in a secret (**any** long string) that is **only available to you and your server**. No third-party entities should have access, because it is used to encode (sign) and decode your token.

Add the secret to your environment variables in the *.env* file:

.env

```
DATABASE=postgres
DATABASE_USER=postgres
DATABASE_PASSWORD=postgres


SECRET=wr3r23fwfwefwekwself.2456342.dawqdq
```

Then, in the *src/index.js* file, pass the secret via Apollo Server's context to all resolver functions:

src/index.js

```
const server = new ApolloServer({
  typeDefs: schema,
  resolvers,
  ...
  context: async () => ({
    models,
    me: await models.User.findByLogin('rwieruch'),
    secret: process.env.SECRET,
  }),
});
```

Next, use it in your `signUp` resolver function by passing it to the token creation. The `sign` method of JWT handles the rest. You can also pass in a third argument for setting an expiration time or date for a token. In this case, the token is only valid for 30 minutes, after which a user has to sign in again.

{{< javascript "hl_lines=1 3 5 6 7 19 27" >}} import jwt from 'jsonwebtoken';

const createToken = async (user, secret, expiresIn) ⇒ { const { id, email, username } = user; return await jwt.sign({ id, email, username }, secret, { expiresIn, }); };

export default { Query: { ... },

Mutation: { signUp: async (parent, { username, email, password }, { models, secret },) ⇒ { const user = await models.User.create({ username, email, password, });

```
  return { token: createToken(user, secret, '30m') };
},
```

},

... };

Now you have secured your information in the token as well. If you would want to decode it, in order to access the secured data (the first argument of the `sign` method), you would need the secret again. Furthermore, the token is only valid for 30 minutes.

That's it for the registration: you are creating a user and returning a valid token that can be used from the client application to authenticate the user. The server can decode the token that comes with every request and allows the user to access sensitive data. You can try out the registration with GraphQL Playground, which should create a user in the database and return a token for it. Also, you can check your database with `psql` to test if the use was created and with a hashed password.

Login (Sign In) with GraphQL

Before you dive into the authorization with the token on a per-request basis, let's implement the second mutation for the authentication mechanism: the `signIn` mutation (or login mutation). Again, first we add the GraphQL mutation to your user's schema in the *src/schema/user.js* file:

src/schema/user.js

```
import { gql } from 'apollo-server-express';

export default gql`
  ...

  extend type Mutation {
    signUp(
      username: String!
```

```
    email: String!
    password: String!
  ): Token!

  signIn(login: String!, password: String!): Token!
}

type Token {
  token: String!
}

...
`;
```

Second, add the resolver counterpart to your *src/resolvers/user.js* file:

src/resolvers/user.js

```
import jwt from 'jsonwebtoken';
import { AuthenticationError, UserInputError } from 'apollo-server';

...

export default {
  Query: {
    ...
  },

  Mutation: {
    signUp: async (...) => {
      ...
    },

    signIn: async (
      parent,
      { login, password },
      { models, secret },
    ) => {
      const user = await models.User.findByLogin(login);

      if (!user) {
        throw new UserInputError(
          'No user found with this login credentials.',
        );
```

```
    }

    const isValid = await user.validatePassword(password);

    if (!isValid) {
      throw new AuthenticationError('Invalid password.');
    }

    return { token: createToken(user, secret, '30m') };
    },
  },

  ...
};
```

Let's go through the new resolver function for the login step by step. As arguments, the resolver has access to the input arguments from the GraphQL mutation (login, password) and the context (models, secret). When a user tries to sign in to your application, the login, which can be either the unique username or unique email, is taken to retrieve a user from the database. If there is no user, the application throws an error that can be used in the client application to notify the user. If there is an user, the user's password is validated. You will see this method on the user model in the next example. If the password is not valid, the application throws an error to the client application. If the password is valid, the `signIn` mutation returns a token identical to the `signUp` mutation. The client application either performs a successful login or shows an error message for invalid credentials. You can also see specific Apollo Server Errors used over generic JavaScript Error classes.

Next, we want to implement the `validatePassword()` method on the user instance. Place it in the *src/models/user.js* file, because that's where all the model methods for the user are stored, same as the `findByLogin()` method.

src/models/user.js

```
import bcrypt from 'bcrypt';

const user = (sequelize, DataTypes) => {
  ...

  User.findByLogin = async login => {
    let user = await User.findOne({
      where: { username: login },
    });

    if (!user) {
      user = await User.findOne({
```

```
      where: { email: login },
    });
  }

  return user;
};

User.beforeCreate(async user => {
  user.password = await user.generatePasswordHash();
});

User.prototype.generatePasswordHash = async function() {
  const saltRounds = 10;
  return await bcrypt.hash(this.password, saltRounds);
};

User.prototype.validatePassword = async function(password) {
  return await bcrypt.compare(password, this.password);
};

  return User;
};

export default user;
```

Again, it's a prototypical JavaScript inheritance for making a method available in the user instance. In this method, the user (this) and its password can be compared with the incoming password from the GraphQL mutation using bcrypt, because the password on the user is hashed, and the incoming password is plain text. Fortunately, bcrypt will tell you whether the password is correct or not when a user signs in.

Now you have set up registration (sign up) and login (sign in) for your GraphQL server application. You used bcrypt to hash and compare a plain text password before it reaches the database with a Sequelize hook function, and you used JWT to encrypt user data with a secret to a token. Then the token is returned on every sign up and sign in. Then the client application can save the token (e.g. local storage of the browser) and send it along with every GraphQL query and mutation as authorization.

The next section will teach you about authorization in GraphQL on the server-side, and what should you do with the token once a user is authenticated with your application after a successful registration or login.

Exercises:

- Confirm your source code for the last section[237]
- Register (sign up) a new user with GraphQL Playground
- Check your users and their hashed passwords in the database with `psql`
- Read more about JSON web tokens (JWT)[238]
- Login (sign in) a user with GraphQL Playground
  - copy and paste the token to the interactive token decoding on the JWT website (conclusion: the information itself isn't secure, that's why you shouldn't put a password in the token)

---

[237]https://github.com/the-road-to-graphql/fullstack-apollo-react-express-boilerplate-project/tree/831ab566f0b5c5530d9270a49936d102f7fdf73c

[238]https://jwt.io/

Authorization with GraphQL and Apollo Server

In the last section, you set up GraphQL mutations to enable authentication with the server. You can register a new user with bcrypt hashed passwords and you can login with your user's credentials. Both GraphQL mutations related to authentication return a token (JWT) that secures non-sensitive user information with a secret.

The token, whether its obtained on registration or login, is returned to the client application after a successful GraphQL `signIn` or `signUp` mutation. The client application must store the token somewhere like the browser's session storage[239]. Every time a request is made to the GraphQL server, the token has to be attached to the HTTP header of the HTTP request. The GraphQL server can then validate the HTTP header, verify its authenticity, and perform a request like a GraphQL operation. If the token is invalid, the GraphQL server must return an error for the GraphQL client. If the client still has a token locally stored, it should remove the token and redirect the user to the login page.

Now we just need to perform the server part of the equation. Let's do it in the *src/index.js* file by adding a global authorization that verifies the incoming token before the request hits the GraphQL resolvers.

src/index.js

```
import jwt from 'jsonwebtoken';
import {
  ApolloServer,
  AuthenticationError,
} from 'apollo-server-express';
...

const getMe = async req => {
  const token = req.headers['x-token'];

  if (token) {
    try {
      return await jwt.verify(token, process.env.SECRET);
    } catch (e) {
      throw new AuthenticationError(
        'Your session expired. Sign in again.',
      );
    }
  }
};

const server = new ApolloServer({
```

---

[239]https://www.robinwieruch.de/local-storage-react

```
  typeDefs: schema,
  resolvers,
  ...
  context: async ({ req }) => {
    const me = await getMe(req);

    return {
      models,
      me,
      secret: process.env.SECRET,
    };
  },
});
```

...

In this general authorization on the server-side, you are injecting the me user, the authenticated user from the token, with every request to your Apollo Server's context. The me user is encoded in the token in the createToken() function. It's not a user from the database anymore, which spares the additional database request.

In the getMe() function, you extract the HTTP header for the authorization called "x-token" from the incoming HTTP request. The GraphQL client application sends the token obtained from the registration or login with every other request in an HTTP header, along with the payload of the HTTP request (e.g. GraphQL operation). It can then be checked to see if there is such an HTTP header in the function or not. If not, the function continues with the request, but the me user is undefined. If there is a token, the function verifies the token with its secret and retrieves the user information that was stored when you created the token. If the verification fails because the token was invalid or expired, the GraphQL server throws a specific Apollo Server Error. If the verification succeeds, the function continues with the me user defined.

The function returns an error when the client application sends an HTTP header with an invalid or expired token. Otherwise, the function waves the request through, because users must be checked at the resolver level to see if they're allowed to perform certain actions. A non-authenticated user–where the me user is undefined–might be able to retrieve messages but not create new ones. The application is now protected against invalid and expired tokens.

That's the most high-level authentication for your GraphQL server application. You are able to authenticate with your GraphQL server from a GraphQL client application with the signUp and signIn GraphQL mutations, and the GraphQL server only allows valid, non-expired tokens from the GraphQL client application.

GraphQL Authorization on a Resolver Level

A GraphQL HTTP request comes through the getMe() function, even if it has no HTTP header for a token. This is good default behavior, because you want to register new users and login to the application without a token for now. You might want to query messages or users without being authenticated with the application. It is acceptable and sometimes necessary to wave through some requests without authorization token, to grant different levels of access to different user types. There will be an error only when the token becomes invalid or expires.

However, certain GraphQL operations should have more specific authorizations. Creating a message should only be possible for authorized users. Otherwise, or there would be no way to track the messages' authors. The createMessage GraphQL mutation can be protected, or "guarded", on a GraphQL resolver level. The naive approach of protecting the GraphQL operation is to guard it with an if-else statement in the *src/resolvers/message.js* file:

src/resolvers/message.js

```
import { ForbiddenError } from 'apollo-server';

export default {
  Query: {
    ...
  },

  Mutation: {
    createMessage: async (parent, { text }, { me, models }) => {
      if (!me) {
        throw new ForbiddenError('Not authenticated as user.');
      }

      return await models.Message.create({
        text,
        userId: me.id,
      });
    },

    ...
  },

  ...
};
```

You can imagine how this becomes repetitive and error prone if it is used for all GraphQL operations that are accessible to an authenticated user, as it mixes lots of authorization logic into the resolver functions. To remedy this, we introduce an authorization abstraction layer for protecting GraphQL operations, with solutions called **combined resolvers** or **resolver middleware**. Let's install this node package:

Command Line

```
npm install graphql-resolvers --save
```

Let's implement a protecting resolver function with this package in a new *src/resolvers/authorization.js* file. It should only check whether there is a me user or not.

src/resolvers/authorization.js

```
import { ForbiddenError } from 'apollo-server';
import { skip } from 'graphql-resolvers';

export const isAuthenticated = (parent, args, { me }) =>
  me ? skip : new ForbiddenError('Not authenticated as user.');
```

The isAuthenticated() resolver function acts as middleware, either continuing with the next resolver (skip), or performing another action, like returning an error. In this case, an error is returned when the me user is not available. Since it is a resolver function itself, it has the same arguments as a normal resolver. A guarding resolver can be used when a message is created in the *src/resolvers/message.js* file. Import it with the combineResolvers() from the newly installed node package. The new resolver is used to protect the resolvers by combining them.

src/resolvers/message.js

```
import { combineResolvers } from 'graphql-resolvers';

import { isAuthenticated } from './authorization';

export default {
  Query: {
    ...
  },

  Mutation: {
    createMessage: combineResolvers(
      isAuthenticated,
      async (parent, { text }, { models, me }) => {
        return await models.Message.create({
          text,
          userId: me.id,
        });
```

```
    },
  ),

  . . .

  },

. . .

};
```

Now the `isAuthenticated()` resolver function always runs before the resolver that creates the message associated with the authenticated user in the database. The resolvers get chained to each other, and you can reuse the protecting resolver function wherever you need it. It only adds a small footprint to your actual resolvers, which can be changed in the *src/resolvers/authorization.js* file.

Permission-based GraphQL Authorization

The previous resolver only checks if a user is authenticated or not, so it is only applicable to the higher level. Cases like permissions require another protecting resolver that is more specific than the one in the *src/resolvers/authorization.js* file:

src/resolvers/authorization.js

```
. . .

export const isMessageOwner = async (
  parent,
  { id },
  { models, me },
) => {
  const message = await models.Message.findById(id, { raw: true });

  if (message.userId !== me.id) {
    throw new ForbiddenError('Not authenticated as owner.');
  }

  return skip;
};
```

This resolver checks whether the authenticated user is the message owner. It's a useful check before deleting a message, since you only want the message creator to be able to delete it. The guarding resolver retrieves the message by id, checks the message's associated user with the authenticated user, and either throws an error or continues with the next resolver.

Let's protect a resolver with this fine-tuned authorization permission resolver in the *src/resolvers/message.js* file:

src/resolvers/message.js

```
import { combineResolvers } from 'graphql-resolvers';

import { isAuthenticated, isMessageOwner } from './authorization';

export default {
  Query: {
    ...
  },

  Mutation: {
    ...

    deleteMessage: combineResolvers(
      isMessageOwner,
      async (parent, { id }, { models }) => {
        return await models.Message.destroy({ where: { id } });
      },
    ),
  },

  ...
};
```

The `deleteMessage` resolver is protected by an authorization resolver now. Only the message owner, i.e. the message creator, is allowed to delete a message. If the user isn't authenticated, you can stack your protecting resolvers onto each other:

src/resolvers/message.js

```
import { combineResolvers } from 'graphql-resolvers';

import { isAuthenticated, isMessageOwner } from './authorization';

export default {
  Query: {
    ...
  },

  Mutation: {
    ...

    deleteMessage: combineResolvers(
```

```
    isAuthenticated,
    isMessageOwner,
    async (parent, { id }, { models }) => {
      return await models.Message.destroy({ where: { id } });
    },
  ),
},


  ...
};
```

As an alternate tactic, you can also use the isAuthenticated resolver directly in the isMessageOwner resolver; then, you can avoid handling it in the actual resolver for deleting a message. I find being explicit to be more practical than hiding knowledge within the authorization resolver. The alternative route is still explained in the role-based authorization section, however.

The second combined resolver is for permission checks, because it decides whether or not the user has permission to delete the message. This is just one way of doing it, though. In other cases, the message could carry a boolean flag that decides if the active user has certain permissions.

Role-based GraphQL Authorization

We went from a high-level authorization to a more specific authorization with permission-based resolver protection. Now we'll cover yet another way to enable authorization called **roles**. The next code block is a GraphQL mutation that requires role-based authorization, because it has the ability to delete a user. This allows you to create users with admin roles.

Let's implement the new GraphQL mutation first, followed by the role-based authorization. You can start in your *src/resolvers/user.js* file with a resolver function that deletes a user in the database by identifier:

src/resolvers/user.js

```
...

export default {
  Query: {
    ...
  },

  Mutation: {
    ...

    deleteUser: async (parent, { id }, { models }) => {
```

```
      return await models.User.destroy({
        where: { id },
      });
    },
  },


  ...
};
```

New GraphQL operations must be implemented in the resolvers and schema. Next, we'll add the new mutation in the *src/schema/user.js* file. It returns a boolean that tells you whether the deletion was successful or not:

src/schema/user.js

```
import { gql } from 'apollo-server-express';

export default gql`
  extend type Query {
    ...
  }

  extend type Mutation {
    signUp(
      username: String!
      email: String!
      password: String!
    ): Token!

    signIn(login: String!, password: String!): Token!
    deleteUser(id: ID!): Boolean!
  }


  ...
`;
```

Before you can implement role-based protections for it, you must introduce the actual roles for the user entities. Add a role entry to your user's entity in the *src/models/user.js* file:

src/models/user.js

```
...

const user = (sequelize, DataTypes) => {
  const User = sequelize.define('user', {
    ...
    password: {
      type: DataTypes.STRING,
      allowNull: false,
      validate: {
        notEmpty: true,
        len: [7, 42],
      },
    },
    role: {
      type: DataTypes.STRING,
    },
  });

  ...

  return User;
};

export default user;
```

Add the role to your GraphQL user schema in the *src/schema/user.js* file too:

src/schema/user.js

```
import { gql } from 'apollo-server-express';

export default gql`
  ...

  type User {
    id: ID!
    username: String!
    email: String!
    role: String
    messages: [Message!]
  }
`;
```

Since you already have seed data in your *src/index.js* file for two users, you can give one of them a role. The admin role used in this case will be checked if the user attempts a delete operation:

src/index.js

```
...

const createUsersWithMessages = async () => {
  await models.User.create(
    {
      username: 'rwieruch',
      email: 'hello@robin.com',
      password: 'rwieruch',
      role: 'ADMIN',
      messages: [
        {
          text: 'Published the Road to learn React',
        },
      ],
    },
    {
      include: [models.Message],
    },
  );

  ...
};
```

Because you are not retrieving the actual me user from the database in the *src/index.js* file, but the user from the token instead, you must add the role information of the user for the token when it's created in the *src/resolvers/user.js* file:

src/resolvers/user.js

```
const createToken = async (user, secret, expiresIn) => {
  const { id, email, username, role } = user;
  return await jwt.sign({ id, email, username, role }, secret, {
    expiresIn,
  });
};
```

Next, protect the new GraphQL mutation with a role-based authorization. Create a new guarding resolver in your *src/resolvers/authorization.js* file:

src/resolvers/authorization.js

```
import { ForbiddenError } from 'apollo-server';
import { combineResolvers, skip } from 'graphql-resolvers';

export const isAuthenticated = (parent, args, { me }) =>
  me ? skip : new ForbiddenError('Not authenticated as user.');

export const isAdmin = combineResolvers(
  isAuthenticated,
  (parent, args, { me: { role } }) =>
    role === 'ADMIN'
      ? skip
      : new ForbiddenError('Not authorized as admin.'),
);

export const isMessageOwner = async (
  parent,
  { id },
  { models, me },
) => {
  const message = await models.Message.findById(id, { raw: true });

  if (message.userId !== me.id) {
    throw new ForbiddenError('Not authenticated as owner.');
  }

  return skip;
};
```

The new resolver checks to see if the authenticated user has the ADMIN role. If it doesn't, the resolver returns an error; if it does, the next resolver is called. Unlike the isMessageOwner resolver, the isAdmin resolver is already combined, using the isAuthenticated resolver. Put this check in your actual resolver, which you are going to protect in the next step:

src/resolvers/user.js

```
import jwt from 'jsonwebtoken';
import { combineResolvers } from 'graphql-resolvers';
import { AuthenticationError, UserInputError } from 'apollo-server';

import { isAdmin } from './authorization';

...

export default {
  Query: {
    ...
  },

  Mutation: {
    ...

    deleteUser: combineResolvers(
      isAdmin,
      async (parent, { id }, { models }) => {
        return await models.User.destroy({
          where: { id },
        });
      },
    ),
  },

  ...
};
```

That's the basics of role-based authorization in GraphQL with Apollo Server. In this example, the role is only a string that needs to be checked. In a more elaborate role-based architecture, the role might change from a string to an array that contains many roles. It eliminates the need for an equal check, since you can check to see if the array includes a targeted role. Using arrays with a roles is the foundation for a sophisticated role-based authorization setup.

Setting Headers in GraphQL Playground

You set up authorization for your GraphQL application, and now you just need to verify that it works. The simplest way to test this type of application is to use GraphQL Playground to run through different scenarios. The user deletion scenario will be used as an example, but you should test all the remaining scenarios for practice.

Before a user can perform a delete action, there must be a sign-in, so we execute a `signIn` mutation in GraphQL Playground with a non admin user. Consider trying this tutorial with an admin user later to see how it performs differently.

GraphQL Playground

```
mutation {
  signIn(login: "ddavids", password: "ddavids") {
    token
  }
}
```

You should receive a token after logging into GraphQL Playground. The token needs to be set in the HTTP header for the next GraphQL operation. GraphQL Playground has a panel to add HTTP headers. Since your application is checking for an x-token, set the token as one:

GraphQL Playground

```
{
  "x-token": "eyJhbGciOiJIUzI1NiIsInR5cCI6IkpXVCJ9.eyJpZCI6MiwiZW1haWwiOiJoZWxsb0BkY\
XZpZC5jb20iLCJ1c2VybmFtZSI6ImRkYXZpZHMiLCJpYXQiOjE1MzQ5MjM4NDcsImV4cCI6MTUzNDkyNTY0N\
30.ViGU6UUY-XWpWDJGfXqES2J1lEr-Uye8XDQ79lAvByE"
}
```

Your token will be different than the one above, but of a similar format. Since the token is set as an HTTP header now, you should be able to delete a user with the following GraphQL mutation in GraphQL Playground. The HTTP header with the token will be sent with the GraphQL operation:

GraphQL Playground

```
mutation {
  deleteUser(id: "2")
}
```

Instead of a successful request, you will see the following GraphQL error after executing the GraphQL mutation for deleting a user. That's because you haven't logged in as a user with an admin role.

GraphQL Playground

```
{
  "data": null,
  "errors": [
    {
      "message": "Not authorized as admin.",
      "locations": [
        {
          "line": 2,
          "column": 3
        }
      ],
      "path": [
        "deleteUser"
      ],
      "extensions": { ... }
    }
  ]
}
```

If you follow the same sequence as an admin user, you can delete a user entity successfully.

We've added basic authorization for this application. It has the global authorization before every request hits the GraphQL resolvers; and authorization at the resolver level with protecting resolvers. They check whether a user is authenticated, whether the user is able to delete a message (permission-based authorization), and whether a user is able to delete a user (role-based authorization).

If you want to be even more exact than resolver level authorization, check out **directive-based authorization** or **field level authorization** in GraphQL. You can apply authorization at the data-access level with an ORM like Sequelize, too. Your application's requirements decide which level is most effective for authorization.

Exercises:

- Confirm your source code for the last section[240]
- Read more about GraphQL authorization[241]
- Work through the different authorization scenarios with GraphQL Playground
- Find out more about field level authorization with Apollo Server and GraphQL
- Find out more about data access level authorization with Apollo Server and GraphQL

---

[240]https://github.com/the-road-to-graphql/fullstack-apollo-react-express-boilerplate-project/tree/4f6e8e6e7b899faca13e1c8354fe59637e7e23a6
[241]https://graphql.github.io/learn/authorization/

GraphQL Custom Scalars in Apollo Server

So far, you have used a couple of scalars in your GraphQL application, because each field resolves eventually to a scalar type. Let's add a String scalar for the date when a message got created. First, we'll extend the *src/schema/message.js* which uses this field for a message:

src/schema/message.js

```
import { gql } from 'apollo-server-express';

export default gql`
  extend type Query {
    messages(cursor: String, limit: Int): [Message!]!
    message(id: ID!): Message!
  }

  extend type Mutation {
    createMessage(text: String!): Message!
    deleteMessage(id: ID!): Boolean!
  }

  type Message {
    id: ID!
    text: String!
    createdAt: String!
    user: User!
  }
`;
```

Second, adjust the seed data in the *src/index.js* file. At the moment, all seed data is created at once, which applies to the messages as well. It would be better to have each message created in one second intervals. The creation date should differ for each message.

src/index.js

```
...

sequelize.sync({ force: eraseDatabaseOnSync }).then(async () => {
  if (eraseDatabaseOnSync) {
    createUsersWithMessages(new Date());
  }

  app.listen({ port: 8000 }, () => {
    console.log('Apollo Server on http://localhost:8000/graphql');
```

```
  });
});

const createUsersWithMessages = async date => {
  await models.User.create(
    {
      username: 'rwieruch',
      email: 'hello@robin.com',
      password: 'rwieruch',
      role: 'ADMIN',
      messages: [
        {
          text: 'Published the Road to learn React',
          createdAt: date.setSeconds(date.getSeconds() + 1),
        },
      ],
    },
    {
      include: [models.Message],
    },
  );

  await models.User.create(
    {
      username: 'ddavids',
      email: 'hello@david.com',
      password: 'ddavids',
      messages: [
        {
          text: 'Happy to release ...',
          createdAt: date.setSeconds(date.getSeconds() + 1),
        },
        {
          text: 'Published a complete ...',
          createdAt: date.setSeconds(date.getSeconds() + 1),
        },
      ],
    },
    {
      include: [models.Message],
    },
  );
};
```

Now you should be able to query the `createdAt` of a message in your GraphQL Playground:

GraphQL Playground

```
query {
  message(id: "1") {
    id
    createdAt
    user {
      username
    }
  }
}


// query result
{
  "data": {
    "message": {
      "id": "1",
      "createdAt": "1540978531448",
      "user": {
        "username": "rwieruch"
      }
    }
  }
}
```

You may have noticed something odd: While the date returned from a GraphQL Playground has a unix timestamp (e.g. 1540978531448), the date the database for a message (and other entities) has another format (e.g. 2018-10-31 17:35:31.448+08). Check it yourself with psql. That's the internal working of GraphQL which uses its internal formatting rules for dates. You can change this behavior by adding a custom scalar. First, install a popular GraphQL node package for custom date scalars.

Command Line

```
npm install graphql-iso-date --save
```

Second, introduce a `Date` scalar in your schema in the *src/schema/index.js* file:

src/schema/index.js

```
const linkSchema = gql`
  scalar Date

  type Query {
    _: Boolean
  }

  type Mutation {
    _: Boolean
  }

  type Subscription {
    _: Boolean
  }
`;
```

Third, define the scalar with the help of the installed node package in your *src/resolvers/index.js* file:

src/resolvers/index.js

```
import { GraphQLDateTime } from 'graphql-iso-date';

import userResolvers from './user';
import messageResolvers from './message';

const customScalarResolver = {
  Date: GraphQLDateTime,
};

export default [
  customScalarResolver,
  userResolvers,
  messageResolvers,
];
```

And last but not least, change the scalar type from String to Date for your message schema in the *src/schema/message.js*:

src/schema/message.js

```
import { gql } from 'apollo-server-express';

export default gql`
  extend type Query {
    messages(cursor: String, limit: Int): [Message!]!
    message(id: ID!): Message!
  }

  extend type Mutation {
    createMessage(text: String!): Message!
    deleteMessage(id: ID!): Boolean!
  }

  type Message {
    id: ID!
    text: String!
    createdAt: Date!
    user: User!
  }
`;
```

Now, query again your messages. The output for the `createdAt` date should be different.

GraphQL Playground

```
{
  "data": {
    "message": {
      "id": "1",
      "createdAt": "2018-10-31T11:57:53.043Z",
      "user": {
        "username": "rwieruch"
      }
    }
  }
}
```

It's in a readable format now. You can dive deeper into the date formatting that can be adjusted with this library by checking out their documentation[242].

---

[242]https://github.com/excitement-engineer/graphql-iso-date

Exercises:

- Confirm your source code for the last section[243]
- Read more about custom scalars in GraphQL[244]

---

[243]https://github.com/the-road-to-graphql/fullstack-apollo-express-postgresql-boilerplate/tree/709a406a8a94e15779d2e93cfb847d49de5aa6ca
[244]https://www.apollographql.com/docs/apollo-server/features/scalars-enums.html

Pagination in GraphQL with Apollo Server

Using GraphQL, you will almost certainly encounter a feature called **pagination** for applications with lists of items. Stored user messages in a chat application become long lists, and when the client application request messages for the display, retrieving all messages from the database at once can lead to severe performance bottlenecks. Pagination allows you to split up a list of items into multiple lists, called pages. A page is usually defined with a limit and an offset. That way, you can request one page of items, and when a user wants to see more, request another page of items.

You will implement pagination in GraphQL with two different approaches in the following sections. The first approach will be the most naive approach, called **offset/limit-based pagination**. The advanced approach is **cursor-based pagination**. one of many sophisticated ways to allow pagination in an application.

Offset/Limit Pagination with Apollo Server and GraphQL

Offset/limit-based pagination isn't too difficult to implement. The limit states how many items you want to retrieve from the entire list, and the offset states where to begin in the whole list. Using different offsets, you can shift through the entire list of items and retrieve a sublist (page) of it with the limit.

We set the message schema in the *src/schema/message.js* file to consider the two new arguments:

src/schema/message.js

```
import { gql } from 'apollo-server-express';

export default gql`
  extend type Query {
    messages(offset: Int, limit: Int): [Message!]!
    message(id: ID!): Message!
  }

  extend type Mutation {
    createMessage(text: String!): Message!
    deleteMessage(id: ID!): Boolean!
  }

  type Message {
    id: ID!
    text: String!
    createdAt: Date!
    user: User!
```

```
  }
`;
```

Then you can adjust the resolver in the *src/resolvers/message.js* file to handle the new arguments:

src/resolvers/message.js

```
...

export default {
  Query: {
    messages: async (
      parent,
      { offset = 0, limit = 100 },
      { models },
    ) => {
      return await models.Message.findAll({
        offset,
        limit,
      });
    },
    message: async (parent, { id }, { models }) => {
      return await models.Message.findById(id);
    },
  },

  Mutation: {
    ...
  },

  ...
};
```

Fortunately, your ORM (Sequelize) gives you everything you need for internal offset and limit functionality. Try it in GraphQL Playground yourself by adjusting the limit and offset.

GraphQL Playground

```
query {
  messages(offset: 1, limit: 2){
    text
  }
}
```

Even though this approach is simpler, it comes with a few disadvantages. When your offset becomes very long, the database query takes longer, which can lead to a poor client-side performance while the UI waits for the next page of data. Also, offset/limit pagination cannot handle deleted items in between queries. For instance, if you query the first page and someone deletes an item, the offset would be wrong on the next page because the item count is off by one. You cannot easily overcome this problem with offset/limit pagination, which is why cursor-based pagination might be necessary.

Cursor-based Pagination with Apollo Server and GraphQL

In cursor-based pagination, the offset is given an identifier called a **cursor** rather counting items like offset/limit pagination. The cursor can be used to express "give me a limit of X items from cursor Y". A common approach to use dates (e.g. creation date of an entity in the database) to identify an item in the list. In our case, each message already has a createdAt date that is assigned to the entity when it is written to the database and we expose it already in the schema of the message entity. That's the creation date of each message that will be the cursor.

Now we have to change the original pagination to cursor-based in the *src/schema/message.js* file. You only need to exchange the offset with the cursor. Instead of an offset that can only be matched implicitly to an item in a list and changes once an item is deleted from the list, the cursor has a stable position within, because the message creation dates won't change.

src/schema/message.js

```
import { gql } from 'apollo-server-express';

export default gql`
  extend type Query {
    messages(cursor: String, limit: Int): [Message!]!
    message(id: ID!): Message!
  }

  extend type Mutation {
    createMessage(text: String!): Message!
    deleteMessage(id: ID!): Boolean!
  }
```

```
  type Message {
    id: ID!
    text: String!
    createdAt: Date!
    user: User!
  }
`;
```

Since you adjusted the schema for the messages, reflect these changes in your *src/resolvers/message.js* file as well:

src/resolvers/message.js

```
import Sequelize from 'sequelize';

...

export default {
  Query: {
    messages: async (parent, { cursor, limit = 100 }, { models }) => {
      return await models.Message.findAll({
        limit,
        where: {
          createdAt: {
            [Sequelize.Op.lt]: cursor,
          },
        },
      });
    },
    message: async (parent, { id }, { models }) => {
      return await models.Message.findById(id);
    },
  },

  Mutation: {
    ...
  },

  ...
};
```

Instead of the offset, the cursor is the createdAt property of a message. With Sequelize and other ORMs it is possible to add a clause to find all items in a list by a starting property (createdAt) with less than (lt) or greater than (gt, which is not used here) values for this property. Using a date as a cursor, the where clause finds all messages **before** this date, because there is an lt Sequelize operator. There are two more things to make it work:

src/resolvers/message.js

```
. . .

export default {
  Query: {
    messages: async (parent, { cursor, limit = 100 }, { models }) => {
      return await models.Message.findAll({
        order: [['createdAt', 'DESC']],
        limit,
        where: cursor
          ? {
              createdAt: {
                [Sequelize.Op.lt]: cursor,
              },
            }
          : null,
      });
    },
    message: async (parent, { id }, { models }) => {
      return await models.Message.findById(id);
    },
  },

  Mutation: {
    . . .
  },

  . . .
};
```

First, the list should be ordered by createdAt date, otherwise the cursor won't help. However, you can be sure that requesting the first page of messages without a cursor will lead to the most recent messages when the list is ordered. When you request the next page with a cursor based on the previous page's final creation date, you get the next page of messages ordered by creation date. That's how you can move page by page through the list of messages.

Second, the ternary operator for the cursor makes sure the cursor isn't needed for the first page request. As mentioned, the first page only retrieves the most recent messages in the list, so you can use the creation date of the last message as a cursor for the next page of messages.

You can also extract the where clause from the database query:

src/resolvers/message.js

```
...

export default {
  Query: {
    messages: async (parent, { cursor, limit = 100 }, { models }) => {
      const cursorOptions = cursor
        ? {
            where: {
              createdAt: {
                [Sequelize.Op.lt]: cursor,
              },
            },
          }
        : {};

      return await models.Message.findAll({
        order: [['createdAt', 'DESC']],
        limit,
        ...cursorOptions,
      });
    },
    message: async (parent, { id }, { models }) => {
      return await models.Message.findById(id);
    },
  },

  Mutation: {
    ...
  },

  ...
};
```

Now you can test what you've learned in GraphQL Playground to see it in action. Make the first request for the most recent messages:

GraphQL Playground

```
query {
  messages(limit: 2) {
    text
    createdAt
  }
}
```

Which may lead to something like this (be careful, dates should be different from your dates):

GraphQL Playground

```
{
  "data": {
    "messages": [
      {
        "text": "Published a complete ...",
        "createdAt": "2018-10-25T08:22:02.484Z"
      },
      {
        "text": "Happy to release ...",
        "createdAt": "2018-10-25T08:22:01.484Z"
      }
    ]
  }
}
```

Now you can use the `createdAt` date from the last page to request the next page of messages with a cursor:

GraphQL Playground

```
query {
  messages(limit: 2, cursor: "2018-10-25T08:22:01.484Z") {
    text
    createdAt
  }
}
```

The result gives the last message from the seed data, but the limit is set to 2 messages. This happens because there are only 3 messages in the database and you already have retrieved 2 in the last pagination action:

GraphQL Playground

```
{
  "data": {
    "messages": [
      {
        "text": "Published the Road to learn React",
        "createdAt": "2018-10-25T08:22:00.484Z"
      }
    ]
  }
}
```

That's a basic implementation of a cursor-based pagination using the creation date of an item as a stable identifier. The creation date is a common approach, but there are alternatives you should explore as well.

Cursor-based Pagination: Page Info, Connections and Hashes

In this last section about pagination in GraphQL, we advance the cursor-based pagination with a few improvements. Currently, you have to query all creation dates of the messages to use the creation date of the last message for the next page as a cursor. GraphQL connections add only a structural change to your list fields in GraphQL that allow you to pass meta information. Let's add a GraphQL connection in the *src/schema/message.js* file:

src/schema/message.js

```
import { gql } from 'apollo-server-express';

export default gql`
  extend type Query {
    messages(cursor: String, limit: Int): MessageConnection!
    message(id: ID!): Message!
  }

  extend type Mutation {
    createMessage(text: String!): Message!
    deleteMessage(id: ID!): Boolean!
  }

  type MessageConnection {
    edges: [Message!]!
    pageInfo: PageInfo!
  }
```

```
  type PageInfo {
    endCursor: Date!
  }

  type Message {
    id: ID!
    text: String!
    createdAt: Date!
    user: User!
  }
`;
```

You introduced an intermediate layer that holds meta information with the PageInfo type with the list of items in an edges field. In the intermediate layer, you can introduce the new information such as an endCursor (createdAt of the last message in the list). Then, you won't need to query every createdAt date of every message, only the endCursor. Place these changes in the *src/resolvers/message.js* file:

src/resolvers/message.js

```
...

export default {
  Query: {
    messages: async (parent, { cursor, limit = 100 }, { models }) => {
      const cursorOptions = cursor
        ? {
            where: {
              createdAt: {
                [Sequelize.Op.lt]: cursor,
              },
            },
          }
        : {};

      const messages = await models.Message.findAll({
        order: [['createdAt', 'DESC']],
        limit,
        ...cursorOptions,
      });

      return {
        edges: messages,
```

```
        pageInfo: {
          endCursor: messages[messages.length - 1].createdAt,
        },
      };
    },
    message: async (parent, { id }, { models }) => {
      return await models.Message.findById(id);
    },
  },

  Mutation: {
    ...
  },


  ...
};
```

You gave the result a new structure with the intermediate edges and pageInfo fields. The pageInfo field now has the cursor of the last message in the list, and you should be able to query the first page the following way:

GraphQL Playground

```
query {
  messages(limit: 2) {
    edges {
      text
    }
    pageInfo {
      endCursor
    }
  }
}
```

The result may look like the following:

GraphQL Playground

```
{
  "data": {
    "messages": {
      "edges": [
        {
          "text": "Published a complete ..."
        },
        {
          "text": "Happy to release ..."
        }
      ],
      "pageInfo": {
        "endCursor": "2018-10-25T08:29:56.771Z"
      }
    }
  }
}
```

Use the last cursor to query the next page:

GraphQL Playground

```
query {
  messages(limit: 2, cursor: "2018-10-25T08:29:56.771Z") {
    edges {
      text
    }
    pageInfo {
      endCursor
    }
  }
}
```

Again, this will only return the remaining last message in the list. You are no longer required to query the creation date of every message, only to query the cursor for the last message. The client application doesn't need the details for the cursor of the last message, as it just needs endCursor now.

You can add relevant information in the intermediate GraphQL connection layer. Sometimes, a GraphQL client needs to know whether there are more pages of a list to query, because every list is finite. Let's add this information to the schema for the message's connection in the *src/schema/message.js* file:

src/schema/message.js

```
import { gql } from 'apollo-server-express';

export default gql`
  extend type Query {
    messages(cursor: String, limit: Int): MessageConnection!
    message(id: ID!): Message!
  }

  extend type Mutation {
    createMessage(text: String!): Message!
    deleteMessage(id: ID!): Boolean!
  }

  type MessageConnection {
    edges: [Message!]!
    pageInfo: PageInfo!
  }

  type PageInfo {
    hasNextPage: Boolean!
    endCursor: Date!
  }

  ...
`;
```

In the resolver in the *src/resolvers/message.js* file, you can find this information with the following:

src/resolvers/message.js

```
...

export default {
  Query: {
    messages: async (parent, { cursor, limit = 100 }, { models }) => {
      ...

      const messages = await models.Message.findAll({
        order: [['createdAt', 'DESC']],
        limit: limit + 1,
        ...cursorOptions,
      });
```

```
      const hasNextPage = messages.length > limit;
      const edges = hasNextPage ? messages.slice(0, -1) : messages;

      return {
        edges,
        pageInfo: {
          hasNextPage,
          endCursor: edges[edges.length - 1].createdAt,
        },
      };
    },
    message: async (parent, { id }, { models }) => {
      return await models.Message.findById(id);
    },
  },

  Mutation: {
    ...
  },

  ...
};
```

You only retrieve one more message than defined in the limit. If the list of messages is longer than the limit, there is a next page; otherwise, there is no next page. You return the limited messages, or all messages if there is no next page. Now you can include the hasNextPage field in the pageInfo field. If you query messages with a limit of 2 and no cursor, you get true for the hasNextPage field. If query messages with a limit of more than 2 and no cursor, the hasNextPage field becomes false. Then, your GraphQL client application knows that the list has reached its end.

The last improvements gave your GraphQL client application a more straightforward GraphQL API. The client doesn't need to know about the cursor being the last creation date of a message in a list. It only uses the endCursor as a cursor argument for the next page. However, the cursor is still a creation date property, which may lead to confusion on the GraphQL client side. The client shouldn't care about the format or the actual value of the cursor, so we'll ask the cursor with a hash function that uses a base64 encoding:

src/resolvers/message.js

```
...

const toCursorHash = string => Buffer.from(string).toString('base64');

const fromCursorHash = string =>
  Buffer.from(string, 'base64').toString('ascii');

export default {
  Query: {
    messages: async (parent, { cursor, limit = 100 }, { models }) => {
      const cursorOptions = cursor
        ? {
            where: {
              createdAt: {
                [Sequelize.Op.lt]: fromCursorHash(cursor),
              },
            },
          }
        : {};

      ...

      return {
        edges,
        pageInfo: {
          hasNextPage,
          endCursor: toCursorHash(
            edges[edges.length - 1].createdAt.toString(),
          ),
        },
      };
    },
    message: async (parent, { id }, { models }) => {
      return await models.Message.findById(id);
    },
  },

  Mutation: {
    ...
  },
```

```
  . . .
};
```

The returned cursor as meta information is hashed by the new utility function. Remember to stringify the date before hashing it. In addition, the endCursor in the *src/schema/message.js* file isn't a Date anymore, but a String scalar again.

src/schema/message.js

```
import { gql } from 'apollo-server-express';

export default gql`
  . . .

  type MessageConnection {
    edges: [Message!]!
    pageInfo: PageInfo!
  }

  type PageInfo {
    hasNextPage: Boolean!
    endCursor: String!
  }

  . . .
`;
```

The GraphQL client receives a hashed endCursor field. The hashed value can be used as a cursor to query the next page. In the resolver, the incoming cursor is reverse hashed to the actual date, which is used for the database query.

Hashing the cursor is a common approach for cursor-based pagination because it hides the details from the client. The (GraphQL) client application only needs to use the hash value as a cursor to query the next paginated page.

Exercises:

- Confirm your source code for the last section[245]
- Read more about GraphQL pagination[246]

---

[245]https://github.com/the-road-to-graphql/fullstack-apollo-react-express-boilerplate-project/tree/810907cde43b460231b9ed3a2172e62528f81ba4
[246]https://graphql.github.io/learn/pagination/

GraphQL Subscriptions

So far, you used GraphQL to read and write data with queries and mutations. These are the two essential GraphQL operations to get a GraphQL server ready for CRUD operations. Next, you will learn about GraphQL Subscriptions for real-time communication between GraphQL client and server.

Next, you will implement real-time communication for created messages. If a user creates a message, another user should get this message in a GraphQL client application as a real-time update. To start, we add the Subscription root level type to the *src/schema/message.js* schema:

src/schema/message.js

```
import { gql } from 'apollo-server-express';

export default gql`
  extend type Query {
    ...
  }

  extend type Mutation {
    ...
  }

  ...

  type Message {
    id: ID!
    text: String!
    createdAt: Date!
    user: User!
  }

  extend type Subscription {
    messageCreated: MessageCreated!
  }

  type MessageCreated {
    message: Message!
  }
`;
```

As a naive GraphQL consumer, a subscription works like a GraphQL query. The difference is that the subscription emits changes (events) over time. Every time a message is created, the subscribed

GraphQL client receives the created message as payload. A subscription from a GraphQL client for the schema would look like this:

GraphQL Playground

```
subscription {
  messageCreated {
    message {
      id
      text
      createdAt
      user {
        id
        username
      }
    }
  }
}
```

In the first part, you'll set up the subscription architecture for your application; then, you'll add the implementation details for the created message subscription. The first step need only be completed once, but the latter will be a recurring when more GraphQL subscriptions are added to your application.

Apollo Server Subscription Setup

Because we are using Express as middleware, expose the subscriptions with an advanced HTTP server setup in the *src/index.js* file:

src/index.js

```
import http from 'http';

...

server.applyMiddleware({ app, path: '/graphql' });

const httpServer = http.createServer(app);
server.installSubscriptionHandlers(httpServer);

const eraseDatabaseOnSync = true;

sequelize.sync({ force: eraseDatabaseOnSync }).then(async () => {
  if (eraseDatabaseOnSync) {
```

```
      createUsersWithMessages(new Date());
  }

  httpServer.listen({ port: 8000 }, () => {
    console.log('Apollo Server on http://localhost:8000/graphql');
  });
});
```

...

For the context passed to the resolvers, you can distinguish between HTTP requests (GraphQL mutations and queries) and subscriptions in the same file. HTTP requests come with a req and res object, but the subscription comes with a connection object, so you can pass the models as a data access layer for the subscription's context.

src/index.js

...

```
const server = new ApolloServer({
  typeDefs: schema,
  resolvers,
  ...
  context: async ({ req, connection }) => {
    if (connection) {
      return {
        models,
      };
    }

    if (req) {
      const me = await getMe(req);

      return {
        models,
        me,
        secret: process.env.SECRET,
      };
    }
  },
});
```

...

To complete the subscription setup, you'll need to use one of the available PubSub engines[247] for publishing and subscribing to events. Apollo Server comes with its own by default, but there are links for other options should you find it lacking. In a new *src/subscription/index.js* file, add the following:

src/subscription/index.js

```
import { PubSub } from 'apollo-server';

export default new PubSub();
```

This PubSub instance is your API which enables subscriptions in your application. The overarching setup for subscriptions is done now.

Subscribing and Publishing with PubSub

Let's implement the specific subscription for the message creation. It should be possible for another GraphQL client to listen to message creations. For instance, in a chat application it should be possible to see a message of someone else in real-time. Therefore, extend the previous *src/subscription/index.js* file with the following implementation:

src/subscription/index.js

```
import { PubSub } from 'apollo-server';

import * as MESSAGE_EVENTS from './message';

export const EVENTS = {
  MESSAGE: MESSAGE_EVENTS,
};

export default new PubSub();
```

And add your first event in a new *src/subscription/message.js* file, which we used earlier:

src/subscription/message.js

```
export const CREATED = 'CREATED';
```

This folder structure allows you to separate your events at the domain level. By exporting all events with their domains, you can import all events elsewhere and make use of the domain-specific events.

The only piece missing is using the event and the PubSub instance in your message resolver. In the beginning of this section, you added the new subscription to the message schema. Now you have to implement its counterpart in the *src/resolvers/message.js* file:

---

[247]https://www.apollographql.com/docs/apollo-server/v2/features/subscriptions.html#PubSub-Implementations

src/resolvers/message.js

```
...

import pubsub, { EVENTS } from '../subscription';

...

export default {
  Query: {
    ...
  },

  Mutation: {
    ...
  },

  Message: {
    ...
  },

  Subscription: {
    messageCreated: {
      subscribe: () => pubsub.asyncIterator(EVENTS.MESSAGE.CREATED),
    },
  },
};
```

The subscribe's function signature has access to the same arguments as the other resolver functions. Models from the context can be accessed here, but it isn't necessary for this application.

The subscription as resolver provides a counterpart for the subscription in the message schema. However, since it uses a publisher-subscriber mechanism (PubSub) for events, you have only implemented the subscribing, not the publishing. It is possible for a GraphQL client to listen for changes, but there are no changes published yet. The best place for publishing a newly created message is in the same file as the created message:

src/resolvers/message.js

```
...

import pubsub, { EVENTS } from '../subscription';

...

export default {
  Query: {
    ...
  },

  Mutation: {
    createMessage: combineResolvers(
      isAuthenticated,
      async (parent, { text }, { models, me }) => {
        const message = await models.Message.create({
          text,
          userId: me.id,
        });

        pubsub.publish(EVENTS.MESSAGE.CREATED, {
          messageCreated: { message },
        });

        return message;
      },
    ),

    ...
  },

  Message: {
    ...
  },

  Subscription: {
    messageCreated: {
      subscribe: () => pubsub.asyncIterator(EVENTS.MESSAGE.CREATED),
    },
  },
};
```

You implemented your first subscription in GraphQL with Apollo Server and PubSub. To test it, create a new message with a logged in user. You can try both these GraphQL operations in two separate tabs in GraphQL Playground to compare their output. In the first tab, execute the subscription:

GraphQL Playground

```
subscription {
  messageCreated {
    message {
      id
      text
      createdAt
      user {
        id
        username
      }
    }
  }
}
```

Results will indicate the tab is listening for changes. In the second tab, log in a user:

GraphQL Playground

```
mutation {
  signIn(login: "rwieruch", password: "rwieruch") {
    token
  }
}
```

Copy the token from the result, and then paste it to the HTTP headers panel in the same tab:

GraphQL Playground

```
{
  "x-token": "eyJhbGciOiJIUzI1NiIsInR5cCI6IkpXVCJ9.eyJpZCI6MSwiZW1haWwiOiJoZWxsb0Byb\
2Jpbi5jb20iLCJ1c2VybmFtZSI6InJ3aWVydWNoIiwicm9sZSI6IkFETUlOIiwiaWF0IjoxNTM0OTQ3NTYyL\
CJleHAiOjE1MzQ5NDkzNjJ9.mg4M6SfYPJkGf_Z2Zr7ztGNbDRDLksRWdhhDvTbmWbQ"
}
```

Then create a message in the second tab:

GraphQL Playground

```
mutation {
  createMessage(text: "Does my subscription work?") {
    text
  }
}
```

Afterward, check your first tab again. It should show the created message:

GraphQL Playground

```
{
  "data": {
    "messageCreated": {
      "message": {
        "id": "4",
        "text": "Does my subscription work?",
        "createdAt": "2018-10-25T08:56:04.786Z",
        "user": {
          "id": "1",
          "username": "rwieruch"
        }
      }
    }
  }
}
```

You have implemented GraphQL subscriptions. It can be a challenge to wrap your head around them, but once you've worked through some basic operations, you can use these as a foundation to create real-time GraphQL applications.

Exercises:

- Confirm your source code for the last section[248]
- Read more about Subscriptions with Apollo Server[249]
- Watch a talk about GraphQL Subscriptions[250]

---

[248]https://github.com/the-road-to-graphql/fullstack-apollo-react-express-boilerplate-project/tree/eeb50f34a2569fa85141bf8ec3f8e9baaf670170
[249]https://www.apollographql.com/docs/apollo-server/v2/features/subscriptions.html
[250]http://youtu.be/bn8qsi8jVew

Testing a GraphQL Server

Testing often get overlooked in programming instruction, so this section will focus on to end-to-end (E2E) testing of a GraphQL server. While unit and integration tests are the fundamental pillars of the popular testing pyramid, covering all standalone functionalities of your application, E2E tests cover user scenarios for the entire application. An E2E test will assess whether a user is able to sign up for your application, or whether an admin user can delete other users. You don't need to write as many E2E tests, because they cover larger and more complex user scenarios, not just basic functionality. Also, E2E tests cover all the technical corners of your application, such as the GraphQL API, business logic, and databases.

GraphQL Server E2E Test Setup

Programs called Mocha and Chai are really all you need to test the application we've created. Mocha is a test runner that lets you execute tests from an npm script, while providing an organized testing structure; Chai gives you all the functionalities to make assertions, e.g. "Expect X to be equal to Y" based on real-world scenarios and run through them.

Command Line

```
npm install mocha chai --save-dev
```

To use these programs, you must first install a library called axios[251] for making requests to the GraphQL API. When testing user sign-up, you can send a GraphQL mutation to the GraphQL API that creates a user in the database and returns their information.

Command Line

```
npm install axios --save-dev
```

Mocha is run using npm scripts in your *package.json* file. The pattern used here matches all test files with the suffix *.spec.js* within the *src/* folder.

---

[251]https://github.com/axios/axios

package.json

```
{
  ...
  "scripts": {
    "start": "nodemon --exec babel-node src/index.js",
    "test": "mocha --require @babel/register 'src/**/*.spec.js'"
  },
  ...
}
```

Don't forget to install the babel node package with `npm install @babel/register --save-dev`. That should be sufficient to run your first test. Add a *src/tests/user.spec.js* to your application. and write your first test there:

src/tests/user.spec.js

```
import { expect } from 'chai';

describe('users', () => {
  it('user is user', () => {
    expect('user').to.eql('user');
  });
});
```

The test is executed by typing `npm test` into the command line. While it doesn't test any logic of your application, the test will verify that Mocha, Chai, and your new npm script are working.

Before you can write end-to-end tests for the GraphQL server, the database must be addressed. Since the tests run against the actual GraphQL server, so you only need to run against a test database rather than the production database. Add an npm script in the *package.json* to start the GraphQL server with a test database:

package.json

```
{
  ...
  "scripts": {
    "start": "nodemon --exec babel-node src/index.js",
    "test-server": "TEST_DATABASE=mytestdatabase npm start",
    "test": "mocha --require @babel/register 'src/**/*.spec.js'"
  },
  ...
}
```

The script must be started before the E2E GraphQL server tests. If the TEST_DATABASE environment flag is set, you have to adjust the database setup in the *src/models/index.js* file to use the test database instead:

src/models/index.js

```
import Sequelize from 'sequelize';

const sequelize = new Sequelize(
  process.env.TEST_DATABASE || process.env.DATABASE,
  process.env.DATABASE_USER,
  process.env.DATABASE_PASSWORD,
  {
    dialect: 'postgres',
  },
);

...
```

You also need to make sure to create such a database. Mine is called *mytestdatabase* in the npm script, which I added in the command line with psql and createdb or CREATE DATABASE.

Finally, you must start with a seeded and consistent database every time you run a test server. To do this, set the database re-seeding flag to depend on the set test database environment variable in the *src/index.js* file:

src/index.js

```
...

const isTest = !!process.env.TEST_DATABASE;

sequelize.sync({ force: isTest }).then(async () => {
  if (isTest) {
    createUsersWithMessages(new Date());
  }

  httpServer.listen({ port: 8000 }, () => {
    console.log('Apollo Server on http://localhost:8000/graphql');
  });
});

...
```

Now you are ready to write tests against an actual running test sever (`npm run test-server`) that uses a consistently seeded test database. If you want to use async/await in your test environment, adjust your *.babelrc* file:

.babelrc

```
{
  "presets": [
    [
      "@babel/preset-env", {
        "targets": {
          "node": "current"
        }
      }
    ]
  ]
}
```

Now you can write tests with asynchronous business logic with async/await.

Testing User Scenarios with E2E Tests

Every E2E test sends an actual request with axios to the API of the running GraphQL test server. Testing your user GraphQL query would look like the following in the *src/tests/user.spec.js* file:

src/tests/user.spec.js

```
import { expect } from 'chai';

describe('users', () => {
  describe('user(id: String!): User', () => {
    it('returns a user when user can be found', async () => {
      const expectedResult = {
        data: {
          user: {
            id: '1',
            username: 'rwieruch',
            email: 'hello@robin.com',
            role: 'ADMIN',
          },
        },
      };

      const result = await userApi.user({ id: '1' });
```

```
    expect(result.data).to.eql(expectedResult);
  });
 });
});
```

Each test should be as straightforward as this one. You make a GraphQL API request with axios, expecting a query/mutation result from the API. Behind the scenes, data is read or written from or to the database. The business logic such as authentication, authorization, and pagination works in between. A request goes through the whole GraphQL server stack from API to database. An end-to-end test and doesn't test an isolated unit (unit test) or a smaller composition of units (integration test), but the entire pipeline.

The userApi function is the final piece needed to set up effective testing for this application. It's not implemented in the test, but in another *src/tests/api.js* file for portability. In this file, you will find all your functions which can be used to run requests against your GraphQL test server.

src/tests/api.js

```
import axios from 'axios';

const API_URL = 'http://localhost:8000/graphql';

export const user = async variables =>
  axios.post(API_URL, {
    query: `
      query ($id: ID!) {
        user(id: $id) {
          id
          username
          email
          role
        }
      }
    `,
    variables,
  });
```

You can use basic HTTP to perform GraphQL operations across the network layer. It only needs a payload, which is the query/mutation and the variables. Beyond that, the URL of the GraphQL server must be known. Now, import the user API in your actual test file:

src/tests/user.spec.js

```
import { expect } from 'chai';

import * as userApi from './api';

describe('users', () => {
  describe('user(id: String!): User', () => {
    it('returns a user when user can be found', async () => {
      const expectedResult = {
        ...
      };

      const result = await userApi.user({ id: '1' });

      expect(result.data).to.eql(expectedResult);
    });
  });
});
```

To execute your tests now, run your GraphQL test server in the command line with `npm run test-server`, and execute your tests in another command line tab with `npm test`. The output should appear as such:

Command Line

```
users
  user(id: ID!): User
    ✓ returns a user when user can be found (69ms)


1 passing (123ms)
```

If your output is erroneous, the console logs may help you figure out what went wrong. Another option is to take the query from the axios request and put it into GraphQL Playground. The error reporting in Playground might make it easier to find problems.

That's your first E2E test against a GraphQL server. The next one uses the same API, and you can see how useful it is to extract the API layer as reusable functions. In your *src/tests/user.spec.js* file add another test:

src/tests/user.spec.js

```
import { expect } from 'chai';

import * as userApi from './api';

describe('users', () => {
  describe('user(id: ID!): User', () => {
    it('returns a user when user can be found', async () => {
      const expectedResult = {
        ...
      };

      const result = await userApi.user({ id: '1' });

      expect(result.data).to.eql(expectedResult);
    });

    it('returns null when user cannot be found', async () => {
      const expectedResult = {
        data: {
          user: null,
        },
      };

      const result = await userApi.user({ id: '42' });

      expect(result.data).to.eql(expectedResult);
    });
  });
});
```

It is valuable to test the common path, but also less common edge cases. In this case, the uncommon path didn't return an error, but null for the user.

Let's add another test that verifies non-admin user authorization related to deleting messages. Here you will implement a complete scenario from login to user deletion. First, implement the sign in and delete user API in the *src/tests/api.js* file:

src/tests/api.js

```
...

export const signIn = async variables =>
  await axios.post(API_URL, {
    query: `
      mutation ($login: String!, $password: String!) {
        signIn(login: $login, password: $password) {
          token
        }
      }
    `,
    variables,
  });

export const deleteUser = async (variables, token) =>
  axios.post(
    API_URL,
    {
      query: `
        mutation ($id: ID!) {
          deleteUser(id: $id)
        }
      `,
      variables,
    },
    {
      headers: {
        'x-token': token,
      },
    },
  );
```

The `deleteUser` mutation needs the token from the `signIn` mutation's result. Next, you can test the whole scenario by executing both APIs in your new E2E test:

src/tests/user.spec.js

```
import { expect } from 'chai';

import * as userApi from './api';

describe('users', () => {
  describe('user(id: ID!): User', () => {
    ...
  });

  describe('deleteUser(id: String!): Boolean!', () => {
    it('returns an error because only admins can delete a user', async () => {
      const {
        data: {
          data: {
            signIn: { token },
          },
        },
      } = await userApi.signIn({
        login: 'ddavids',
        password: 'ddavids',
      });

      const {
        data: { errors },
      } = await userApi.deleteUser({ id: '1' }, token);

      expect(errors[0].message).to.eql('Not authorized as admin.');
    });
  });
});
```

First, you are using the signIn mutation to login a user to the application. The login is fulfilled once the token is returned. The token can then be used for every other GraphQL operation. In this case, it is used for the deleteUser mutation. The mutation still fails, however, because the current user is not admin. You can try the same scenario on your own with an admin to test the simple path for reusing APIs.

Command Line

```
users
  user(id: String!): User
    ✓ returns a user when user can be found (81ms)
    ✓ returns null when user cannot be found
  deleteUser(id: String!): Boolean!
    ✓ returns an error because only admins can delete a user (109ms)


3 passing (276ms)
```

These E2E tests cover scenarios for user domains, going through the GraphQL API over business logic to the database access. However, there is still plenty of room for alternatives. Consider testing other user domain-specific scenarios such as a user sign up (registration), providing a wrong password on sign in (login), or requesting one and another page of paginated messages for the message domain.

This section only covered E2E tests. With Chai and Mocha at your disposal, you can also add smaller unit and integration tests for your different application layers (e.g. resolvers). If you need a library to spy, stub, or mock something, I recommend Sinon[252] as a complementary testing library.

Exercises:

- Confirm your source code for the last section[253]
- Implement tests for the message domain similar to the user domain
- Write more fine-granular unit/integration tests for both domains
- Read more about GraphQL and HTTP[254]
- Read more about Mocking with Apollo Server[255]

---

[252]https://sinonjs.org
[253]https://github.com/the-road-to-graphql/fullstack-apollo-react-express-boilerplate-project/tree/d11e0487085e014170146ec7479d0154c4a6fce4
[254]https://graphql.github.io/learn/serving-over-http/
[255]https://www.apollographql.com/docs/apollo-server/v2/features/mocking.html

Batching and Caching in GraphQL with Data Loader

The section is about improving the requests to your database. While only one request (e.g. a GraphQL query) hits your GraphQL API, you may end up with multiple database reads and writes to resolve all fields in the resolvers. Let's see this problem in action using the following query in GraphQL Playground:

GraphQL Playground

```
query {
  messages {
    edges {
      user {
        username
      }
    }
  }
}
```

Keep the query open, because you use it as a case study to make improvements. Your query result should be similar to the following:

GraphQL Playground

```
{
  "data": {
    "messages": {
      "edges": [
        {
          "user": {
            "username": "ddavids"
          }
        },
        {
          "user": {
            "username": "ddavids"
          }
        },
        {
          "user": {
            "username": "rwieruch"
          }
        }
      ]
```

```
      }
   }
}
```

In the command line for the running GraphQL server, four requests were made to the database:

Command Line

```
Executing (default): SELECT "id", "text", "createdAt", "updatedAt", "userId" FROM "m\
essages" AS "message" ORDER BY "message"."createdAt" DESC LIMIT 101;

Executing (default): SELECT "id", "username", "email", "password", "role", "createdA\
t", "updatedAt" FROM "users" AS "user" WHERE "user"."id" = 2;

Executing (default): SELECT "id", "username", "email", "password", "role", "createdA\
t", "updatedAt" FROM "users" AS "user" WHERE "user"."id" = 2;

Executing (default): SELECT "id", "username", "email", "password", "role", "createdA\
t", "updatedAt" FROM "users" AS "user" WHERE "user"."id" = 1;
```

There is one request made for the list of messages, and three requests for each individual user. That's the nature of GraphQL. Even though you can nest your GraphQL relationships and query structure, there will still be database requests. Check the resolvers for the message user in your *src/resolvers/message.js* file to see where this is happening. At some point, you may run into performance bottlenecks when nesting GraphQL queries or mutations too deeply, because a lot of items need to be retrieved from your database.

In the following, you will optimize these database accesses with batching. It's a strategy used for a GraphQL server and its database, but also for other programming environments. Compare the query result in GraphQL Playground and your database output in the command line.

There are two improvements that can be made with batching. First, one author of a message is retrieved twice from the database, which is redundant. Even though there are multiple messages, the author of some of these messages can be the same person. Imagine this problem on a larger scale for 100 messages between two authors in a chat application. There would be one request for the 100 messages and 100 requests for the 100 authors of each message, which would lead to 101 database accesses. If duplicated authors are retrieved only once, it would only need one request for the 100 messages and 2 requests for the authors, which reduces the 101 database hits to just 3. Since you know all the identifiers of the authors, these identifiers can be batched to a set where none are repeated. In this case, the two authors a list of [2, 2, 1] identifiers become a set of [2, 1] identifiers.

Second, every author is read from the database individually, even though the list is purged from its duplications. Reading all authors with only one database request should be possible, because at the time of the GraphQL API request with all messages at your disposal, you know all the identifiers of the authors. This decreases your database accesses from 3 to 2, because now you only request the list of 100 messages and its 2 authors in two requests.

The same two principals can be applied to the 4 database accesses which should be decreased to 2. On a smaller scale, it might not have much of a performance impact, but for 100 messages with the 2 authors, it reduces your database accesses significantly. That's where Facebook's open source dataloader[256] becomes a vital tool. You can install it via npm on the command line:

Command Line

```
npm install dataloader --save
```

Now, in your *src/index.js* file you can import and make use of it:

src/index.js

```
import DataLoader from 'dataloader';


...


const batchUsers = async (keys, models) => {
  const users = await models.User.findAll({
    where: {
      id: {
        $in: keys,
      },
    },
  });

  return keys.map(key => users.find(user => user.id === key));
};

const server = new ApolloServer({
  typeDefs: schema,
  resolvers,
  ...
  context: async ({ req, connection }) => {
    if (connection) {

      ...

    }

    if (req) {
      const me = await getMe(req);
```

---

[256]https://github.com/facebook/dataloader

```
      return {
        models,
        me,
        secret: process.env.SECRET,
        loaders: {
          user: new DataLoader(keys => batchUsers(keys, models)),
        },
      };
    }
  },
});
```

```
. . .
```

The loaders act as abstraction on top of the models, and can be passed as context to the resolvers. The user loader in the following example is used instead of the models directly.

Now we'll consider the function as argument for the DataLoader instantiation. The function gives you access to a list of keys in its arguments. These keys are your set of identifiers, purged of duplication, which can be used to retrieve items from a database. That's why keys (identifiers) and models (data access layer) are passed to the `batchUser()` function. The function then takes the keys to retrieve the entities via the model from the database. By the end of the function, the keys are mapped in the same order as the retrieved entities. Otherwise, it's possible to return users right after their retrieval from the database, though they have a different order than the incoming keys. As a result, users need to be returned in the same order as their incoming identifiers (keys).

That's the setup for the loader, an improved abstraction on top of the model. Now, since you are passing the loader for the batched user retrieval as context to the resolvers, you can make use of it in the *src/resolvers/message.js* file:

src/resolvers/message.js

```
. . .

export default {
  Query: {
    . . .
  },

  Mutation: {
    . . .
  },

  Message: {
    user: async (message, args, { loaders }) => {
```

```
      return await loaders.user.load(message.userId);
    },
  },

  Subscription: {
    ...
  },
};
```

While the `load()` function takes each identifier individually, it will batch all these identifiers into one set and request all users at the same time. Try it by executing the same GraphQL query in GraphQL Playground. The result should stay the same, but you should only see 2 instead of 4 requests to the database in your command-line output for the GraphQL server:

Command Line

```
Executing (default): SELECT "id", "text", "createdAt", "updatedAt", "userId" FROM "m\
essages" AS "message" ORDER BY "message"."createdAt" DESC LIMIT 101;

Executing (default): SELECT "id", "username", "email", "password", "role", "createdA\
t", "updatedAt" FROM "users" AS "user" WHERE "user"."id" IN (2, 1);
```

That's the benefit of the batching improvement: instead of fetching each (duplicated) user on its own, you fetch them all at once in one batched request with the dataloader package.

Now let's get into caching. The dataloader package we installed before also gives the option to cache requests. It doesn't work yet, though; try to execute the same GraphQL query twice and you should see the database accesses twice on your command line.

Command Line

```
Executing (default): SELECT "id", "text", "createdAt", "updatedAt", "userId" FROM "m\
essages" AS "message" ORDER BY "message"."createdAt" DESC LIMIT 101;
Executing (default): SELECT "id", "username", "email", "password", "role", "createdA\
t", "updatedAt" FROM "users" AS "user" WHERE "user"."id" IN (2, 1);

Executing (default): SELECT "id", "text", "createdAt", "updatedAt", "userId" FROM "m\
essages" AS "message" ORDER BY "message"."createdAt" DESC LIMIT 101;
Executing (default): SELECT "id", "username", "email", "password", "role", "createdA\
t", "updatedAt" FROM "users" AS "user" WHERE "user"."id" IN (2, 1);
```

That's happening because a new instance of the dataloader is created within the GraphQL context for every request. If you move the dataloader instantiation outside, you get the caching benefit of dataloader for free:

src/index.js

```
. . .

const userLoader = new DataLoader(keys => batchUsers(keys, models));

const server = new ApolloServer({
  typeDefs: schema,
  resolvers,
  . . .
  context: async ({ req, connection }) => {
    if (connection) {
      . . .
    }

    if (req) {
      const me = await getMe(req);

      return {
        models,
        me,
        secret: process.env.SECRET,
        loaders: {
          user: userLoader,
        },
      };
    }
  },
});

. . .
```

Try to execute the same GraphQL query twice again. This time you should see only a single database access, for the places where the loader is used; the second time, it should be cached.

Command Line

```
Executing (default): SELECT "id", "text", "createdAt", "updatedAt", "userId" FROM "m\
essages" AS "message" ORDER BY "message"."createdAt" DESC LIMIT 101;
Executing (default): SELECT "id", "username", "email", "password", "role", "createdA\
t", "updatedAt" FROM "users" AS "user" WHERE "user"."id" IN (2, 1);

Executing (default): SELECT "id", "text", "createdAt", "updatedAt", "userId" FROM "m\
essages" AS "message" ORDER BY "message"."createdAt" DESC LIMIT 101;
```

In this case, the users are not read from the database twice, only the messages, because they are not using a dataloader yet. That's how you can achieve caching in GraphQL with dataloaders. Choosing a caching strategy isn't quite as simple. For example, if a cached user is updated in between actions, the GraphQL client application still queries the cached user.

It's difficult to find the right timing for invalidating the cache, so I recommended performing the dataloader instantiation with every incoming GraphQL request. You lose the benefit of caching over multiple GraphQL requests, but still use the cache for every database access with one incoming GraphQL request. The dataloader package expresses it like this: *"DataLoader caching does not replace Redis, Memcache, or any other shared application-level cache. DataLoader is first and foremost a data loading mechanism, and its cache only serves the purpose of not repeatedly loading the same data in the context of a single request to your Application."* If you want to get into real caching on the database level, give Redis[257] a shot.

Outsource the loaders into a different folder/file structure. Put the batching for the individual users into a new *src/loaders/user.js* file:

src/loaders/user.js

```
export const batchUsers = async (keys, models) => {
  const users = await models.User.findAll({
    where: {
      id: {
        $in: keys,
      },
    },
  });

  return keys.map(key => users.find(user => user.id === key));
};
```

And in a new *src/loaders/index.js* file export all the functions:

---

[257]https://redis.io/

src/loaders/index.js

```
import * as user from './user';

export default { user };
```

Finally, import it in your *src/index.js* file and use it:

src/index.js

```
...
import DataLoader from 'dataloader';

...
import loaders from './loaders';

...

const server = new ApolloServer({
  typeDefs: schema,
  resolvers,
  ...
  context: async ({ req, connection }) => {
    if (connection) {
      ...
    }

    if (req) {
      const me = await getMe(req);

      return {
        models,
        me,
        secret: process.env.SECRET,
        loaders: {
          user: new DataLoader(keys =>
            loaders.user.batchUsers(keys, models),
          ),
        },
      };
    }
  },
});

...
```

Remember to add the loader to your subscriptions, in case you use them there:

src/index.js

```
...

const server = new ApolloServer({
  typeDefs: schema,
  resolvers,
  ...
  context: async ({ req, connection }) => {
    if (connection) {
      return {
        models,
        loaders: {
          user: new DataLoader(keys =>
            loaders.user.batchUsers(keys, models),
          ),
        },
      };
    }

    if (req) {
      ...
    }
  },
});

...
```

Feel free to add more loaders on your own, maybe for the message domain. The practice can provide useful abstraction on top of your models to allow batching and request-based caching.

Exercises:

- Confirm your source code for the last section[258]
- Read more about GraphQL and Dataloader[259]
- Read more about GraphQL Best Practices[260]

---

[258]https://github.com/the-road-to-graphql/fullstack-apollo-react-express-boilerplate-project/tree/9ff0542f620a0d9939c1adcbd21951f8fc1693f4
[259]https://www.apollographql.com/docs/graphql-tools/connectors.html#dataloader
[260]https://graphql.github.io/learn/best-practices/

GraphQL Server + PostgreSQL Deployment to Heroku

Eventually you want to deploy the GraphQL server online, so it can be used in production. In this section, you learn how to deploy a GraphQL server to Heroku, a platform as a service for hosting applications. Heroku allows PostgreSQL as well.

This section guides you through the process in the command line. For the visual approach check this GraphQL server on Heroku deployment tutorial[261] which, however, doesn't include the PostgreSQL database deployment.

Initially you need to complete three requirements to use Heroku:

- Install git for your command line and push your project to GitHub[262]
- Create an account for Heroku[263]
- Install the Heroku CLI[264] for accessing Heroku's features on the command line

In the command line, verify your Heroku installation with `heroku version`. If there is a valid installation, sign in to your Heroku account with `heroku login`. That's it for the general Heroku setup. In your project's folder, create a new Heroku application and give it a name:

Command Line

```
heroku create graphql-server-node-js
```

Afterward, you can also install the PostgreSQL add-on for Heroku on the command line for your project:

Command Line

```
heroku addons:create heroku-postgresql:hobby-dev
```

It uses the hobby tier[265], a free application that can be upgraded as needed. Output for the PostgreSQL add-on installation should be similar to:

[261]https://www.apollographql.com/docs/apollo-server/deployment/heroku.html
[262]https://www.robinwieruch.de/git-essential-commands/
[263]https://www.heroku.com/
[264]https://devcenter.heroku.com/articles/heroku-cli
[265]https://devcenter.heroku.com/articles/heroku-postgres-plans#hobby-tier

Command Line

```
Creating heroku-postgresql:hobby-dev on ⬡ graphql-server-node-js... free
Database has been created and is available
 ! This database is empty. If upgrading, you can transfer
 ! data from another database with pg:copy
Created postgresql-perpendicular-34121 as DATABASE_URL
Use heroku addons:docs heroku-postgresql to view documentation
```

Check the Heroku PostgreSQL documentation[266] for more in depth instructions for your database setup.

You are ready to take your application online. With the PostgreSQL add-on, you received a database URL as well. You can find it with `heroku config`. Now, let's step into your GraphQL server's code to make a couple of adjustments for production. In your *src/models/index.js*, you need to decide between development (coding, testing) and production (live) build. Because you have a new environment variable for your database URL, you can use this to make the decision:

src/models/index.js

```
import Sequelize from 'sequelize';

let sequelize;
if (process.env.DATABASE_URL) {
  sequelize = new Sequelize(process.env.DATABASE_URL, {
    dialect: 'postgres',
  });
} else {
  sequelize = new Sequelize(
    process.env.TEST_DATABASE || process.env.DATABASE,
    process.env.DATABASE_USER,
    process.env.DATABASE_PASSWORD,
    {
      dialect: 'postgres',
    },
  );
}

...
```

If you check your *.env* file, you will see the DATABASE_URL environment variable isn't there. But you should see that it is set as Heroku environment variable with `heroku config:get DATABASE_URL`. Once your application is live on Heroku, your environment variables are merged with Heroku's

[266]https://devcenter.heroku.com/articles/heroku-postgresql

environment variables, which is why the DATABASE_URL isn't applied for your local development environment.

Another environment variable used in the *src/index.js* file is called *SECRET* for your authentication strategy. If you haven't included an *.env* file in your project's version control (see .gitignore), you need to set the SECRET for your production code in Heroku using `heroku config:set SECRET=wr3r23fwfwefwekwself.2456342.dawqdq`. The secret is just made up and you can choose your own custom string for it.

Also, consider the application's port in the *src/index.js* file. Heroku adds its own PORT environment variable, and you should use the port from an environment variable as a fallback.

src/index.js

```
...

const port = process.env.PORT || 8000;

sequelize.sync({ force: isTest }).then(async () => {
  if (isTest) {
    createUsersWithMessages(new Date());
  }

  httpServer.listen({ port }, () => {
    console.log(`Apollo Server on http://localhost:${port}/graphql`);
  });
});

...
```

Finally, decide whether you want to start with a seeded database or an empty database on Heroku PostgreSQL. If it is to be seeded, add an extra flag to the seeding:

src/index.js

```
...

const isTest = !!process.env.TEST_DATABASE;
const isProduction = !!process.env.DATABASE_URL;
const port = process.env.PORT || 8000;

sequelize.sync({ force: isTest || isProduction }).then(async () => {
  if (isTest || isProduction) {
    createUsersWithMessages(new Date());
  }
```

```
  httpServer.listen({ port }, () => {
    console.log(`Apollo Server on http://localhost:${port}/graphql`);
  });
});
```

```
...
```

Remember to remove the flag after, or the database will be purged and seeded with every deployment. Depending on development or production, you are choosing a database, seeding it (or not), and selecting a port for your GraphQL server. Before pushing your application to Heroku, push all recent changes to your GitHub repository. After that, push all the changes to your Heroku remote repository as well, since you created a Heroku application before: `git push heroku master`. Open the application with `heroku open`, and add the `/graphql` suffix to your URL in the browser to open up GraphQL Playground. If it doesn't work, check the troubleshoot area below.

Depending on your seeding strategy, your database will either be empty or contain seeded data. If its empty, register a user and create messages via GraphQL mutations. If its seeded, request a list of messages with a GraphQL query.

Congratulations, your application should be live now. Not only is your GraphQL server running on Heroku, but your PostgreSQL database. Follow the exercises to learn more about Heroku.

Heroku Troubleshoot

It can happen that the GraphQL schema is not available in GraphQL Playground for application in production. It's because the `introspection` flag for Apollo Server is disabled for production. In order to fix it, you can set it to true:

src/index.js

```
const server = new ApolloServer({
  introspection: true,
  typeDefs: schema,
  resolvers,
  ...
});
```

Another issue may be that Heroku doesn't install the dev dependencies for production. Although it does install the dev dependencies for building the application on Heroku, it purges the dev dependencies afterward. However, in our case, in order to start the application (npm start script), we rely on a few dev dependencies that need to be available in production. You can tell Heroku to keep the dev dependencies:[267]

---

[267]https://devcenter.heroku.com/articles/nodejs-support#package-installation

Command Line

```
heroku config:set NPM_CONFIG_PRODUCTION=false YARN_PRODUCTION=false
```

In a real world scenario, you would want to use something else to start your application and not rely on any dev dependencies.

Exercises:

- Confirm your source code for the last section[268]
- Feedback whether the troubleshooting area for Heroku was useful is very appreciated
- Create sample data in your production database with GraphQL Playground
- Get familiar with the Heroku Dashboard[269]
    - Find your application's logs
    - Find your application's environment variables
- access your PostgreSQL database on Heroku with `heroku pg:psql`

<hr class="section-divider">

You built a sophisticated GraphQL server boilerplate project with Express and Apollo Server. You should have learned that GraphQL isn't opinionated about various things, and about authentication, authorization, database access, and pagination. Most of the operations we learned were more straightforward because of Apollo Server over the GraphQL reference implementation in JavaScript. That's okay, because many people are using Apollo Server to build GraphQL servers. Use this application as a starter project to realize your own ideas, or find my starter project with a GraphQL client built in React in this GitHub repository[270].

---

[268]https://github.com/the-road-to-graphql/fullstack-apollo-react-express-boilerplate-project/tree/9dbfb30226cdc4843adbcc09d16871b2a902a4d3
[269]https://dashboard.heroku.com/apps
[270]https://github.com/rwieruch/fullstack-apollo-react-express-boilerplate-project

Final Thoughts

The last chapters of this book are to inspire you to apply what you've learned. So far, the book has taught you how to use GraphQL in JavaScript on the client and server-side. You used React on the client-side and Express on the server-side. On both ends you used Apollo for a sophisticated GraphQL library between both entities. However, there is plenty of room to explore the ecosystem. If you haven't completed all the exercises from the book or read all the articles, you should start with these. Otherwise, let's see what else you can do to advance your GraphQL skills.

Further Learning Paths

You built a couple of applications in this book. While reading the chapters, you adapted the applications to apply advanced techniques (permission-based authorization), tools (GraphQL Playground) or features (GitHub commenting). Perhaps you even followed all of the exercises closely in the book. But that's not the end. There are many more features, techniques, and tools that you can apply to these applications. Be creative and challenge yourself by implementing these on your own. I am curious what you come up with, so don't hesitate to reach out to me.

We used React on the client-side and Express on the server-side. As GraphQL and also the Apollo libraries are framework agnostic, you can couple them with any other solution. If you are familiar with Angular or Vue, you can transfer what you've learned about GraphQL and Apollo for building client-side applications with these frameworks. If you are more into Koa or Hapi on the server-side, you can use these middleware libraries instead of Express as you have done in the book. The same applies for the database used for the GraphQL server application. In this book, you used PostgreSQL with the Sequelize ORM to connect your GraphQL resolvers to the PostgreSQL database. It's up to you to substitute PostgreSQL and Sequelize with something else like MongoDB and Mongoose. Also, the Apollo client and server libraries can be substituted with other libraries from the ecosystem. You read about them in the introductory chapters of this book. You can also use Yoga GraphQL[271] and Prisma[272] to get your GraphQL server up and running. None of the technologies used in this book are set in stone, and you can substitute of them to build GraphQL applications with JavaScript.

My ultimate recommendation would be to continue with the Apollo Server application that you built in this book, as it's an ideal starter kit to realize your own ideas. As mentioned, you are free to substitute the technologies used under the hood, but it would be great to focus on the features for your application. Since the user management is implemented for you, you can start to add your own features.

---

[271]https://github.com/prisma/graphql-yoga
[272]https://www.prisma.io/

Never stop Learning

The Learning Pyramid shows the relation between retention rates and mental activities, proving usable data for both teaching and learning. It is one of the most effective ways to measure effective lessons since I started teaching programming. This is how typical mental activities break down according to retention rates:

- **5% Lecture**
- **10% Reading** - This book is a great start!
- **20% Audiovisual** - Screencasts are an excellent source of hands-on learning.
- **30% Demonstration** - Code was demonstrated throughout this book.
- **50% Discussion** (FYI: There is a Slack Group[273] where you can participate)
- **75% Practice by Doing** - Use the practical chapters and purchase the source code to extend your understanding.
- **90% Teach Others** - Assist your peers in Slack communities, Open Source, or on platforms like Facebook Groups and Reddit.

In the beginning of the book, I mentioned that no one masters programming by reading a book, and throughout I have emphasized application of the lessons is the best way to retain them. The last item in the pyramid that has the biggest return of investment: teaching Others. I had the same experience when I started blogging about my experiences in web development, answered questions on Quora, Reddit, Slack Overflow, and wrote books. Teaching others forces you to dive deeper into topics, so you learn about the nuances because you want to teach them the right way. Think of friends, coworkers, or online peers from Stack Overflow or Reddit who are keen to learn about state management in modern applications with React, Redux, and MobX. Schedule a get-together, and teach them state management in modern applications with React. Both mentor and student will grow from the experience.

---

[273]https://slack-the-road-to-learn-react.wieruch.com/

Thank You

So now we've reached the end of The Road to GraphQL. I hope you enjoyed reading it, and I hope it helped you to gain some traction in GraphQL. If you liked the book, share it as a way to learn GraphQL with your friends. It should be used as giveaway. Also, a review on Amazon[274] or Goodreads[275] can really help improve future projects.

Foremost, I want to thank you for reading this book or taking the full course. My greatest wish is that you had a great learning experience with the material. I hope you feel empowered now to build your own applications that uses GraphQL. I strive to go in the direction of education, so I depend on your feedback, both positive and critical.

Visit my website[276] to find more topics about software and web development, and I have updates are available by subscription[277]. The updates will be in-depth content, but never spam.

If you liked the learning experience, I hope you share it with others. Think about people in your life who want to learn more about this topic. I believe developers need to align on this topic to reach the next level with modern applications.

Thanks for reading, Robin.

---

[274]https://www.amazon.com/s/?field-keywords=The+Road+to+GraphQL
[275]https://www.goodreads.com/book/show/42641103-the-road-to-graphql
[276]https://www.robinwieruch.de/
[277]https://www.getrevue.co/profile/rwieruch

Printed in Great Britain
by Amazon